From Tin Pan Alley
To The Yellow Brick Road

Keith Hayward

ELTON JOHN

From Tin Pan Alley
To The Yellow Brick Road

Keith Hayward

WP
WYMER
PUBLISHING
Bedford, England

First published in Great Britain in 2015
by Wymer Publishing
Bedford, England
www.wymerpublishing.co.uk
Tel: 01234 326691
Wymer Publishing is a trading name of Wymer (UK) Ltd

First edition. Copyright © 2015 Keith Hayward / Wymer Publishing.

ISBN 978-1-908724-51-9

Edited by Lynn Baker.

Every effort has been made to trace the copyright holders of the
photographs in this book but some were unreachable. We would
be grateful if the photographers concerned would contact us.

Typeset by Wymer
Printed and bound in Great Britain by
Clays Ltd, Bungay, Suffolk

A catalogue record for this book is available from the British Library.

Cover design by Wymer.
Cover photos © Steve Emberton.

Contents

Preface

This book is the second in a two part series about the music business from the mid sixties through to the end of the seventies but told through the career of Elton John.

The first book; *Tin Pan Alley: The Rise of Elton John* focussed on the world of Denmark Street, the centre of the British music business, affectionately nicknamed Tin Pan Alley. It was a street of music publishers and songwriters, churning out three-minute songs for the publishers to buy and convert into sheet music or for the singers of the day to sing. It also describes the lives of musicians travelling up and down the roads of England on a hectic schedule of gigs just to keep the momentum of their search for fame and fortune going.

If you haven't seen a copy of *Tin Pan Alley: The Rise of Elton John*, then shame on you. But don't worry you can still make sense of this book without it and I hope you will find it as equally interesting about Elton John in his heyday, as well as an historic record of a time when the music business was different.

The seventies saw the music publishing world of the sixties give way to charts and records; and Tin Pan Alley songwriters replaced by singer songwriters, writing for themselves. It was a time when radio DJ's were as big, if not bigger, than the singers and bands whose records they were playing and music producers were as important as the songwriters and musicians who created the music. The small family publisher who frequented the small street in London was gradually replaced by the independent record label that did everything from publishing to selling records, then towards to end of the seventies all were swallowed up whole by the large corporate companies who saw music as commodity to be traded on the stock exchange.

Elton John was just one of the artists that crossed the divide from the sixties to the seventies alongside David Bowie, Marc Bolan, Sandy Denny, and John Martyn to name a few; all who followed the lead of Lennon and McCartney and Jagger and Richards. It was, arguably one of the most exciting times in the history of the music business where change was a way of life. I hope this book gives you a glimpse of that way of life.

The author would like to thank the following contributors who made this book possible: John Reid, Gavin Sutherland, Linda Lewis, David Larkham, Mick Inkpen, Jim Cregan, Kiki Dee, Rick Wakeman, Tony King, Stuart Epps, Chrissie Cremore, David Hockman, Andy Hill, Gary Osborne, Roger Pope, Kenny Passarelli, Harry Barter, Steve Brown, Jerry Donahue, Stephen James, Danny Hutton, Tony Taupin, Dave Glover, B.J. Cole, Ian Duck, Caleb Quaye, Noel Murphy, Chris Simpson, Jean Luc Ponty, Bryan Forbes, Del Newman, Martyn Ford, Phil Greenfield, Chris Charlesworth, Beryl Virtue, Sue Cooke, John Carsello, Anett Murray, Doug Ayris. I must give very special thanks to Richard Gale who spent many hours putting together the list of concerts from 1970 to 1979: "A monumental task and one that the author appreciates immensely". And to Nick Warburton who helped enormously with the Bluesology gig guide.

This book is dedicated to the memory of Roger Pope who I had the honour to call my friend alongside his long time partner and later, wife Sue. Together they taught me what true friendship and lasting love should be like through good and difficult times. Alongside them I credit the inspiration for this book to Sarah Johnson who has kept my idea alive when I really didn't have the stamina to go on. Finally to my family; to Lucy my beautiful granddaughter and Mark and Rachael who are brilliant parents to her; to Stevie, may your demons pass and you continue to be the loving, sensitive man you are; to Ashleigh, may your child's happiness continue into adulthood and to my beloved Nicole, who makes me smile every day.

Prologue

Reg Dwight was a talented young man from Northwood, a northerly suburb of the UK's capital, London Town. Learning to play the piano by ear and listening to his mother's records by Bill Hayley and Elvis Presley, he honed his skills after being spotted by his piano teacher at Pinner County Grammar School and was picked out of hundreds of hopefuls from Schools in the London area for a scholarship at the Royal Academy of Music in the heart of London. Under the tutelage of a young Helen Piena he learnt the rudiments of piano playing. Piena deserves much credit for her perseverance with a young boy who preferred to play the blues than classical music. In fact Reg had already dabbled with the blues with his teenage pals and formed a band called The Corvettes; the group of school chums used to rehearse in a local pub or at the School across the playing fields from Reg's home at Frome Court in Northwood. If the powers that be at the Academy had known he was playing in such a band then they would have surely expelled him; it was not the sort of thing a student at the Academy should be doing.

The Corvettes didn't last long and Reg turned his hand at playing in a local pub, The Northwood Hills Hotel, having been given his first real chance at performing by the landlord George Hill. Whilst it took Reg a while to get the customers to warm to him he would eventually earn enough in wages and tips to buy his first electric piano and that was the cue for him to join his next band; Bluesology, again with his teenage pals from Corvettes and a couple of other hopefuls who liked the same sort of music as Reg. Although he continued his treks into Central London every

Saturday morning to learn his trade at the Academy he didn't do as well as Piena had hoped but still learnt enough to pass his exams. Not so his school work though. Whilst Reg had started his exams he decided not to finish them and instead opted to go and work in London's Tin Pan Alley; Denmark Street - the UK's equivalent to New York's Tin Pan Alley in America; where Reg yearned to be a successful singer songwriter alongside Bill Martin, Phil Coulter, Tony Hiller, Rogers Cooke and Greenaway, and Tony Hatch to name a few. He set out to make his mark in the music publishing world under the guidance of Cyril Gee at Mills Music; where, as a sheet music packer and all round gopher and tea boy, he would be in the centre of the British music business rubbing shoulders with songwriters, publishers and musicians and listening to the latest sounds, which he quickly absorbed; storing it all up to be used later in his own compositions.

Bluesology became a success in its own right and Reg and his pals were soon offered work with an agency that booked American R&B acts to tour the UK. They were to be the backing band for the very acts that Reg admired as a boy due to his own musical tastes. That was the cue for Reg to turn professional and take the next step in the career of a budding Elton John; that of keyboard player and backing singer to Stu Brown's lead vocals - something that Reg would become frustrated with as the life of Bluesology flourished. Even though the band would taste some of Reg's early musical compositions like 'Come Back Baby' and 'Mr Frantic', (even though the words he was singing were far removed from the Tin Pan Alley lyricists of the day and from the lyrics a young Bernie Taupin would write); songs that gave the young keyboard player his chance to stretch his vocal chords with the band, although he still wasn't the first choice vocalist.

The success of Bluesology soon attracted the charismatic and popular Long John Baldry who saw the ever-changing line up of Bluesology as an ideal backing band for his cabaret circuit. It also gave the band the opportunity for the first time to earn a steady living as well as having roadies to help them instead of Reg and Co. humping their own kit around. However it was to push Reg further and further behind in the singing stakes as Stu Brown as well as Marsha Hunt, Baldry and others took turns in the vocal show. Reg was still just the keyboard player and his own compositions took a back seat; neither was his voice to surface in public, except as a backing vocalist.

Although Reg probably felt that his career as a singer songwriter would be seriously hampered by Baldry they developed a strong mutual respect and Baldry became a mentor for Reg's musical career. By the time Baldry had his hit 'Let the Heartaches Begin', Reg had been introduced to a young upstart from Lincolnshire called Bernard Taupin who could write really good poems. After both Reg and Bernie had answered the advert in *New Musical Express* for 'young talent' for Liberty Records, they were put together by the entrepreneurial Ray Williams and the song writing partnership grew and developed. But first Reg was to be reunited with an acquaintance he had met whilst he was a gopher at Mills Music. Caleb Quaye had been a gopher alongside him but whilst Reg was playing the musician with Bluesology, Caleb was developing a broad career in the music business. As well as being an accomplished guitarist, who Eric Clapton would later claim to be the best guitarist in the world, he was forging a career as an engineer and studio manager at Dick James Music in New Oxford Street. DJM, as it was known, was the home of one of the most successful Tin Pan Alley publishers in the UK. Dick James had the publishing rights for The Beatles songs; but in the ever changing music world the days of sheet music and Tin Pan Alley songs were fast disappearing and the advent of producers, artists and record labels started becoming the focus of the music business. Times were changing and the publishers were being overtaken by independent record labels like Island Records and The Beatles Apple label. DJM started its own studio and then its own label under Dick James son Stephen James who looked to Caleb to use his skills to develop the talent of young musicians who had signed for the new label. Little did the James's know that Caleb was letting young talent use the studios for free late at night; this was where Reg and Bernie were writing their songs and using the musicians and studio around them to practice their art and to turn it into sounds.

Through a quirk of fate those late night sessions not only lead to Reg and Bernie cementing their own musical relationship but it was to provide them with their first contract as songwriters. The DJM offices were situated above a bank and the rule was that if there was going to be any activity in the studio then the banks security guards were to be told about it - one night they weren't. The DJM office manager was disturbed from his sleep and told of the sessions. The next morning he complained to Stephen James about his rude awakening. Caleb was called in to Dick James office and asked to answer for his actions. Having admitted to his sins and fearing his dismissal and the end of his music career, he asked James to listen to the work of two young composers. An angry James agreed. He liked what he heard. He quickly signed the pair as staff songwriters and Caleb was given a reprieve. During the day Reg and Bernie were writing songs to emulate the Tin Pan Alley songwriters of the day but getting nowhere fast. A classic example was 'I Can't Go On Living Without You', which came last of six in *A Song for Europe*, to find the British entry for the Eurovision Song Contest. At night Reg was gigging with Bluesology and then going into the studio to record his own songs.

Eventually the new deal with DJM gave Reg the opportunity to give up his gigging with Bluesology but not before engaging Caleb as guitarist in the band for a final tour with Baldry. It was during that tour that Caleb and Reg planned the future for Reg and Bernie's songs and that was for Reg to record them himself. After all he was an accomplished pianist and could sing. They had little success persuading many other artists to buy the songs and James was beginning to lose faith in his new acquisitions. It was during an arduous journey home from a Bluesology gig that Reg decided to use the name of two of his band mates, Elton Dean and John Baldry to create the stage name Elton John, after Caleb joked that Reg Dwight was an unlikely name for a rock star.

Having completed his commitments with Bluesology, and having found a girlfriend Linda Woodrow, who was now his fiancée, Elton embarked on trying to sell his songs as well as earning money doing session work for other artists: Most notably The Hollies, as well as providing vocals and piano for some budget albums of covers. Despite being in demand for these sessions Elton felt he was going nowhere fast as a staff songwriter writing songs he hated. His songwriting career was not developing as he'd hoped and he didn't want to remain a session musician all his life. He was also having second thoughts about his impending marriage to Linda with whom he and Bernie now lived in North London. The cry for help came when Reg made a pathetic attempt at suicide. He wanted out of his relationship with Linda and out of his contract with DJM. The first was to come during his stag night at the Bag O Nails night club in London where John Baldry, a gay man himself, suggested that Reg was too. Reg went home to Linda and told her the wedding was off, called his stepfather Fred and was home the next morning at Frome Court never to see Linda again. Bernie followed Reg back to Frome Court soon after.

Getting out of the contract was a bit trickier. Despite attempts by Island Records to persuade Dick James to give up on Reg he resisted but things were to change at DJM for the better. Steve Brown was brought in as label manager and he saw massive potential in the Elton John sounding songs. He encouraged Elton and Bernie to write the songs that they wanted to write and then persuaded Dick James to invest in an album, which Brown produced. The album *Empty Sky* had critical acclaim and so did the single 'Lady Samantha'. Neither bothered the UK charts but nevertheless it was a good start.

The breakthrough for Elton John came when Steve Brown introduced him to Paul Buckmaster, who had just completed the arrangements for David Bowie's 'Space Oddity', and who in turn introduced the team to Gus Dudgeon. The idea was to produce an orchestral arrangement for the next album. Until this point Reg had developed a close relationship and friendship with a band called Hookfoot: Roger Pope, Caleb Quaye, Ian Duck and David Glover. Elton would often sit in on Hookfoot gigs where they played some of his songs. They were also the recording band for his demos as well as the iconic Elton John albums and singles: *Empty Sky*, 'Lady Samantha' and then *Tumbleweed Connection* and *Madman Across the Water* before the band moved off to earn its own critical acclaim in the USA. Before that though they were in Trident Studios laying down the demo tracks for the album that was soon to be called *Elton John* that included the classic single 'Your Song' which would launch Elton John to worldwide acclaim.

By now Ray Williams had left Liberty Records and was working for Dick James, and managing Elton. Despite his efforts to promote this newly created masterpiece arranged by Buckmaster and produced by Dudgeon the album did little to impress the British public. During a tour of the UK, which culminated in a washout gig at the Krumlin Festival in Yorkshire, England, Williams managed to secure a short promotional tour in the US which was to start at the Los Angeles Troubadour owned by the entrepreneur Doug Weston. At the same time the word had got to Russ Regan, the head man at UNI Records in America, about this young guy from the UK who had created such a unique album. He duly listened to it and was impressed. The American public were looking for something new and it seemed to Regan that this was it. He put his whole weight behind the Elton John project and signed Elton to a deal with UNI and made sure that the promotional tour was a success. It was. A star was born.

1

The Short
Fuse Arrives

In the spring of 1970, a short time before Elton John's first career
defining US trip, John Reid and Reg Dwight, as he was still known to
his friends, met for the first time. Considering that the pair were to
become one of pop music's most powerful partnerships, the first meeting
wasn't exactly an earth-shattering moment.

David Croker, the label manager for Bell Records at EMI, and Elton
were friends and one day he ushered the singer into Reid's office. The
latter, who performed similar duties to Croker for Motown UK, recalled
that, "There was this very shy guy standing in the doorway, with little
round glasses, wearing a jump suit and a sparkly tee shirt. He was looking
for some American records, so I gave him a couple of singles. He told me
that he had made a record and offered me a copy."

What Reid received was a white label copy of the as yet unreleased
Elton John album. "I put it on the side, and thanked him. We chatted for a
while, and I thought no more of it. About two or three weeks later, I
played it and I thought it was amazing." What surprised Reid most was
how an awkward shy guy had composed and played on such a moving
album. "It was fresh, very good, very different and poignant. At the time,
the combination of orchestral and rock had never been done before. I
always thought 'Your Song' was the single especially as, at the time, my
role with Tamla Motown was choosing songs as singles." Reid, of course,
was right when the single later hit the charts on both sides of the Atlantic
and put the singer firmly on the musical map.

Reid promptly forgot about Reg Dwight after the chance meeting at EMI, but the next meeting was to be different. It would prove to be the start of a long-term partnership on both a personal and professional level that, arguably, became the most significant pairing in the music business since Elvis Presley and Colonel Tom Parker.

"I flew off to Tamla Motown's 10th Anniversary Convention in San Francisco, and we had a riotous time," continued Reid. "Barney Ales [Motown Sales Director at the time] said I could go as long as I wore my kilt. So I went down to Scotch House and got one." This was to be the first time that Reid had visited San Francisco, and only the second time he had been to the States. Not only did he have the thrill of visiting America, he also had the excitement of meeting and mixing with some of the *Motown* stars, something he could only dream about in his dance hall days in Paisley; stars like Diana Ross [who threw a 12th birthday party for Michael Jackson], Smokey Robinson, Marvin Gaye, The Temptations and Berry Gordy, the legendary founder of *Motown*. Reid must have wanted to pinch himself to make sure he really was there at soul music's Mount Olympus.

However, not all was, as it seemed at the bash. It totally surprised Reid to note that even at *Motown* segregation was alive and well with blacks and whites not mixing, except when they were on stage receiving awards or performing their music.

The morning after the party, Reid received a telephone call that would change his life and musical direction forever: "This voice on the other end of the phone said 'Hello it's Reg.' Somewhat miffed, I asked, 'Reg? Reg who?' He replied, 'Reg, Dave Croker's friend'." Reid realised at that point that the caller was a very elated Elton John, who had just finished a gig at the Troubadour club in Los Angeles. "I'm in LA and David said you were going to be in San Francisco but I've just done a gig at the Troubadour and I've had all these great reviews."

Reid believed that Elton had only called him because he had no-one else to speak to about his success. "He told me he was coming to San Francisco to do a gig the following night and would I like to meet up with him? And of course, I agreed. He came and we went to see another gig, and we stayed together during his time in San Francisco and that is where our personal relationship started."

When Reid went home to his native Scotland for his 21st birthday party, Elton stayed on in America to continue his mini-promotional tour and by the time he had returned to the UK Elton John was known across the States and a star was born, essentially from the publicity started by influential music critic Robert Hilburn of the *Los Angeles Times*.

Steve Brown, Elton's musical mentor at Dick James Music (DJM) and friend took up the story: "The second week of the mini tour that launched Elton's career was when Elton met John Reid in San Francisco. He had told me previously that he was gay and I asked him why he thought that. I didn't know anyone who was gay. He said that when he was coming into work on the London Underground every morning he found himself looking at the guy opposite him rather than the girl. I thought that it was a fair indication of the way he was predisposed. At the point when Elton was playing the Troubadour he was wearing a beard. When we were in San Francisco he told me that he had met John Reid, who I had never heard of at the time, who was working for Tamla Motown and he had invited Reg over to see him. Reg asked me whether he should go and I said 'Why not', Elton said, 'Well I think he is gay'. I said 'Well he is probably just inviting you over for a drink or a chat so you should go.' He went and came back the next day without a beard and said 'I definitely am gay'."

"Elton always had his suspicions that he was gay," recalled David Larkham, Elton's friend and Art Director for DJM. And John was probably the sort of person who would not have hidden his gay nature, so Elton and John Reid got together, and to Elton this was a big deal." Not only had Bernie found a new partner Maxine Feibleman that he had met by chance before Elton's gigs at The Troubadour, but so had Elton. Although it was too early for Maxine to fly back to the UK with Bernie, the relationship grew from a distance and by the time Elton went on his second tour of the US later that year, Bernie was smitten, and so, it seemed, was Elton.

John Reid's career had begun when he had headed south to London in the mid to late 1960s after he had studied Marine Engineering at Stowe

College, Glasgow. It was during these teenage student days that he discovered the music of Tamla Motown and decided there and then that he wanted to be involved with the music business and Motown in particular. On the spur of the moment he left Glasgow and his education to try and get a job in music. And it was really down to television producer David Bell who made it happen. It also helped that Bell had known Reid for some years and was, at the time, producing *Juke Box Jury*. Bell thought he would make a good song plugger, even though Reid had never heard of such a job and hadn't a clue what it entailed.

"Bell gave me a list of contacts in record companies and music publishers and I went round for a couple of months just knocking on doors trying to find a job as a plugger," remembered Reid. And then, just before Christmas of 1968, Reid got lucky, and was invited back for a further meeting at Ardmore & Beechwood, who had offices above the HMV shop in London's Oxford Street.

Ardmore & Beechwood was an EMI-owned music publishing company and were the original publishers for the Beatles' songs, which they eventually lost to Dick James because they showed little interest in the Fab Four and even less in the group's first single 'Love Me Do'.

Reid was hired by Ardmore & Beechwood as a song plugger with the grandiose title Head of Exploitation. It was a job title he didn't care much for, not that he was too worried – at least he had got his foot inside the door of the British music business. "I started work straight after Christmas 1968, and I was just thrown into the deep end. I knew nothing about publishing, but they gave me the entire Neil Diamond catalogue to exploit and so I learnt as I went along. As the company was owned by EMI, I frequently used go to their famous offices in Manchester Square and got to know all the people there such as song pluggers who in turn helped me a great deal by taking me to the BBC to get contacts and generally to pick things up quickly." It was something that he enjoyed immensely and clearly had an aptitude for.

After Reid had been with Ardmore & Beechwood for twelve months, EMI bought Keith Prowse Music. This involved a consolidation of accommodation at EMI, which saw Reid and his colleagues move into

Denmark Street and the hustle and bustle of Tin Pan Alley. Reid recalls this period as a very exciting time. He began to learn the rudiments of music publishing alongside his newfound skills as a plugger from Jimmy Phillips, who had his own music publishing set up called Peter Maurice Music. Phillips had found Tommy Steele and writer Lionel Bart in a long and illustrious Denmark Street career. "Jimmy was in his eighties then and still went into his offices. He taught me a lot about the world of publishing and I had a great time in Tin Pan Alley."

Reid also got to know the writers in Tin Pan Alley, and how the whole world of publishing worked. "Being in the promotions end of the business, there were very few avenues to promote, so I used to go round the pubs and clubs and I managed to get a key for the juke boxes and put my records on them. It was not really hard graft and there was no payola despite what is often said, although it did go on later on during the seventies. But the business back then was very small and the outlets for promotion were very narrow and you had to fight your corner and find your own contacts and outlets. Getting in with the radio producers and DJs, like Tony Blackburn, was all part and parcel of it. I was given a £25 per month expense account to wine and dine all these music business people in the best restaurants in London, and you could do it with that sum back then. This was a real eye opener for a young man from Scotland," smiles Reid.

Not that his *modus operandi* always met with the approval of his staid employers at EMI. "I took my holidays at Christmas one year, and got a 'bucket ticket' to New York and went to meet a music publisher, whose catalogue I dealt with for Ardmore & Beechwood. EMI didn't want me to go, so it led to a big bust up with L.G. Wood [EMI Managing Director]. I wined and dined the publisher and when I got back to the UK and put my expenses claim in for about $40 Wood refused to sign it." Not that it mattered as Reid thought there would come a time when he would get it back. And he did, eight years after he had formed Rocket Records with Elton. It was during a deal he was setting up with EMI; he refused to sign anything until he received his long-lost expenses from 1968. Needless to say, he received them!

Reid though, still had his sights on Tamla Motown and so when the

5

label manager's role became vacant he decided to apply for it at the tender age of 18. Deciding that Reid was too young for such an important role, Motown gave the job to someone else. Disappointed but not downhearted, Reid continued his work as a plugger and built up his contact book which by now included Barney Ales at Motown, who were distributed by EMI. Six months after accepting the job at Motown, the label manager left leaving the position vacant once again. "I got to know Barney Ales very well, and he said to the recruiters 'Give it to John Reid'; this was an order not a request! And so I landed my dream job when I was just 19, and having only been in the business for a year at the most."

Having received his letter from Roy Featherstone, EMI's Director of Repertoire, offering him the job as Head of Tamla Motown UK on the heady salary of £1,607 a year, Reid went off to make his mark with the label. "At Motown, there were hits 'coming off the walls'. Every Tuesday I'd go to the EMI label managers' meeting, and we'd sit and play the up-and-coming releases, and discuss what we could do with them. It was a great training ground."

Most of the material that Reid got hold of was from America. He was tasked with scheduling the UK release date, organising the promotion, and was generally head cook and bottle washer as it was essentially him and a shared secretary who were responsible for the whole of Tamla Motown UK. All of the American Motown artists – such as Diana Ross and Stevie Wonder – were coming in at the time trying to break the UK, and Reid was their main point of contact when they arrived.

Being as starstruck as he was, Reid thought he had died and gone to heaven. After all, these were his idols and now he was promoting them. He would spend most of his time attending gigs and organising promotional appearances on programmes like *Top Of The Pops,* as well as his daily trawl of the artists' repertoire looking for that elusive hit single.

One of the artists who Reid promoted in his early days at Motown was Smokey Robinson who, at the time, hadn't had a hit for some time. "I was listening to an old Smokey album and I came across 'Tears Of A Clown' and I thought it would make a good single, and so I scheduled it for release and out it went. Because I didn't ask anyone, I got an irate call from

Motown in Detroit asking me who gave me permission to release it, and I told them that no-one said I couldn't, so I did, and, by the way - it's No.1."

Reid was eventually congratulated by Berry Gordy himself and his star was in the ascendency at Tamla Motown on both sides of the Atlantic. Reid continued in his role at Motown, and didn't really have any interest or exposure to the business end of the music industry until he became a manager, and his first client in that role was Reg, soon-to-be Elton John - superstar.

"When he came back to the UK we got together again and the first time I saw him perform was at a DJM album launch for *Tumbleweed Connection* at the Revolution Club," remembered Reid. "It was a typical lunchtime launch, which consisted of a short gig, with Nigel and Dee, and a reception of wine, beer and crisps." All the same and despite his position at Motown, here Reid was the new boy on the block; he hadn't met Dee and Nigel, or Steve Brown, and in fact, he hadn't met anyone from DJM.

"I saw him play the piano and he was doing handstands on it, and I just couldn't get my head around this guy. He had this *Elton John* album out which gave the impression of a sombre piano player and singer, but he was such an outrageous performer on stage. And yet, he was such a shy person, but as soon as he got on the piano he was a complete lunatic." But the launch wasn't the only time he watched Elton perform live in those early days of their relationship. "I went to see him play at the Albert Hall supporting Fotheringay, and after that, I met his mother and stepdad and of course, Bernie."

During the early days of his personal relationship with Elton, Reid continued working for EMI and Motown. He was also seeing more and more of Elton; so much so that they decided to move in together in an exclusive apartment off the Edgware Road, London known as the Water Gardens. However, being 23, and with no credit record of his own to speak of, Elton was turned down for a mortgage. Being quite miffed about it, James got Geoffrey Ellis to sort it out with an estate agent he was friendly with, and in no time at all, the flat was his.

At the same time, Dick James had parted company with Elton's former manager Ray Williams on less than amicable terms, and Elton was now relying on DJM's Steve Brown to be his manager and mentor. The problem was that Brown had a young family and didn't really want to be out on the road all the time in addition to managing DJM's new record label. The task of managing Elton's career, which had exploded overnight, was a full time job in itself.

♪

Steve Brown was always interested in music. "My parents were very religious and I was not allowed to listen to pop music but just classical music so I used to do what a lot of kids did then and listen to Radio Luxembourg under the sheets at night time." The first song he was allowed to listen to was 'Mary's Boy Child' by the Beverley Sisters. "I just about got away with that as long as I didn't play it too loudly: it was just about acceptable to my parents" joked Brown. But he really wanted to hear pop music and so he went to see Ray Charles at the Hammersmith Odeon having bought his EP. Charles was relatively unknown at the time in the UK. "I was about 17 years old and I came out and thought I had seen God. He completely changed my life. It was like a religious conversion I just couldn't believe what I had seen. I just wanted to be part of that; it was what I wanted to do."

When Brown left school he got a job in Potters music shop selling records. He then learnt to play the saxophone and played with Emile Ford and the Checkmates with whom he toured across Scandinavia for 6 to 9 months. "When the tour finished I decided I wasn't a musician; as much as I wanted to be it was not really what I was cut out to do." Brown had some contacts at the BBC and got to know some radio producers and through them he ended up with a job at EMI as a plugger. "I was shy so I didn't really suit that job but because of my friendships at the BBC I did fairly well." Brown had, by then, built up friendships with half a dozen DJs and producers and eventually got a job at DJM having been involved with the promotion of The Beatles at EMI. "It wasn't that difficult to promote The Beatles at the BBC so I had it easy," he joked. His job at Dick James Music was to promote the songs in his publishing repertoire but essentially doing the same job as he did at EMI.

Elton John and Bernie Taupin used to go into the DJM Studio most days but they didn't have any songs published by Dick James so Brown had no reason to have any contact with them as his job was to promote the songs being published by Dick James. "We used to chat about music and that, but I had nothing to do with them creatively at that time. I knew they had written a song called 'Skyline Pigeon' that had been covered by Roger Cooke and had done well but that was the extent of my knowledge."

Steve Brown's creative input first started when, for no reason at all, Bernie approached Brown and announced that he and Reg had made an album called *Sergeant Zippo,* which had been produced by Zack Lawrence who was a staff producer and arranger at the Dick James studios. "They asked me if I wanted to hear it; I said sure and I went into the studio. He gave me the album and asked me what I thought. I said it was not my cup of tea. It was nice and it was good but it's not the sort of music I would listen to so I was not the right person to judge. Reg went off and sulked and was very pissed off at me at this point. Eventually after a few days he came back and said to 'okay so what should I be doing; what sort of music should I be writing.' I said 'listen there is nothing wrong with it, it's pop music but it's not my taste.'" Brown had noticed that it was not much different to the poppy tunes being written by the other Tin Pan Alley writers of the day and it was not the sort of music he was listening to. "I reminded Elton that when we had talked previously the sort of music we discussed was Pink Floyd, Leonard Cohen and The Beatles. So I said that none of that was reflected in his song writing. I said it was strange as he was writing pop, but he was listening to and liked something entirely different."

When Brown first met Elton he was trying to write songs for other people. Just like most Tin Pan Alley songwriters of the time these were poppy songs with memorable tunes. The Rolling Stones, The Kinks and The Beatles were writing their own songs and these songs were becoming contemporary. The songs that were emerging were not 'whistle along to' songs but they had more depth to them and Brown's aim for Elton was to get him to rethink this aspect of his career.

Elton went away and came back with a totally new set of songs, which reflected what he liked and Brown was completely blown away. "Elton then said what do we do now? So I said we should record them." At that point in his career Elton didn't see himself as a recording artist but as a songwriter and it was possibly to do with the way he looked. "He wasn't Elvis Presley that's for sure," laughed Brown. "I said I quite liked a song he had written called 'Lady Samantha' but Elton said that Zack Lawrence wasn't the right person to produce it." Brown offered to do it having never been into a studio in his life. They all went into a little Dick James recording 4-track studio and started working. "I remember we finished the track quite late at night. By this time we had become very close friends and when I asked him what he thought he simply smiled at me and said 'as a producer you probably make a very good manager!' and I said, 'Okay'" laughed Brown. "But I quite liked my first effort and he did too but he wasn't quite sure of the end result." Brown suggested Elton searched for another producer. However on his way out he bumped into Tony King, a close friend of Larry Page, who owned the record label Page One - which was loosely a part of the Dick James Music Empire - and he played 'Lady Samantha' to him. Tony said it was a great record and he should release it. "So Elton decided it wasn't that bad after all and decided to release it," laughed Brown.

As a result of his past few jobs in the music business Brown knew all the DJ's and producers; "I pulled in all the favours I could, Tony Blackburn played it to death and so did John Peel," explained Brown. The song became a huge turntable hit but hardly sold anything. "We went off and released another song called 'It's Me That You Need' which didn't do much better either," said Brown in amusement. Elton still persevered with Brown producing. Brown was prepared to try one last time to get his protégé a hit record. So they embarked on an ambitious project to record an album. "We stayed up all night every night for a week and recorded *Empty Sky*, which was great fun," recalled Brown. "My Father worked for the Salvation Army and we would go back there after sessions and Elton would sleep on the floor of the flat in Oxford Street, or we would go to the Golden Egg Cafe at one or two in the morning, because it was the only place open. We'd have breakfast or whatever meal it was." Although Brown didn't have any production knowledge he tried to do what he could with the limited knowledge he had but using his creative imagination. "On 'Skyline Pigeon' I couldn't get the voice sound I wanted or was happy with so I ended up recording it on the fire escape by the studio," he explained. "Because of the echo from the concrete on the fire escape it created the sound that I wanted. We knew that the facilities in the studio were very limited; I remember that if we wanted to do a harmony or a double track then Elton would have to sing live with the mix so if he messed up or we got the levels wrong he would have to go back into the studio and sing live again."

The album was completed and released and everyone who created it was happy with the results including Brown and Elton. "Dick James was also pleased and he sent it to Russ Regan at MCA in America" enthused Brown. "Russ said he liked it and that he would release it in America". The album didn't see the light of day in America for some years after Elton John became a success but it was released in the UK and, like 'Lady Samantha' received a lot of airplay but few record sales.

Soon after *Empty Sky* was completed, Elton went back into DJM to see Brown with another batch of songs written with Bernie and asked Brown whether he would like to hear them. "I recall there were four songs and one of them was 'Your Song', so I was probably one of the first people to hear that song being played for the first time other than Bernie," he proudly stated. "I really liked it and I said to Elton, look *Empty Sky* hasn't done well but you should continue and record 'Your Song'. I will produce it if you want me too as I am sure the song will be a great success." Brown told him that if it didn't work out then Elton should find another producer. "Reg said that he was happy with what I was doing and was prepared to let me produce 'Your Song'. I decided I wanted to use strings and an original string arrangement. I had heard David Bowie's 'Space Oddity' and I really liked the string arrangement on that. I got in touch with Paul Buckmaster I asked him whether he would consider doing the strings; he said he'd consider it so I sent him some demos." Buckmaster liked them and so he went into Brown's DJM office and told him he would do the arrangements. "Paul said he really liked the song and some of the others as well so I played him even more songs most of which eventually appeared on the *Elton John* and *Madman Across the Water* albums, as they were all written at about the same time."

"Paul said that the songs were incredible and we really had a good thing going here and we should do more than two tracks, he said he thought that we should have an orchestra and brass and tympani and arrange and record at least half a dozen songs. I told Elton that I was really out of my depth and didn't feel confident to produce this complicated piece of work that Paul was suggesting." To put things into perspective, Brown had completed *Empty Sky* in a studio with limited scope on a budget of £400 and now they were looking at booking an orchestra and another bigger, more technically equipped studio. "I told Elton that he should look at getting a new producer and he reluctantly agreed. I went back to Paul and asked him if he could recommend one." Buckmaster had worked with many excellent producers but he recommended Gus Dudgeon with whom he had worked with on 'Space Oddity'. "I set up a meeting with Gus and played him some of the demos. He said he was interested so, we arranged a second meeting. I took along Elton and Bernie. I remember it well because I recall going to meet Gus initially and introducing Elton and Bernie; he was pleased with what he had heard and got on well with them both. I arranged a further meeting but Gus hadn't worked out which one was Bernie and which was Elton which caused a bit of upset but it was soon laughed off." With the new team of Brown, Buckmaster, Dudgeon, Elton and Bernie they set out to make the album. "Gus had a bit of a successful track record so we went to Dick (James) and to his credit he said he would back it and put his money behind it," explained Brown. "At the time Elton was an unknown artist and didn't really look like a rock or pop star, so it was a bit of a risk. The team booked Trident Studios and made the album with Brown taking the role of creative director instead of producer. "We planned it in meticulous detail as we only had a limited budget" recalled Brown. "We did two tracks every day for three hours each a day until they were completed."

When they finished the album they all knew it was something special. "We obviously didn't expect Elton's career to develop the way it did but we all agreed it wasn't just another pop record." When the album was finished it was sent off to the guys in America who got very excited and asked Elton to go over to play on a mini tour organised by Russ Regan and his PR guru Norman Winter. "At this point, he had only played to about

50 to 100 people in small club venues. He was trying out his own songs and people weren't and still aren't for that matter, used to listening to new material."

Brown's married life was frequently interrupted by Elton and Bernie, who would visit his marital home to socialise and talk music and Brown became a close friend and musical mentor to Elton at DJM. "Elton and Bernie used to come down to my house with a bottle of Mateus Rose wine and a box of After Eight mints," laughed Brown. "We would spend all our time together at the office and he would call me on the telephone every night and that went on for years. We couldn't have been closer. His only other friend was Bernie. He had other acquaintances but we were real friends all day every day. Our shared love of the same type of music and other interests in common brought us together and we were both very committed to his talent. When he developed his writing I suddenly realised it was something exceptional and he wasn't just another songwriter."

♫

Although Dick James held the management, publishing and recording contracts for Elton John, he was also aware that, sooner or later, something was going to have to give, so he decided to separate out the management contract. That's when Elton approached Reid and asked, "Why don't you come and work for Dick and when the contract has expired come and take over?"

Initially, Reid agreed, although he knew he had no experience of managing an artist, and it was very clear that if Elton's career kept growing exponentially he would need to hit the ground running. The other issue that Elton probably hadn't considered was whether or not Reid actually wanted to jump ship at EMI. Reid had, by now, become friendly with the Chairman, Joseph Lockwood, and he, together with Barney Ales and Berry Gordy, had big plans for the young Scot.

"They had given me a chance and I was really enjoying what I was doing," recalled Reid. "Reluctantly, and with some trepidation as to where the Elton John thing was going, I gave my notice into EMI and then all hell broke loose. I got a real bollocking from Barney, so I withdrew my resignation." Elton was obviously upset to hear that news, and soon after his mother, Sheila, went to see Reid, to persuade him to reconsider withdrawing the withdrawal request. "She said: At the time, Elton and Reid were becoming incredibly close and so it created a huge dilemma for everyone concerned. Reid recalled how Elton said "He was going back to LA in a couple of weeks' time to interview some managers, and invited me to go with him." They both went to LA, just two months after returning from San Francisco, and suddenly everything for them was like a whirlwind; all the breakneck speed changes that were happening.

"I went with Elton to all these meetings with possible managers, and I don't know what they thought my role was, and nor did I, but we came out thinking 'These guys are not right.' Elton John is English and based in the UK and these managers are in LA. Yes they were throwing everything at him but he needed a UK-based manager." At the end of the meetings, Elton told Reid that there was no one he liked, and again asked him to take on the role. Being in an almost impossible situation, given their personal relationship, Reid once again agreed to manage Elton, though he still had reservations. However, it had to be strictly on Reid's terms.

"I took a deep breath, and went to see Dick James, and thought 'I know how I can get out of this.' So Dick and I went through all the deal and then we got to salary. I was making £1,607 a year, and Roy Featherstone was making about £3,000. So I said to Dick, 'I want £6,000 a year', and much to my shock he agreed straight away. This was my only way out and I had called his bluff and it had backfired."

At this point, Reid knew that he had painted himself into a corner and was now going to have to live with it. "Salary was my big out and Dick called my bluff and that's how we kicked off. From that experience, I learnt that you could never start negotiations too high." It was a weapon that Reid, later on in his career when he was negotiating multi-million pound contract deals with record companies, learned to deploy with significant success.

From the start, Reid and James got on well and, to this day, Reid credits James as being a great tutor when it came to learning about the management side of the music business, which complemented his experiences with *Motown* and EMI. "James described the job to me, and then left me alone to get on with it. He trusted me and he was magnanimous. He knew what was going to happen, that I was going to take the management contract, and that I was going to learn the ropes and then go off and be his adversary, which is what I became. He was a very nice man. Straightforward, good to work for, but he was also a very old fashioned publisher who had created a happy place to work, everyone mucked in and it was like a little cottage industry. When we formed Rocket, we wanted to continue in that same way, which is why we took people like Geoffrey Ellis and Maureen Hillier with us."

"I was supposed to be with Dick James for a year, but I actually stayed just six months. It was clear that I had to leave and take over. I had no money at the time and no business experience, but I had to set up an office and make the transition. I had to borrow money and I don't think I actually slept for a year. I must have read all of Elton John's contracts about 50 times to get used to them, having not read a contract before." Reid formed his own management company, John Reid Enterprises, which in the future would become successful in its own right.

♪

Publicist Tony King had known John Reid before he met Elton. "When Elton started to get successful, after his shows in LA and San Francisco, I was at the BBC one day, and I met John Reid, who said 'I met a friend of yours the other day: Elton.' I asked him where he was when he met him, and he told me he had been in San Francisco where Elton was doing his shows." Reid also told King that he was going to get involved in Elton's career from now on. And later, when Elton called King, he said "I hear you ran into John, and confirmed that he would be working with him on his career. That was really when we started to get close again because John very quickly became his manager. I don't think Dick James was too thrilled with it because Dick thought that he might be more influential in that department, but John had bigger ideas."

According to King, Reid was an amazing go-getter, a terrier of a person, "But he had a very endearing personality, and was very funny with a great deal of ambition. I could see the extent of Elton's ambition, and so when I saw them together, in a business sense, I thought they were a match made in heaven. It didn't end up that way, of course, but it lasted a long time and Reid and Elton did some great things together. Elton would have the ideas and John would make them happen; in fact John made it happen for Elton. He was infuriating, he was bolshie and he could be very disruptive, and you could never quite know whether to trust him, but his ambition was total and dedicated."

What Reid did not expect was how difficult he would find it in getting to know everyone at DJM. Just as Colonel Tom Parker didn't get involved with Elvis Presley's creative process, neither did Reid. The musical aspect of Elton's career was his own. That, however, didn't stop Reid attending recording sessions, something that Colonel Parker was said not to do.

"The first recording session I went to was for the *Madman Across The Water* album, and that is when I met Paul Buckmaster; and the others. For a couple of years, I had a slightly difficult time, because I was the last one in and it took a while for them to fully accept me, especially Steve Brown. What was also different was that Gus was with his wife Sheila, and Steve Brown and his wife Jill, and I was with Elton. They all accepted the gay relationship but it was different. Everyone knew we were gay and in a relationship, and we thought it was funny that it took so long for it to become public. Even Dick James accepted it, and took the view that at least I could get him up in the mornings being his manager and his partner."

Whenever Elton and John Reid were not busy recording, touring or attending one of the many business meetings that surrounded his new-found stardom, they were settled in their new flat. "You pressed a button to call the flat and, when you were greeted, a lift was sent down to collect you which was carpeted and very nice. It took you directly into the flat like an extension of the front door," recalled Mick Inkpen a friend of Elton and Bernie and drummer in the band Bluesology.

"My wife and I had been married a while, and Elton had moved out of Frome Court where he and Bernie had been living with Elton's mother Sheila and his stepfather Fred Farebrother. He was now very busy and we didn't see much of him and Bernie. He called me and told me he was living in a flat at the Water Gardens, Edgware Road near Marble Arch. I wasn't told who owned the flat, but it became clear that he and John Reid had set up home together. We were invited to see the place. It was quite small, but nicely furnished with modern furniture of the day. There was a piano, of course, and Elton told me that only a few days before he had Neil Young round and he had played on that very instrument."

The completion of the *Elton John* album and the subsequent success of Elton John in America, following the Troubadour gigs and the final Philadelphia gig, secured the reputations of Dudgeon and Buckmaster alongside Bernie Taupin, and of course the man himself, as the creators of the Elton John sound. The final piece of the jigsaw John Reid, was now in place and he was ready, willing and able to take it to the next level.

2

The Times They Are 'A-Changin'

By the end of 1973 the independent record company was the focus of the British music business. Included in the distinguished list were Island Records, Virgin, Chrysalis, A&M and Dick James Music, who had an array of other acts apart from Elton. The Independents were a vibrant part of the business. DJM was to start with, very successful and doing a variety of things, even making movies, and was probably one of the leading independents of its time. One of its legal team was David Hockman who would later join PolyGram and later still Sony Music and be one of the leading executives to change the music business once again in the late seventies and into the eighties when corporate entities and venture capitalists started to see music as a commodity to be traded on the stock market.

But before all that Hockman was working for Dick James and spent most of his time writing contracts for Stephen James who was signing many artists and singer songwriters like Blackfoot Sue, Johnny Guitar Watson, Helen Shapiro and a host of others in the quest to find a replacement for Elton John as the next major artist. "I remember Stephen being very disappointed that he didn't sign Guys 'n' Dolls, a popular boy/girl band formed in 1974 in the UK; even though he had signed the songwriters Chris Arnold, David Martin & Geoff Morrow to publishing who had written the band's first mega hit. The master recording of the song 'Whole Lot of Loving' went to Michael Levy at another independent, Magnet Records and turned into a big hit and there was a lot of angst about that."

Dick James Music had by now turned into a record company rather than just a publisher. James had the foresight to see the times changing so he established the recording arm of the DJM business in 1969 and set up a studio out of disused offices in New Oxford Street. He handed the record company over to his son Stephen to run, much the same as Island and half a dozen other independents of the day had done. However Dick James was a music man and not the sort of swashbuckling entrepreneur that was beginning to emerge onto the music business scene in the guise of the charismatic Richard Branson who formed Virgin Records in 1972. The company eventually became a multi-million dollar enterprise due to Branson's ability to take risks having started as a record retail outfit in Notting Hill Gate, London. Virgin signed a multitude of artists to the label; starting with Mike Oldfield whose album *Tubular Bells* was an instant success and was arguably the cornerstone to Virgin's venture into the music business. To demonstrate Branson's eye for a deal he, much later in the history of Virgin, took a risk and signed The Sex Pistols in 1975, when both A&M and EMI had abandoned the Punk act for being too controversial. Branson allegedly thought Virgin was beginning to lose its edge as a leading progressive independent record label and therefore needed another 'string to its bow.' The gamble paid off and Virgin became the home of punk and post punk bands.

In contrast to Virgin, after Elton had left DJM, it was difficult for the label to adjust to not having a major act. Dick had signed Elton just after he had sold the Beatles, so he was used to having major acts. When Elton left the label shrank back. Dick James just didn't have the same temperament as a Richard Branson and even though he was a very successful businessman he just didn't want to put it all at risk.

Elton's contract with Dick James expired just before David Hockman started with the company in 1973 and his first music copyright was the B-side of 'Step into Christmas' which was the Christmas 1973 release and a song called 'Ho, Ho, Ho, (Who'd Be A Turkey at Christmas)'. It was a split copyright between Dick James and Rocket Music, formed by Elton. The record contract went on for a couple more years until 1975 with the last album being *Rock of the Westies* and Elton then signed for EMI Records. "Elton did talk to Stephen and Dick James about extending the contract but in the final event I think they had outgrown each other. But Dick James had all these lucrative Elton John songs written under contract to Dick James Music," explained Hockman.

The measure of Dick James success was when in 1973, 1976, and 1977 the company was presented with the unique honour of receiving the Queen's Award to Industry for Export Achievement. No other company wholly involved in Pop Music and Records had ever won any such award, let alone three times. However according to Hockman this was as much an honour for Elton John as it was for Dick James: "I suspect that the largest amount of credit for that must go to Elton John." Hockman had a good case for this assumption. In 1971/1972 Elton John and DJM received five gold albums each of which represented more than one million dollars worth of sales in the U.S.A. alone, and a platinum disc for one million sales worldwide of the single 'Rocket Man'. In the U.K. two gold records were awarded for 100,000 sales of the single 'Crocodile Rock'and 'Daniel'. His single 'Daniel' passed the million mark worldwide. The 1974 album *Elton John Greatest Hits* sold over six million in the U.S.A. alone. "I think though that without the investment that Dick made in Elton John then there is a likelihood that Elton John would not have happened. Without Dick James there would not have been an Elton John but there would not have been the same longevity without John Reid. I believe that John was certainly responsible for the longevity and Dick and Stephen were responsible for the launch of Elton John," summised Hockman.

What was also evident from 1975 onwards was that the power pendulum in the music business had changed from the companies to the artists and the writers who owned their own songs. "They didn't own their own masters, they could never control those, and that was a changing world that Dick didn't adapt to but others did," explained David Hockman. The master is the record that was actually recorded and released; the songs are what the publisher put out. "So if you were a songwriter writing a song for say, Frank Sinatra: that was one product, the song; Frank would then record it and the recording was a separate product, the master. When The Beatles came on the scene, the two products merged; if you were a singer songwriter then you had two income streams, publishing and records or masters with the recording being the more lucrative. Someone like Paul McCartney sees himself as a songwriter and his songs are his babies, but then he sees himself as a performer and last of all he sees himself as a recording artist. In fact most singer songwriters would probably say that their songs are the most important part of what they create although they used to make more money from records."

The singer songwriters 'saw off' the small publisher from Tin Pan Alley in Denmark Street as there was no longer the need for a separate publisher to take a song and plug it and get someone else to record it. Much the same as the art of plugging started to die out, a song was no longer a big deal. For instance, there was little point in being a plugger for The Beatles at Northern Songs, after all the company was established for The Beatles songs sung by The Beatles. You didn't need pluggers to go out and get songs for the Beatles or even persuade other artists to record their songs. Hockman suggested that, "When the Independents came along the focus was a one act company in some cases. Certainly when Elton John's label, Rocket Records started it was obviously a one act company and then they signed other artists to the label. However, not much input was credited to the publishing side of the business because they hadn't signed any writers."

It was different for the likes of Island and A&M because they were fully functioning publishing companies as well as record companies even though not all the artists were signed exclusively to both publishing and recording. Hockman agree's; "When you get to the recent super star acts very few of them have set up their own labels. They are huge singer songwriters but they never felt the urge to set up their own labels in the way Elton did with Rocket, and The Beatles did with Apple, and to a lesser extent with Northern Songs."

♪

Denmark Street was to the music business in London as the Brill Building was to the same business in New York; everyone knew each other and the music business was a very small world. Songwriters were hustling to sell a song to a publisher for sheet music for a few pounds to pay the rent at the end of the week and it was still commonplace up to the end of the sixties. Whereas the songwriters would walk the short streets and thoroughfares of Denmark Street in and out of publishers' offices hawking round songs, at the Brill Building the songwriters were sitting in cubicles writing songs all day. The singer songwriter changed all of that. The exception today is Nashville where songwriting is still a 'nine to five' job.

"This method of writing worked for a long period of time but eventually the time came and went. You rarely get people sitting in cubicles writing songs now. In Nashville songs and songwriters come first and the recording act and record company come a long way second. The writers treat it as a job, not in the same way as The Brill Building where it was achieved by creative impulse, but in Nashville it really is more like a job. A writer would show up for work at 10.00am, go out to lunch, go back to work and if they hadn't written three or four songs by the end of the day they had failed and could lose their job." This was certainly the view of Jim Cregan who was a prolific songwriter for Rod Stewart in the late seventies and worked a stint as a songwriter in Nashville.

Although the music world changed, the sense of camaraderie was still around once Tin Pan Alley and the Brill Building songwriters disappeared but it just wasn't evident in one place. Hockman explains; "It came out during events like the Ivor Novello Awards and PPA meetings. There was still that sense of camaraderie amongst many publishers and writers but it was later on, when all the Independents started to get hoovered up, by the major corporate music businesses and that was when things really started to change."

♫

The songwriters who were plying their trade up and down Denmark Street in the sixties to try and sell a song to a publisher were now, in the seventies, left to find an outlet for their creative talent. Songwriters like Bill Martin went on to form his own publishing company with his writing partner Phil Coulter called Martin-Coulter Publishing as well as finding artists to write for. Martin made a significant impact on the music business in the early to mid-seventies with both his song-writing and producing success for the Scottish teen sensations the Bay City Rollers who were billed the next best thing since The Beatles. He also wrote 'My Boy' for Elvis Presley, which was to be the King's last top 20 hit before his untimely death in 1977. Martin's shrewd business skills led to significant success for Martin-Coulter Publishing which built up a heavyweight catalogue which included songs written by Van Morrison, Billy Connolly, Sky and Midge Ure to name a few; as well as the entire catalogue of East/Memphis Music.

Roger Cooke and Roger Greenaway were prised away from Mills Music in Denmark Street by George Martin for his Associated Independent Recording (AIR) production and recording company for their back catalogue, but to also write songs for bands like White Plains, The Pipkins, Blue Mink, Congregation, (featuring Brian Keith from Plastic Penny) and David and Jonathan that were put together specifically to play and sing Greenaway and Cooke songs with some considerable success. The pair also had significant success with AIR on the production side working with such artists as Twiggy. According to Harry Barter, who was a Director managing the publishing side of the business and was a good friend of Cooke and Greenaway, there was an eclectic mix of people signed to AIR from barrow boys to public school boys - and they were all managed by Cooke and Greenaway at one time or another. Even Elton John was nearly prised away from Dick James Music by John Burgess, co-founder of AIR with George Martin after they had both left successful careers at EMI. According to Barter, even though AIR didn't sign Elton John he was very affectionate towards John Burgess as they had worked together before when Elton was a session musician, playing piano and providing backing vocals for AIR artists such as The Hollies and even Roger Cooke. AIR had wanted to sign him but DJM got there before them. Barter remembered when Roger Cooke first decided to use Elton's 'Skyline Pigeon' as a single, "Roger Cooke gave me an acetate demo copy with Elton singing it. We all knew that Elton was a special talent so we covered it. Subsequently, when the song became a hit, Elton went to the Colston Hall in Bristol and played the piano when Roger did it live and he slept on Mrs Cooke's settee in Bristol after he had backed Roger that night."

Like most independent record companies in the seventies AIR had its own studio where AIR artists and others like Bryan Ferry would record either their own songs or songs penned by songwriters from the AIR stable. Barter was responsible for the catalogues of many of the songwriters signed to the Company. "I was responsible for AIR Publishing. I had Mike Hazelwood, Roger Cook and Roger Greenaway, Albert Hammond and Alan Clarke (The Hollies), catalogues and my job was to get covers and get them played on the radio."

During the early seventies the music power base shifted again from the artists and publishers to the radio stations and the disc jockeys (DJ's) who could make or break an artist or a song. According to Barter in those days all the DJ's in the UK were stars; Dave Lee Travis (DLT), Paul Burnett, Johnnie Walker, Peter Powell were all bigger than some of the one hit wonders put together. If you could get a song played on the radio by one of these guys then it would really sell the song to the record buying public. "I remember going to a gig with DLT and it was manic; I also went to a gig with Johnnie Walker and women just threw themselves at him, he was a heartthrob. I remember going to a gig with Annie Nightingale, she just put the record on and people would be screaming, she was a star in her own right." The plugger's job was to be the friend of the radio producer and the DJ. "Even though I was good friends with Johnnie Walker, and he lived across the road from me, if he didn't like the song I was plugging he wouldn't play it and he would never change his mind; John Peel was much the same. John Peel had a slightly different approach as he didn't need a plugger to sell him a song, he would go in search of songs himself and if he found something he would play it if he liked it."

If you couldn't get your song to the radio stations then there was little hope that either the song or artists would get a hit despite its quality. Getting a song played on the major radio stations like the BBC was difficult and there was little hope of a song reaching the playlist unless it had made some impact on the music shops across the country. "Distribution was vital for the independent record companies" recalled Barter, "and in the early seventies the smaller independents had access to equally small distributing companies who could get records in the shops. Towards the end of the seventies the smaller distributors started to be bought up by the corporates so the smaller independent record companies struggled to compete to get their releases into the shops. Without unlimited funds to pay distributors for promotion and marketing and the strike force to get it into the shops the small independent record companies had difficulty plugging records into the radio stations because they had not achieved enough sales for it to chart or at least chart well enough to be of interest to the radio producer. As a result the independent record labels were swallowed up by the large corporates or simply went bust."

A lot of small labels and the 'one man bands' folded before they could build a decent catalogue well enough for them to be an interest to the corporates. "When you owned a small label that was going bust then you had to go down honourably and make sure you paid the artists because it was easy to lose your name in the business if you didn't and your name is all you had left to trade on. If you were known as an honest person then you had a chance to recover, but if you are a corporate it didn't matter as there was no personal identity."

♫

The corporatisation of the music business came when other large businesses who could, for instance, be an electronics company whose Board of Directors is 10,000 miles away from the UK and had little or no footprint in the music business but had decided music publishing was a good income stream. "You are now in a position today where you have got publishers owning 2-3 million copyrights each and with the best will in the world no-one ever dreamt 30/40 years ago that this would have been the case," described Hockman. These corporates expanded the music-publishing base of the business by acquisition, cost saving and growth by employing a significant number of song pluggers who went out in search of new songs.

In 1975 Hockman joined PolyGram, a so called corporate, and the future of the music business in the UK suddenly became clear to him: "I remember going to a conference in Amsterdam and the Head of EMI and the Head of Polygram were there presenting. The Head of EMI said then that he could predict a time when there would only be a handful of 8 or 9 music companies left. His words were met with complete uproar and everyone said it just wasn't true. The audience truly believed that all the energy and vitality came from the Independent sectors and the big companies were considered as vultures that were preying on this creative part of the business." Despite the uproar caused by the comments, the Head of EMI was right.

PolyGram was on the verge of going bankrupt. It had decided to diversify into the movie business and invested heavily. The investment paid off and the company received much acclaim for the success of *Saturday Night Fever* and *Grease*. However the consequence was that the Company did not, it seems, get the financial returns on the investment it needed. "Unfortunately they lost a fortune." recalled Hockman. PolyGram was owned 50/50 between Philips and Siemens and the Siemens Board decided it had enough of bank rolling the losses and wanted out. The only asset that Philips could easily and quickly sell was Chappell, which was PolyGram's publishing operation. So Chappell was sold in 1984/1985. "Because I was the last person left in PolyGram who knew anything about publishing I was asked to set up it's publishing business; I did and in 1986 the first acquisition I made was Dick James Music. I did the deal with Stephen James as Dick had died earlier that year after a long legal battle with Elton John." The essence of the case was focussed on the financial arrangements in the early contracts signed by Elton John before he became a multi-million dollar asset and whether James had knowingly disadvantaged Elton in the arrangements. A report in the Pace International Law Review Volume 8 Issue 1 Winter 1996 (Freedom: Long Term Recording Agreements and the International Music Industry - Karl Zucconi) explained that '*Elton John and Bernie Taupin were minors when they signed an agreement with Dick James Music. After Elton John became a popular recording artist, James sought to renegotiate all of the existing contracts and told John that he wanted him to be represented by legal counsel in future music dealings. Because of this renegotiation, John and Taupin sued DJM on the basis of undue influence, claiming that the publishing agreements should be set aside. The Chancery Court held that the James and DJM were fiduciaries* (trustees). *Thus, the court allowed DJM to retain a percentage of the profits, without ordering the return of copyrights nor the delivery of master recordings*'. (Elton Hercules John v. Richard Leon James; High Court of Justice, Chancery Division, 1982 J.

No. 15026 (November. 29, 1985)).

Dick James died in February 1986 of a heart attack at age 65 and Stephen James claims to this day that the stress of the Court case took its toll on his Father and he never really recovered.

Later the same year James junior decided it was time to draw a line under DJM and sell the business. "I remember that soon after we bought them I thought I had better tell Elton John and John Reid, who I had stayed in touch with over the years," recalled Hockman, "I remember going to LA where Elton was on tour dressed as Mozart and 'Candle in the Wind' had just become a hit for the second time but as a live version." This was fortuitous for PolyGram and Hockman as its success was almost immediately after the Company had bought DJM and made a dent in the losses. "I was at the Universal Amphitheatre when I told them about the purchase of DJM; John Reid was a bit annoyed with me because I hadn't told him that PolyGram were going to do it, as he and Elton might have bought the company had they known. I reminded John that the likelihood of the James family selling them the business was somewhat remote because of the Court battle, which John eventually acknowledged."

Following the purchase of DJM a new relationship emerged between Hockman and Elton John, which some eight to nine years later would lead to a strange but very lucrative deal between the publisher and artist.

Sometime during the early 1980's Hockman recalls receiving a call from John Reid asking him to come to a meeting with him and Elton that Elton and PolyGram. "We had dinner at Bibendum, (a first class restaurant in London); John Reid told me that Elton wanted to sell all his interests in all the songs he had with Dick James Music. I just said 'no he doesn't, that would be a stupid thing to do'. John told me that Elton really wanted to do it. Despite my reluctance to take the offer to buy the songs it was clear that Elton wanted to sell claiming that it was now a part of his life that was over and it was the end of an era and he just wanted to draw a line under it. I told him that I shouldn't be saying this but he would regret doing it. I know my boss should have been kicking me under the table, but I really didn't think it was the right thing for Elton to do and I considered him a friend. It was clear that John (Reid) could do nothing. So I said well if you really want to do it then we will give you the best price and it came to pass and we bought them. About 6 months later he came back to us and said he wanted to sell all his interests in the DJM masters and we bought all of those as well. When Seagram bought PolyGram later on I believe some of the deal was unravelled and Elton bought some of the income stream back again".

Elton sold his royalties to PolyGram and Hockman agreed to the deal provided he could buy Bernie Taupin's royalties as well. Taupin agreed and PolyGram became the owner of the joint royalties of Taupin/John songs during the DJM years.

By the start of the 1990's the major music businesses started to grow even larger by acquiring the independent publishing companies and Hockman added 150 independent publishing companies to his repertoire including Island Records, A&M and Sweden Music – who owned the entire catalogue of the most famous of all of the Eurovision Song Contest winners, ABBA until PolyGram was acquired by Seagram in 1998. During Hockman's reign, PolyGram Publishing was one of the five largest global publishing companies, with turnover in excess of $250,000,000 and profits of more than $40,000,000.

Now there are two major corporates left; Sony and Universal, along with Warners but not to the same scale as the two big players. Some of the Independents still remain today but most have been 'hoovered up' by the likes of Hockman for the larger corporates. There has been a small re-emergence of the independent publishing companies in recent years; being established by writers and producers, but it will never bring it back to the days of Tin Pan Alley. Those days are now over.

3

Rollercoaster Ride

The momentum for Elton John started to build in the second half of 1970 after he had finished the Troubadour gigs and wrapped up the mini-tour of the USA. The British music press was picking up on the positive vibes that were being reported from the States, and both Tin Pan Alley and the music biz were now bathing in the aftermath of Elton's phenomenal success.

"At the time," said Stephen James, "*The Tony Blackburn Show* on Radio 1 was the biggest show on a Saturday morning, and I recall that one of the promotions people came to me and said that if DJM released 'Your Song' in August, then Tony Blackburn would make it his Record of the Week because he had a slot available. That was a huge deal, and so we released it to coincide with what had been promised." The song took the charts by storm and reached No.7 in the British top ten and No. 8 in the *Billboard Top 100* as the B side to 'Take Me To The Pilot'; helping build Elton's future on both sides of the Atlantic.

With the success of the single, and the news from America that Britain had a star in the making, Elton played one of his biggest gigs, at the Royal Albert Hall supporting Sandy Denny's Fotheringay on 2 October 1970, coinciding with the release of *Tumbleweed Connection*. The tracks had been recorded in demo form by Elton and Hookfoot and played live at Hookfoot gigs long before the *Elton John* album was recorded and released, and prior to Elton's unexpected success in Los Angeles. In fact, most of the songs for the next album after *Tumbleweed Connection*, were written and recorded during what is now described as the productive period with Hookfoot. "I remember when *Tumbleweed Connection* came out, I was staying with Elton and Bernie and coming back on the underground to Pinner. We were all very excited about its release," said Tony Taupin, Bernie's older brother.

♪

Some would say that the gig at the Albert Hall with Fotheringay was just as important as the gigs at The Troubadour in LA, which broke Elton John in America. He still hadn't made much of an impact on UK audiences and this was his big chance to show his talent in a large and prestigious auditorium supporting one of the best singer songwriters to emerge from the sixties folk rock scene, Sandy Denny.

Denny first left folk rock band Fairport Convention at the end of 1969, after her producer and manager, Joe Boyd, tried to convince her that her future lay in a solo career. His advice was understandable, as she had just won the *Melody Maker* Poll for best female vocalist of the year in 1970. However Denny had other ideas and she wanted to join forces with her then partner since 1969 and future husband Trevor Lucas. Lucas had just left the band Eclection where he was bass guitarist with fellow band mate Gerry Conway on drums. Jerry Donahue, later became the guitarist for Fotheringay recalled that: "Part of the reason she left Fairport was because Eclection had also broken up. Trevor was in a relationship with Sandy and they wanted to do something together. She didn't have the outlet for her songs and she was really prolific as well. So when Eclection was about to break up she and Trevor started talking about doing something together and this was the golden moment. Joe tried to persuade her not to but he backed off because he didn't want to lose her as she was so adamant she was going to work with Trevor and that collaboration was eventually to become Fotheringay."

Towards the end of September 1970, Fotheringay, without Denny and Lucas, were asked to join Joe Boyd in the Island Studio's to record a session to cover some Nick Drake songs, with Linda Peters, (later to become Linda Thompson), and Reg Dwight (aka Elton John). Elton and Peters would be sharing the vocals and Elton would be playing the piano. "I remember that Linda was very nervous about doing the vocals" laughed

Donahue. "We did about 13 tracks in one afternoon and I remember how wonderful Elton, was as a piano player and a singer."

Elton also played some of his own compositions and the session musicians were knocked out by what they heard. Fotheringay were in the middle of a tour and had been billed to headline the Royal Albert Hall in London on 2nd October 1970, but at this point they didn't have a support act. "We talked about Elton with Sandy and Trevor and recounted our experiences in the studio with him at the Joe Boyd/Nick Drake sessions, and how lovely his songs were. Gerry and I thought he was a tasteful player and a good opening act for us. Apart from doing the Nick Drake stuff he was doing his own as well and his piano playing was fantastic. It was all laid back stuff and we though 'man this guy would be perfect for us'."

In fact the session guys had met before when Donahue, Pat Donaldson and one of Elton's pals from Bluesology, Pete Gavin - who played drums – were invited to join Elton as the backing band for Thelma Houston on a television show to promote Houston's soon to be released album. Although Houston had released a couple of singles with Capital records in 1967 her hit debut album *Sunshower* was to launch her career. It was recorded and released on Dunhill Records in 1969 but recorded in late 1968 and produced by the iconic songwriter Jimmy Webb. It was likely that the television show was to showcase the songs from the album.

"Trevor had heard of Elton vaguely but essentially he trusted us. We had other possible people who had supported us before, like Nick Drake and Humblebums, (featuring Billy Connolly), but none of them were available and so we chose Elton even though we knew he didn't have much of a following. Trevor called him and offered him the gig," remembered Donahue.

Little did they know what would happen on that night. Prior to the gig Elton had made a considerable impact with his stage antics and songs in his inaugural trip to the USA and was now ready to conquer the UK. Fotheringay were to be the fall guys in front of a packed Albert Hall.

Jerry Donahue took up the story of that fateful night: "Sandy and Trevor were out in the audience and Pat, Gerry and I were backstage as we had already seen Elton play in the studio and we were expecting him to do something similar. If we'd have known that he was going to do what he did and blow us off the stage then we wouldn't have chosen him. When Sandy went backstage after the Elton set had finished she was really shaken and making comments like 'how are we supposed to go out there now.' She was even mindful not to do the gig. She had to do it, obviously, but she had no desire to go on the stage after that. It was unfair really as we didn't want to have a battle of the bands, we were a folk rock band but it was gentle rock, the hardest rock we did was a cover of 'Long Distance Information' which was a fifties song, but only as a fun thing to do. We did what we did and it wasn't appropriate any longer when he came off the stage. Everyone was disappointed and I was disappointed in everyone's performance including mine. I didn't think my performance was particularly good but I knew I had done the best I could under the circumstances. I thought that Pat and Gerry played fine; the ones that suffered the most though were Sandy and Trevor because Trevor relied on Sandy's magic to pull the best out of him, and no one knew her better than he did because they were an item. She was still very shaken during and after the gig and we thought then what a dreadful, dreadful mistake we'd made. We could tell on stage that Sandy didn't have her full heart in it. When Sandy was left to sing in her magical way, that nobody else could quite do, then it brought the best out of the band and she raised us to the highest level. We were on stage with this gift from God; like an angel when she sang and we could do no wrong. But on this night it was like trying to carry on when somebody had an injury, or trying to do your best when you have a cold. Something traumatic happened that night but no one blamed us at all for it, as everyone could see what had happened and felt sorry for us. It was unfair because everyone knew what sort of band we were. Normally our set was like a piece of magic, but that magic was compromised big time by what had taken place before. In his heart I think Elton probably knew that he was not what we were looking for as a support, so it was a bit unfair of him, but he was thinking of himself and he needed to show a room full of people that he was a star too. I can understand his intentions, as it probably helped his career that he was in front of a packed house at the Albert Hall so he just took control of the audience. We sounded weak compared to what they had just witnessed; but Elton had probably just played one of the best rock shows ever. Elton didn't stay after his gig and it may have been because of the reaction he had received and he probably didn't want to make it worse for us."

The gig at the Albert Hall hurt the band temporarily but they recovered and went back into the studio to start making plans for the second album. "We broke for Christmas and planned to resume work in the studio early in January 1971". But by then the *Melody Maker* Polls had come in and it was announced that Sandy Denny had won top female singer of the year award for the second year running. That was when Joe Boyd really did insist on her going solo.

♪

When Elton returned to Britain from America, it was clear that he was already on the road to success, both professionally and financially. "I got a call to come in to do some photographs and publicity for *Music Week*," remembered David Larkham. "I took photographs of Elton and Bernie signing their new recording contract with Dick and Stephen James, Dick's son and heir. It was a huge advance that they were given, probably because both Elton and Dick had now only become too aware that their earnings were soon going to be flooding in from record sales." It was soon after the photo shoot, in Steve Brown's office, that Elton realised he was going to be a star with opportunities that he previously could only have dreamt of.

Elton decided to replace his old car with an Aston Martin which had a tasteful lavender/mauve livery. "We met Elton again at the Cromwellian one night, just after he had made it," remembered Len Crawley, who had toured with Bluesology in Germany during Elton's period with the band, "and he told us that he had been to see his accountants and they had told him that he had to be careful." Elton had started earning money but he was, as yet, not as rich as Croesus. The bean-counters had warned him not to spend too much because of the British tax system. "He told us he had ignored them and gone out and bought himself a new car. He was proud of the fact that he had ignored the accountants and was now going to enjoy his money. He was an absolutely terrible driver though." reckoned Crawley.

Even though Elton had broken America, he had his feet on the ground and felt comfortable working with everyone at DJM, whom he considered his family. The feeling it seemed was mutual. One of the things that struck Stuart Epps, Elton's personal assistant, the most was that everyone at DJM was honest with each other, and were essentially friends working together in a changing music environment. "If we didn't like something we would say so, and if it was about Elton and his music then he would listen and take the criticism, and use it to his advantage."

The girls in the promotions and publicity team at DJM were all excited and aware of his overnight success but to them he was nothing special. According to Chrissie Cremore, DJM's publicist, "He was just known as Reg, and he came in to talk to us just like anyone else. It was somewhere he could go and be with friends. When he was not in the studio he would get out the ginger biscuits and I would make the tea and we would sit and chat, and when he was bored he would sit with me and stuff envelopes. We saw him more as a brother than the famous Elton John, songwriter and musician. If anything," Cremore continued, "we were far more interested in people like Edward Woodward and Telly Savalas who were both signed to the DJM label. I remember when Woodward recorded one of Elton's demos as a single. It was called 'The Tide Will Turn For Rebecca', but it had failed to make any significant impact on the charts."

Despite his success, Elton always treated his colleagues as friends and family, even during their difficult times. "I had saved up for a year to go on holiday to Spain, it cost me £70 and the travel company went bust," said Cremore. "I went to work and told everyone what had happened, and Elton heard about it, and when I next saw him in the office he asked me about it and I told him I would be missing my holiday as I couldn't afford to go. A little later he handed me a cheque for £100. I refused it at first because I was used to Elton not having any money, but Steve Brown said, 'Don't worry, take it, he's alright'." An incredibly generous act nonetheless though.

By this time, of course, the money had started to roll in from the American tours and album sales and Elton was becoming financially secure. Not that it changed him when it came to helping others. Cremore remembers when she was publicising two sisters called Doreen and Irene

Chanter who were signed to DJM and called themselves Birds of a Feather. Being part of the DJM family, the sisters had worked with Elton on an earlier tour of the UK as backing singers. In return for their support, Elton played and sang on their album *Birds Of A Feather* as a thank you.

Everyone at DJM was delighted for Elton and his newfound success; after all, they were very fond of him. It wasn't however until he appeared on prime time TV that he was actually considered a star by his colleagues. "We knew he had taken off when he went on *Top Of The Pops,* and then, of course, he became attractive! He had big glasses and long hair." recounted Cremore. "We all went into Dick's room after work and emptied his drinks cupboard while we were watching *Top Of The Pops*. And the next day, when Elton came in, we were really excited for him."

It was after that appearance that the great British public finally sat up and took notice; the tours started to sell out and fan mail started to arrive at DJM by the sack load. It was down to Cremore to deal with the mail and reply to all the letters requesting autographs. In fact, she learned how to sign Elton's autograph so that when he wasn't available, she could sign them *in absentia*. That was how crazy the demand had suddenly become. "There are some people who were requesting signed photographs who are now going to be disappointed because I signed a lot of his stuff as I had his signature down to a fine art." So think again before you take that signed photo of Elton onto *Antiques Roadshow*!

All of a sudden, everyone wanted a piece of Elton, from the music press to photographers. One photographer who did end up with the task of taking some of the earliest publicity shots was Terry O'Neill, already an established leading chronicler of sixties pop culture. He had long been on the lookout for a budding new star to take the place of the Beatles, whom he had photographed on a regular basis since he had turned 21 during his Fleet Street years with the now-defunct *Daily Sketch*.

His first brush with the world of pop music was when he photographed the Beatles and the Rolling Stones, which were among the first ever pictures to show a more natural and human side to both groups. It was enough to start a long and successful relationship with his subjects who have included everyone from Laurence Olivier to members of the Royal Family and prominent politicians.

O'Neill was the first photographer to snap Elton professionally. "I came back to England as I was working between Hollywood and London. The Beatles had finished, and the Stones had lost some impact at the time, but their pictures were never as popular as the Beatles in any case. Basically, I needed someone to promote through my photography and was commissioned by a newspaper to go and find someone who was going to be the next big thing. And I remember I was listening to the radio when I heard 'Take Me To The Pilot', and immediately thought what a great voice the singer had and, at the same time, thought I must find this guy."

He scoured all the record shops trying to find out the identity of the singer he had heard on the radio that morning. In the end, he came across the track on the album, *Elton John*. Not only was he thrilled that he had found the singer and the song, but was equally thrilled to discover that Elton John was British. It was exactly what he was looking for.

"I called Dick James and I said I'd like to photograph your singer Elton John. They were really pleased, because in those days there was a great deal of respect afforded to photographers." O'Neill was invited to DJM by John Reid and was asked to take some photographs of Elton in action. "I went into the studio and photographed him on the piano, doing handstands." But despite O'Neill's enthusiasm and great pictures, it was not all plain sailing. "Everyone saw pop stars as handsome, but he didn't fall into that category. It didn't matter to me, but it did to newspapers; so no newspaper would publish the shots. So then I took them to *Vogue* who published a shot of Elton with a ring as an eye, and that was the start of it."

Although the very first photographs of Elton were shot with him in the studio, O'Neill was invited to the flat in the Water Gardens to take more. "When I first photographed him he lived in a little flat in Edgware Road and I said I loved his music and he could really play the piano. He gave me a tape called *17/11/70*, which I thought was really good and the fact he was English just drove me on to get this guy some publicity."

Above all else, O'Neill really believed in what Elton was doing and then when he met Bernie he really started to believe in the whole Elton John thing. "I started working with them all the time through John Reid. Elton never really liked being photographed but we got on as friends and we did it quickly and he just got through it. Many of the early photographs were taken in his homes or on tour." O'Neill was to remain in the Elton John entourage for the remainder of the seventies and the photographs of Elton, in particular those from the Dodger Stadium gigs, would become regarded as some of the most iconic.

♫

While O'Neill was busy shooting photographs of Elton, across the Atlantic Russ Regan and UNI were planning how to get Elton back to the States as soon as possible. A tour was hastily arranged by the Howard Rose Agency. [Rose himself had become a good friend to Elton who, in turn, became Godfather to Rose's child, who was given the middle name of Umbrella]. Unlike the last tour, Rose was now able to secure bigger, 3,000 seater auditoria and, better yet, he was now able fill them.

The tour started in November 1970 and the audiences were enthralled. At Elton's shows, they witnessed him becoming more theatrical as his confidence increased with every new date. In echoes of a Jerry Lee Lewis performance, Elton was now crawling under the piano to play it as well as doing handstands on the keyboard. Although the audiences lapped it up with screams, clapping and cheering, certain quarters of the American music press were not that impressed.

It was interesting to watch the development of his stage act. When the tour reached the Civic Auditorium in Santa Monica on 15 November 1970, where Elton would share the bill with Odetta and Ry Cooder, his antics were seen as a breath of fresh air. Not that the music purists would agree. One journalist, in particular, took umbrage to the whole thing after sitting through Elton's show at Santa Monica. In his review he was quick to point out that 'Elton John needed to balance his music with his on-stage antics.' If he didn't, then he was destined to become a 'stage freak'. None of it, of course, was helped by Elton's attire. Yellow overalls that concealed a purple jersey, shorts and a leotard, while prancing around the stage and doing head stands on his piano, was hardly what rock legends were made of. Even though Elton's musical ability was praised, the general consensus was that he needed to choose between being a clown or a serious musician. Not that audiences cared; quite the opposite in fact. They seemed to be at their wildest during most of Elton's set, especially when he covered hits by others. The Beatles' 'Get Back' was a particular crowd pleaser.

Prior to the gigs, Elton got together with his old mate Danny Hutton lead singer with Three Dog Night. "Elton knew me and, I guess, because he was relatively unknown over here, I was his American contact," recalled Hutton, who became Elton's mentor in the days leading up to, and during, the tour. "On his first night in town, I took him to Billy James' restaurant called the Black Rabbit. James was Bob Dylan's publicist, and then we went back to my place in Laurel Canyon and I called my friend Van Dyke Parks and told him to come over and hear a future star." When Parks arrived Elton played them all the songs that would later make him famous including a new song called 'Tiny Dancer'. The room where Elton played was the same room that was to feature on the sleeve of Three Dog Night's *It Ain't Easy* album. "I also recall him coming to the studio wearing a jumpsuit with a Mickey Mouse button on the crotch that lit up when you pushed it." Prior to meeting Hutton in the studio, Elton and his entourage had been to Disneyland and no doubt that is where he got the jumpsuit from.

One of the highlights of Elton's Los Angeles trip was when Hutton introduced him to Brian Wilson of the Beach Boys: "Being a good friend of Brian's, we were invited to his house in Bel Air. It was a house once owned by Edgar Rice Burroughs, who wrote the *Tarzan* books, but Brian had it painted purple until the neighbours complained and he had to change the colour. The house had its own studio so Brian decided to call his engineer and have him play the Beach Boys latest recording to Elton. By the end of the hour, Elton was completely blown away. I told Brian that he should listen to what Elton could do on the piano and after convincing Elton that this was a good idea, we set him up with a grand piano and he played 'Amoreena', the song having been newly written by Elton and Bernie especially for Ray Williams' daughter. Brian is a very direct person, who speaks his mind and his approach to music takes a lot of getting used to. After a couple of verses of 'Amoreena', Brian stopped Elton and said 'Great, great, Elton, but now play something else.' This happened a couple of times, and by then, Elton was looking and, no doubt, feeling very nervous that Brian Wilson didn't like his music. In fact, Brian was knocked out by what he had heard and just wanted to hear more. Brian only needed to listen to music for a short time to make an assessment of its quality and he was very impressed with Elton."

♪

Meanwhile one of the first things that Messrs Taupin and Larkham did when they landed in LA was to reacquaint themselves with their partners, Maxine and Janice. "I remember going over with Elton and staying with Ed Caraeff [a prominent rock and roll photographer] and, during the tour, Bernie's romance with Maxine really took off," recounted Larkham. "For Bernie and I washed denim jeans with patches were the in thing, so we wanted to get patches for our denim and pre-faded jeans, or that was the excuse to get Janice and Maxine to take us out to Ventura Boulevard to a special shop that sold them."

That visit to the shops was to become the influence for the next album cover for *Madman Across The Water*. In between supporting Elton on his hectic tour, Bernie and David spent the days between dates being driven around in either Maxine or Janice's car, and that is when Bernie's romance with Maxine reached a new level – much the same as David's relationship with Janice turned from being good friends to something more serious. Being fans of Jack Kerouac's *On The Road*, the pair decided to recreate the journey with Janice and Maxine and took the route on the magical Pacific Coast Highway.

On his return to the UK, Bernie came back with Maxine in tow and they started living together with Steve Brown and his wife Jill at their flat in Whyteleafe, Surrey. Bernie would later admit he was pretty shy when he met Maxine, but she was confident and instilled some of that confidence in him.

They were married at the Holyrood Catholic Church in Market Rasen, in April 1971, where a few years earlier he regularly went to Mass with his parents, and had been an altar boy. "I came back from Spain and was an usher," remembered Tony King. "It was quite an event for the sleepy market town of Market Rasen and the Holyrood Church; the place was besieged with journalists and photographers who turned the whole affair into headline news, including a front page leader in the *Lincolnshire Echo*."

The wedding reception was held at the local Market Rasen Racecourse followed by a private dinner for the respective families at the Limes Hotel. The bride wore a simple white Tudor style dress and Bernie wore a white velvet suit with a lilac shirt, much like the Aston Martin that Elton had lent him for the day to take him to the church. Elton was the best man, resplendent in a wedding suit embroidered with large blue, red and yellow flowers made of rhinestones costing 250 guineas, topped off with a silver silk top hat. Father Hoban, who presided over the church ceremony, must have wondered what he had got himself into when Elton's entourage arrived with police escorts and security.

"When Bernie and Maxine got married, and we went to the wedding and reception afterwards," remembered Mick Inkpen, "I joined the other guests from DJM outside of DJM's offices in New Oxford Street and we chartered a coach to take us to Market Rasen. There were musicians and engineers, all dressed in wedding attire. I think it was the first time I had seen any of them out of their usual jeans and T-shirts. I remember how Jeff Dexter, a big time radio DJ at the time, had this amazing long white hair, and came decked out in a full morning suit with waistcoat, gloves, spats and a cane. It was quite a sight to see. The journey to the church," continued Inkpen, "took about two hours so we were pretty much in an alcohol and drug influenced haze by the time we arrived. After checking into our respective guest houses, we made our way to the church which was decked out in romantic candlelight. And then, when Elton entered, the candlelight and suit were connected, and his suit flickered and lit up. He looked more like the bride than the best man, and it was the first time I had seen Bernie in a suit."

The paparazzi, of course, were having a field day, lining the driveway up to the church entrance outside and, as expectant, fans were clamouring for autographs. "I suddenly realised that the Elton John thing was really going somewhere. After the ceremony, and having made our way through the screaming fans outside, together with all the local people who were fascinated by it all, we went back to Market Rasen on the coach to the reception, where there seemed to be an endless supply of champagne flowing, and a bar for other drinks, but there was so much champagne that you didn't need anything else. I believe Maxine's father was involved with the import of the champagne, which was probably why there was so much of it," recalled David Larkham.

With speeches out of the way, and while still quaffing champers by the bucket load, it was time for party games. There were three hundred people in the room all playing musical chairs to Elton's piano playing. "It was Elton John entertaining us in the racecourse restaurant," said Larkham. "He was showing off all his roots. Songs that influenced him, Winifred Atwell stuff interspersed with his comical impressions."

By the time the wedding and Elton's first major tour were out of the way, Bernie and Maxine settled into married life in the sleepy little village of Tealby which, for Maxine, must have seemed a far cry from the beaches and warm weather of California. But life was very idyllic. What could be better than living in a small cottage that she and Bernie had bought out of one of Bernie's royalty cheques and named Piglet In The Wilds? The couple didn't really ask for anything more, despite the fact that Elton was now scoring hits galore and selling out massive concert tours across Britain and America. If anything, they sat back and remained in relative anonymity away from the spotlight, while Elton got on with the touring part. The only hint that the cottage was owned by celebrities was when it was visited by anyone famous, such as Elton, who used to block any access with his pink Rolls Royce.

"After Bernie and Maxine had been married for a while, they bought a bloodhound puppy from Battersea Dogs Home, which they called Cyril but, in no time at all, it had grown to its full size, and once they started travelling on the tours with Elton, it had to come and live with my parents in Owmby," said Tony. "It was chained to a fence at the corner of the house so it could reach the front and back doors. It was not a vicious dog but being a bloodhound it had a bit of a reputation. He was very playful and would run up to you and knock you over without any trouble at all."

To many, when Bernie met Maxine, it was very much like country boy meets Hollywood girl. "She was quite outrageous and very Hollywood." remembered one of Elton's recording engineers, Stuart Epps. "One minute all he wants is a Landrover and the next minute he wants a pink E-Type Jag for Maxine. In many ways, she was leading him around and spending his money, but she was lovely and I liked her. But it was while they were at Piglet In The Wilds that I noticed a different side to Maxine. She could be very homely and she loved the cottage. In that environment, she made some lovely food, played housewife and they were a lovely couple who were very much in love, but she also loved the glitz and glamour of the Elton John side. On tour, she would dress up and go on stage, but she was usually the only woman around."

After Piglet In The Wilds Maxine and Bernie joined the Virginia Water set where Elton had also moved to. "I found them a house in Virginia Water near Gus and Elton's places." continued Epps, "Even though Elton and Bernie lived close by, outside of the writing, there wasn't much of a relationship between them. It's probably why it lasted so long. Even in those very early days of success, Bernie wasn't there much at all and, by then, he had a different circle of friends. He would rarely hang out with Elton, probably because they were totally different people, and they became more different as it all took off. In fact, Elton had more in common with Gus than he did with Bernie."

♫

The second 1970 tour, which included two nights at the Fillmore West and then the Fillmore East for the legendary promoter Bill Graham, followed on from the success of the first one. They also played the Anaheim Convention Centre, LA, where Elton appeared with his boyhood hero Leon Russell. "I was in England," recalled Epps, "but keeping in touch with Steve [Brown], who, whilst normally pretty reserved and not very excitable, was now getting very excited. He said that Elton was going down better than Leon. In fact blowing him off stage is what he said."

The Anaheim gig was also one of the highlights of the tour for both Elton and Russ Regan, who joined the entourage for the latter stages. "The night before the gig, he came over to my house for dinner. The cold cherry soup was phenomenal, and so we served it whilst I was barbecuing. In fact, the soup was so good that Elton was flipping out over how amazing it tasted. The next night we took a bus load of people to the concert and we sat there and Elton John said, 'Before we start, I want to dedicate this concert to Judy Regan's cold cherry soup'. It's probably the only time an Elton John concert has been dedicated to a bowl of soup!"

The last date of the tour was in San Francisco with The Kinks, but, before returning to London, Elton did a New York radio show which later became his first live album. According to Dudgeon, *17/11/70* was originally broadcast live across the US airwaves from Phil Ramone's studio in New York in front of a lucky studio audience of about 100 people. And after that, while waiting in Los Angeles to fly home just before Christmas, Elton was booked for a guest spot on the *Andy Williams Show* with Mama Cass and his idol Ray Charles. Charles didn't attend the scheduled rehearsals and refused to sing some of the initial suggestions made by the producers of the television show, which probably added to Elton's own frustrations with rehearsals. In the end, though, and after initially refusing, Charles did agree to sing 'Heaven Help Us All', which was apt.

♫

By the time Elton got back from the States, it was clear that there was an increased demand for his material. The New York radio show, for instance, had already been bootlegged, and in an attempt to put a halt to it, Dick James called Gus Dudgeon and asked him if he could make an album of the show. Dudgeon managed to find over 45 minutes of decent material from the tape that James had sent him. It was rushed released in May 1971 as the new Elton John album to prevent the bootleggers ripping off Elton's work – although being bootlegged was a sign of how successful he was becoming.

Elton's next album *Friends*, was not really supposed to be a 'studio' Elton John album but was a throwback to when Ray Williams had signed a contract with Paramount Pictures for Elton and Bernie to write and record three songs for a movie. "I got to know John Gilbert, Lewis Gilbert's son, through the advert that I had placed in the *NME* when I was looking for talent for Liberty Records," explained Williams.

"From the advert we got the band Family, who John was producing, and Liberty released a semi successful single in October 1967 titled 'Scene Through The Eye Of A Lens'. John took them to Warner Brothers/Reprise, but we kept in touch. When I was managing Elton, John came to see me and asked whether Elton would be interested in making an album and creating the soundtrack for a film his father was doing; it was a romantic film about two young people falling in love. He had a £250,000 budget which was considered pretty small in comparison to other films at the time, but I was impressed by the story, so I talked to Elton and Bernie about it and they were up for it. Getting the buy-in from Dick James though was more difficult because the promotions company representative, Leslie Gauld, wanted all the publishing rights to the music, which was normal at the time, but Dick wanted them so he initially refused to allow Elton and Bernie to do it. I continued to persuade Leslie to give way for Elton and Bernie's sake and eventually he did. Dick got the publishing rights and the film went ahead."

Paramount only wanted song segments to last 20/30 seconds long, and a lead song, which Elton insisted on calling 'Friends' even though the original title for the film was *The Intimate Game*. What Elton and Bernie hadn't realised was that writing a film score was entirely different from writing a hit song, and it required significantly more planning than Elton and Bernie's writing style allowed for. Some songs had to be timed to perfection to fit the sequence it related to in the film, which was achieved more by trial and error than planning.

Paramount then insisted on a soundtrack album, which added more complications to the writing and recording process. In the end they recorded the 20/30 second segments for the film in one take and then went into the recording studio and recorded a whole album having re-written some of the songs and added two more. So the album was slightly different to the segments recorded for the film. It was written and recorded in five weeks between September and October 1970. To make it an album length product, Buckmaster was called in to arrange the entire second side. John Gilbert wanted the Elton John sound in the score and source tracks, these being songs that come out of radios and in lifts, and that being the case, both Dudgeon and Buckmaster were responsible for the sound and were the natural choice.

"*Friends* was a total arrangement except for the three source tracks which are 'Michelle's Song', 'Friends' and 'Can I Put You On'. These were all played by Elton and his band, Nigel Olsson and Dee Murray," recalled Buckmaster. "I had to write some extra score for the album because there was not enough music in the film or the film music didn't work by itself and was omitted from the album, so I had to write something that had a bit of interest to it. I didn't know anything about film scoring but Gus knew John Barry, who was primarily a film score composer, and we went to his fabulous two story apartment across from the Tate [Gallery] in London, in a very modern building that was all glass and high ceilings and had sound and projection facilities that were amazing. He didn't have much to offer in terms of advice except he said that I had to get the timing right and the sense of the film's motion. I was with him a couple of hours and I tried to remember all he said. He told me I had the experience for orchestration and that I must not get in the way of the dialogue. It was simple advice like that really."

After that Buckmaster spent endless hours in the editing room in the production office watching film clips and taking notes, followed by meetings with the production teams, consisting of editor and director, during which decisions were made as to where the music would start and end to fit the dialogue and mood of the film.

Buckmaster would then go back to his apartment, armed with his script, his notes and score pad and proceed to put the score together. Elton was less than pleased that the record company started promoting the *Friends* album as it wasn't, as far as he was concerned, an Elton John album. Ruby Mazur who was the Art Director for Paramount Records, was drafted in to produce the sleeve. Under the guidance of a representative from Paramount, he designed a pink cover with a sketch depicting the theme of the film but to cash in on the recent success of Elton in the States, Elton's name was prominently displayed on the sleeve, which didn't best please him.

In an interview for *The Georgia Straight*, Elton was reported to have said, "They came up with that strawberry-coloured rubbish, I suppose I can't blame the Paramount Record Company for putting my name on it in big letters, because I would have probably done that but it's not an Elton John album, believe me." Although it was Buckmaster's first film score and Elton and Bernie's first foray into the celluloid world, the album was a significant success even though the film didn't have the same impact at the box office. However, at the 1972 Grammy Awards, the music was nominated in the Best Original Score Written for a Motion Picture.

4

Back And Forth

With the film soundtrack recording completed, Elton resumed his hectic schedule of live gigs, and by the end of the year supported The Who at the Roundhouse. Chris Charlesworth from *Melody Maker* was there: "I was quite friendly with The Who and I remember seeing Elton backstage and we exchanged words. He was saying how fantastic it was to be supporting The Who and performing to a large crowd. I remember he did a fantastic show and when The Who came on, Townshend introduced *Tommy*, because they were doing *Tommy* then, and dedicated their performance of it to Elton John because he thought he was going to be very big."

After that gig, Elton really broke through in Britain and was now a star on both sides of the Atlantic. He became huge and you couldn't get Elton tickets for love nor money; the market was flooded with Elton products and records, like *Tumbleweed Connection* and *Friends*. At the time he was very prolific, banging out records all the time and, at the end of that year, Elton was one of the biggest names in the business.

It could be said that much of Elton's success in the UK was due to his links with, what was in 1970, the music counter culture underworld, with the likes of David Bowie, Cat Stevens, Marc Bolan, John Martyn and Linda Lewis in a small house in Hampstead in London.

Linda Fredricks (she later took Lewis as her professional surname) first started her singing career following in the footsteps of her mother who was an accomplished singer in her own right. She was first discovered in a Club in Southend UK with John Lee Hooker, where, having been persuaded by her Mother to get up and sing, she sang 'Dancing in the Street', which attracted the interest of a songwriter and producer Ian Samwell who then introduced her to Don Arden, a notorious agent and manager who had established the careers of The Small Faces and The Move amongst many others. Arden based himself in prestigious offices in the famous Carnaby Street in London England. "Here I was in Don Arden's office; a young girl of 15 years of age from the East End of London being thrown into this whole new world of music" laughed Linda.

The Small Faces had just had a hit called 'Whatcha Gonna Do About It' that was written by Samwell who had previously made his name in Tin Pan Alley for writing 'Move It' for Cliff Richard and was the mainstay in Cliff's band from when he was known as Harry Webb and then the Drifters until he lost his spot to Hank Marvin when the band changed its name to The Shadows; but he continued to write songs to enhance Richard's song repertoire. Samwell would become an integral part of Linda's life both professionally and personally.

Linda's first demo was made in Tin Pan Alley, Denmark Street, London with John McLaughlin, who worked with Miles Davies and The Mahavishnu Orchestra on guitar and whose line-up included Jean-Luc Ponty a revolutionary violinist who pioneered the electric violin and would later work with Elton John on the album *Honky Chateau*. "From that I got a recording contract through Don with Polydor." The first single was released under the name of Linda Lewis and was called 'You Turn My Bitter Into Sweet'; "It flopped" laughed Linda, "I thought it was a Northern Soul classic; it had Jimmy Page and John Paul Jones playing on it as session musicians, (both of whom went on to have significant success with Led Zeppelin). I remember promoting it on *Fab 208* with Kiki Dee and some other young up and coming people. We had to go and play netball in these very tiny shorts and look like we were sporty" laughed Linda. *Fab 208* was a music magazine during the 1970's set up by Radio Luxembourg, whose station frequency number was 208 with a strap line of 'Fabulous 208'.

Linda was still very young and at school but was playing clubs and pubs all over the Country, travelling from Manchester to London at the age of 15 making her way in the music business. "My school teachers would say; 'Linda Fredericks why are you looking so tired'. I couldn't really tell them I'd been at the Flamingo Club all night!" amused Linda. After finishing her schooling at the Convent she joined a band called the Q Set and then moved on to another band called White Rabbit. "Lots of people came out of those bands," reflected Linda, "like Junior Marvin who went on the play with Bob Marley and Michael Snow who wrote 'Rosetta'. I just loved singing. I wanted to be famous so I could show all the bullies in school just how wonderful I was. That was one of my motivations to sing would you believe."

In 1968 at the age of 18 Linda left home and moved into a house in Hampstead, London called Hampstead Web with Ian Samwell and some other guys. "It was a communal house with Ian 'Sammy' Samwell, Jeff Dexter - a DJ who regularly played the Roundhouse and Middle Earth and an amazing photographer called Pete Sanders" recalled Linda.

The house and the people who were in it attracted a whole host of other creative people to its doors. "In that environment a lot of people used to come through because it created inspiration," remarked Linda. Some of the young up and coming singer-songwriters who hadn't quite found their escape yet from the Tin Pan Alley era would congregate at the house and share their songs and spend time chatting about their music. "I guess it was people like Ian Samwell, who was, by now, working with Warner Brothers and Jeff Dexter who were an attraction to these people; everyone wanted to be with them and share their songs." Dexter had been involved in the organisation of the very first Glastonbury Festival in 1970 and he invited people from the house to play including Linda. Two other regulars at the house were David Bowie and Marc Bolan who were also on the bill at that first Festival.

"Marc (Bolan) was very flamboyant and he used to come through the house in tap shoes and amazing jackets. Marc was just like a peacock person and a renaissance man, with all the King Arthurs Court type stuff he talked about. We all thought we were Kings and Queens and Princes actually", reflected Linda. "He would always be slinging his hair about; he knew he was gorgeous and he always had something to say about things. I was a very naive person and didn't say much and just listened to him. I lost track of him when he got big but I knew him best when he was in T. Rex and we played Middle Earth together. He had a manager/wife and she kept her beady eye on him as all the girls in the house were in awe of him as they were with Cat (Steve) Stevens. David Bowie was quite shy; I remember David came round and he was wearing all this make-up. I asked him why and he just looked at me and smiled. I didn't know he was getting very big with 'Space Oddity' at the time". Another up and coming star who was a regular at the house was Elton John. "We were all very hippy although Elton was quite down to earth and shy by contrast to Marc. Elton would sit around and soak it up all but not play, he was very inward whereas Marc would be picking up guitars and singing."

Dexter was a regular DJ at The Roundhouse, a popular music venue in London's Chalk Farm near Camden Town. As well as being involved in the organisation of the very first Glastonbury he also organised gigs for the venue and invited Elton John to support The Who on 20 December 1970 at a charity gig at one of Dexter's regular Sunday afternoon gigs known as 'Implosion' - just after Elton's success at The Troubadour in Los Angeles. On the same bill was a British/American band who called themselves America. And within a year of the gig America had a massive hit with 'A Horse with No Name' featuring a soon to be Elton John band member, Ray Cooper, on congas.

It was obvious to Linda and no doubt Elton that the musical inspiration in the house was immense. "I remember Cat Stevens writing 'Moon Shadow' in the living room" laughed Linda. "He just picked up his guitar; I was showing him what I had just written and he said 'I have a song, what do you think of this?' He then played the middle eight of 'Moon Shadow'. I told him it was lovely but it sounded very much like 'Somewhere Over the Rainbow'. He then started singing 'I'm being followed by a moon shadow...' and I said 'yea that sounds really poetic.' I didn't really make any compliments about it because everyone was being creative at the same time and we were listening to these songs all the time. The time and the season and the atmosphere in the house allowed all this creativity so what Cat was creating was just part of that really. We used to spend all day long having breakfast, which would turn into lunch and then into dinner; just sitting around and playing and writing. Cat Stevens and Marc used to jam a lot with the others and me. We didn't wear watches and we were all in this dream state not knowing what time it was."

Gaining confidence from the other songwriters in the house and especially Cat Stevens, who she had started a personal relationship with, Linda started writing her own songs. "I had written some with a band called Ferris Wheel but I didn't really take it seriously until all the singer songwriters came along like Joni Mitchell and Laura Nyro; I was very influenced by that. I was given a Martin guitar by Eric Clapton which had belonged to his girlfriend Alice Ormsby-Gore. There was talk of me and Alice forming an all-girl group and that is possibly why I was given the guitar but it wasn't to be. I've since written dozens and dozens of songs on it."

Other regulars at the house included Robert Wyatt, before his unfortunate accident when he fell out of a fourth floor window which resulted in paralysis from the waist down. According to Linda, Wyatt actually lived at the house for a while. Crosby, Stills and Nash would head for the house during visits to the UK and the Folk guitarist John Martyn was a frequent visitor: "John came all the time, like Marc he was also a peacock type person and was strutting around the house," laughed Linda. "It was John who introduced me to the folk club scene. I used to do Les Cousins in Soho, London which was a folk and blues club in the basement of a Greek restaurant and the first time I played there was down to John. He was playing and he introduced me and asked me to do an impromptu song. I had released a couple of songs by then but didn't have a following and I only knew three guitar chords, but I went down well and after that the resident compere and musician Noel Murphy, (who introduced Elton's future guitarist Davey Johnstone to the London Folk Music Scene) asked me back every week and I gradually started to get a following."

It was during one of the gigs at Les Cousins that Linda was spotted and was introduced to Ian Ralfini from Warner Brothers. "Actually Ian came to see me at the house in Hampstead even though he was the head guy at Warners. He was so intrigued about what was happening at the house and because Sammy was there as well, he actually came around to the house. This was the head of Warner Brothers, he just came round to tea!" laughed

Linda.

Samwell signed Linda to Warners and at the same time signed America who were now jointly managed by Samwell and Jeff Dexter, with Samwell producing the first self-titled album *America*. "The band came and sang on one of my tracks," joked Linda. America was formed by three young teenagers named Gerry Beckley, Dewey Bunnell and Dan Peek. "Dan used to sit at my feet in awe of me and listen to me sing," laughed Linda.

Linda's first album for Warner was *Say No More*. By this time her voice was becoming increasingly well-known both in the house as well as on the radio. She started getting asked by many artists to sing sessions for them and she joined Gary Osborne's pool of session singers. Gary at this time was one of the top vocal contractors in London booking singers for sessions and very lucrative TV commercials. Linda also started working with Manfred Mann, who according to Linda was a perfectionist and wanted everything just right. She also worked with Yes as a backing vocalist along with the more experienced backing vocalists, and successful solo singers, Madeleine Bell, Liza Strike and Lesley Duncan. "I remember doing this session for Yes and they put out the sheet music. I said to Madeleine and Lesley, 'I can't read music'; they replied 'well nor can we but just pretend and you will hear it', so we did it by ear pretending to read the music but we got it right."

Lesley Duncan was a frequent visitor to the house. Duncan had seen moderate success recording wise with several singles to her credit one of which, *Love Song* released in 1969, gave her great critical acclaim and was a particular favourite of Elton John who would cover the song as a duet with Duncan for *Tumbleweed Connection*. "I remember going out searching for flying saucers with Lesley and Jeff Dexter," laughed Linda. "We did a lot of sessions together, but she just didn't want to be famous, she just liked writing and singing her songs. Lesley was very petite and spiritual and wrote some beautiful songs." Scottish born Duncan, whose brother Jimmy managed and produced one of Britain's top R 'n' B bands The Pretty Things, was a regular backing singer for many artists during the sixties and was a regular with Dusty Springfield. By the mid-sixties Duncan had met David Bowie and the two became very close and shared opinions about songwriting. Arguably, Duncan was a big influence on

Bowie's later writing style that would make him a significant songwriting force throughout the seventies. Like Linda Lewis, Duncan lived in a communal house in Hampstead, London, where musicians from Bowie to Alex Harvey used to jam together, compose songs and listen to all sorts of music as well as join together for meditation sessions and talk about flying saucers, lay lines and the concept of peace and love and saving the world and reading books like *The Tibetan Book of the Dead*.

During December 1972, Linda got a call from Trident Studios from her friend David Bowie asking her if she would sing on his album, which would soon become *Aladdin Sane*. "David came in to the studio with loads of make up on," remembered Linda. "He was getting very well known by then. We did three tracks and the only one I remember was 'Panic in Detroit'. David's instructions were basically 'do what you like' so I did and wailed all over it." Despite her view of the wailing the song got great reviews. *Aladdin Sane* made number 1 in the UK and reached number 17 on the American Billboard Charts during 1973.

By the time of *Aladdin Sane*, Lewis had significant success with her single 'Rock-A-Doodle-Doo', which reached number 15 in the UK charts and had toured with her old flame Cat Stevens and sang on his hit album *Catch Bull At Four*.

♬

With Christmas 1970 out of the way, Elton embarked on a British tour, playing small venues culminating in a large gig at the Royal Festival Hall before going back out to the States to emulate his previous success in Los Angeles and New York in the summer. One of his first gigs on the British leg of the tour was in London, (according to Stuart Epps it was at the Town and Country Club) and it got off to a bad start, this time, Elton's temperament got the better of him for all to see.

"When he arrived for the sound check, the piano was in a bit of a state," remembered Epps. "I seem to remember it had an orange box taking the place of one of the legs. He left pretty quickly after seeing it and not looking very happy. Steve Brown came later and the place was really filling up. As Showtime approached, Elton hadn't arrived and when we called him up, he said he wasn't coming. I remember very clearly Steve on the phone in the club trying to persuade him to do the gig. Eventually he was successful, and it turned out to be a great night."

It was during this tour, and as a member of the DJM entourage, that Elton and Bernie attended the MIDEM Festival in Cannes, France. It is essentially a trade show for music publishers and record companies to ply their wares across the music business which, in that year, culminated in a three-hour gala show of artists who represented the respective publishers and record labels. Larkham attended as the DJM photographer and explained: "It was probably second in popularity to the *Eurovision Song Contest* and was broadcast all over Europe. As such, it gave tremendous exposure to new artists, although I don't think it was ever broadcast in Britain."

Larkham contines, "Eric Burdon was second on the bill, appearing just before Elton. He had been an established artist for almost a decade, and must have been truly miffed at having this relatively unknown Johnny-come-lately placed as the star of the show. I can't remember exact times, but let's say that Burdon was allocated fifteen minutes for his slot, and Elton got the final twenty minutes. It was when Burdon launched into his final number, the trouble started. It went on and on, with solos from the lead guitar, the bass player, the drummer and all the while Eric was singing, throwing in scat vocals, and generally pushing the song along well past the fifteen minute slot. It seemed to go into twenty minutes, then into twenty-five, all of which over-ran and was cutting into Elton's time."

"He was livid and, along with the organisers, was screaming for Burdon to stop and get off from the side of the stage. I don't know exactly what finally happened, whether Burdon decided to stop, or whether the organisers had to pull the plug on him, but he finally finished his song and exited the stage."

Because the live show had to finish at a particular time, it left Elton about eight minutes to perform. Not that Elton was unduly worried. After all, he was back in the charts with 'Your Song', which eventually peaked at No.7 in January 1971 and had been awarded a gold disc for the *Elton John* album to recognise one million dollars worth of sales in the States. The *Friends* album was also climbing the charts on both sides of the

Atlantic so all in all, things were looking pretty good. With the tour still rattling on, everything seemed hunky dory but success comes at a price.

When you consider that Elton had been working almost constantly, without any time off, since he had left Bluesology, and also had a great deal happen in both his personal and professional life, it is understandable that the stress he was now under would lead to several dates on the British tour being cancelled. He was worn out, tired and exhausted, and needed time to rest and recuperate. In addition to his own career he was always ready to lend a helping hand to friends, such as his old buddy Long John Baldry. With Rod Stewart he co-produced Baldry's album *It Ain't Easy*. It was released in the US in June 1971, followed by Baldry's American debut at the Fillmore West on June 14.

In many ways, the cracks were already beginning to show under the strain of it all. Even things with his partner and business manager were taking their toll. "John Reid was a big influence on Elton and some say was largely responsible, in a way, for completely turning around Elton's career to the point that Elton probably would have not become the success he did without Reid," reflected Chrissie Cremore. "John made things happen for Elton, but he was a tough cookie, and that put a tremendous pressure on Elton, and he was prone to get angry because of it. On one occasion, I remember, they were in a room at DJM discussing something before going to a gig in Brighton, and John must have said something to upset him, because there was a loud crash and bang, an award was smashed, the door flew open, and Elton stormed off. I got out the dustpan and brush to clear up the mess, and everyone was fussing around including Steve Brown, who was worried about the gig that, once again, Elton was refusing to play. In those days, you couldn't just cancel a gig. Like any job, in or out of the music business, you needed a doctor's certificate, so that's what we did: we told them he was ill."

It didn't help matters that Elton didn't have much time for socialising as he was always too busy, which again denied him a valuable safety valve most of us take for granted. "Well, when you've been travelling all day, sound checking and then the gig, you're pretty knackered," insisted Epps, who by this time was Elton's personal assistant. "And then, there was usually some sort of reception that he would have to be at, to meet the local mayor or something."

The final British gig, prior to the extensive tour of America, was a biggie at the Royal Festival Hall in London on 3 March 1971, which was essentially made up of the musicians from the *Elton John* album. "While Elton was touring, I was busy in the office, helping organise the Festival Hall gig," continued Epps. "I was booking the orchestra, musicians, backing singers, sorting out rehearsals, and making sure there were music stands, and that Buckmaster had access to his special cigarettes. Mr Voike at Steinway was providing the piano."

It was important that the same fiasco that plagued the Town and Country Club gig was not repeated at the Festival Hall, especially as Rick Wakeman and Skaila Kanga were booked to join Elton on stage. "I did the Festival Hall gig wearing a Sari," recalled Kanga. "I spent most of the concert trying to get it out of the pedals!"

Buckmaster was booked to conduct this first of two Festival Hall concerts. "The first gig went well because they were session guys, didn't have an elitist attitude to pop music, and were all very accomplished classical musicians who could grace any orchestra. They were also familiar with the world of rock and pop music." The second gig at the Royal Festival Hall, on 5 February 1972, was with the Royal Philharmonic Orchestra. Buckmaster confessed, "I was very self-conscious and lacking in self-confidence as a conductor and about the art and craft of conducting. I had to teach myself as I didn't even have the guts to go to a teacher and ask how to do it. I feel sorry now that I didn't go to a teacher. To stand in front of one of the greatest orchestras in the world is difficult, even as an accomplished conductor with a great deal of self-confidence, so, when I was asked to recreate the *Elton John* album for the second Festival Hall gig with the Royal Philharmonic, it was very difficult, because not only did I have to conduct an orchestra of the highest standard, I had to rewrite the charts for the gigs. We wrote for the album as we saw fit, never thinking that one day, we would be playing live with a full orchestra."

♫

Elton returned to the States for a gruelling three-month tour in the summer of 1971, ably supported by Hookfoot. "We were the opening act on his gigs which was brilliant for us," recalled bassist Dave Glover. "We were all excited by the experience of going to the US, because of Elton's previous success in LA and in New York. We had everything laid on for us, including limos collecting us from airports, hotels and gigs. We were booked into Holiday Inns for most of the tour, with 24-hour room service, big rooms and swimming pools. It was luxury compared to what we were used to and, of course, we took advantage of the American hospitality as much as we could."

But not everywhere took too kindly to them. "In some of the hotels, or when travelling, we could sometimes get a bit of abuse from the locals." said Epps. "Long hair wasn't looked on favourably by mid-American business types, so we would get the occasional, 'Sorry I thought you were a girl' treatment, and the worst was when you would check into a hotel that had some sort of conference in it with hundreds of what we used to call 'Ernies' all over the place with their photos on their shirts all looking the same."

By this time, of course, Elton was already a well-known name in America, selling millions of albums and playing to packed houses. "I was Elton's personal assistant during the second tour but by then, there was a whole host of people to do everything for him as well," continued Epps. "Everything was very well planned and structured, so we knew what we had to do and where we had to be. When we arrived at the airport there were promoters to meet us and take us to the Holiday Inn. We would sit by the pool, generally have a relaxing time, and then, get ready and go to the gig."

Above all else, as far as Elton was concerned, the audience was the most important thing. Like Elvis, he treated every show and every audience, like it was the first time, and reminded everyone on stage with him, that the crowd had not seen them before. "He wanted to give them a good time," confirmed Epps, "in fact, he went down a storm in almost every place we played. I don't remember any negative reviews at all."

Epps remembered that most times Elton was a great travelling companion, but like anyone else he had his moments. "If someone pissed him off, you knew about it, and part of my job was to recognise when someone had pissed him off. One of those occasions was when we were having breakfast together and there was a knock on the door. It was the tour manager who had popped in to say hello, and we invited him in for a coffee. Then there was another knock on the door and it was one of the roadies. By this time Elton was getting a bit agitated. The next minute another guy came in with a cine camera and started taking pictures and Elton started getting redder and redder. I spotted it, and at some point he just exploded. After that he always had to make a grand exit. On this occasion, he made for the door to the balcony, went out and slammed the door behind him and got stuck on the balcony. I got everyone else out. I then crept out and told Elton that they had all gone, and he went back to his breakfast as if nothing had happened. The point about Elton is that he can look as though he's going to explode, but within five minutes he had gotten it out of his system and would laugh about it. If anything," continued Epps, "Elton was over-committed to his career and was always 100% professional in whatever he did. When he got into the touring, he used to keep records every day of how many people attended the gigs, how many records he sold that day and all manner of information about his career progress. He was completely together in everything he was doing. He had an enormous amount of energy to do the number of gigs he was asked to do, and then he would do interviews every day. He very rarely refused to do interviews at radio stations in every city. He was so focussed on doing promotion as much as possible. To be honest, it was all I could do to keep up with him. He is the most professionally focussed musician I have ever known."

Glover agreed: "Dee and Nigel were now Elton's permanent band and we, as Hookfoot, played as support on the arena part of the tour. We were there for about six weeks and we had a lot of laying around pools and going to parties and drinking, while Elton was doing other gigs on his own or interviews. I remember being in New York and I went out on my own drinking and I got a rollicking for that because New York was dangerous at the time. We had our own manager, John Cokel, and he made sure we acted properly. We did have time to rest and recuperate after a gig in Hawaii, when we spent time on the 'Big Island' of Maui, which had apparently been featured as the backdrop for Elvis's *Blue Hawaii* and *Paradise, Hawaiian Style*. Despite the opportunity to rest, Elton still insisted on contacting the DJM Offices to get all the press cuttings and information relating to the tour. 'Just to keep me informed' wrote Elton in one of his postcards to the girls in the office. It was sort of mad!"

Indeed, it was because the audiences in the US were so good, that Elton started singing and talking with a slight American accent. It was before his flamboyant period, so people were more interested in his music and his playing rather than his stage costumes. Although on the odd occasion he took to wearing novelty shirts and Mickey Mouse ears, it was more to embarrass his band that anything else, and to show off his sense of humour.

Elton was also growing in self-confidence. The more gigs he played and the more the level of adulation increased, the more he gave his all, and expected his band to do the same. He wouldn't come off stage until he had the audience on its feet, and so, more times than not, Nigel would come off soaked in sweat after the hard work he had put into each gig. By the end of the US tour, no one could have disputed that Elton was ranked with some of the other great names in rock. Indeed, one of the final stops on the tour mirrored the prestigious event of the Royal Festival Hall in London when he played the equally illustrious Carnegie Hall in New York.

Not to be left out, Bernie was churning out lyrics faster than Elton could write melodies, so it was not surprising when he announced that he was making his own album, reciting some of his poetry with a musical accompaniment called, logically enough, *Taupin*, also in 1971. It failed to make much of an impact, but it did something that neither Elton nor Bernie had expected. It introduced Davey Johnstone into the fold who, unbeknown to him at the time of meeting Gus Dudgeon at Bernie's album sessions, was about to become a leading player in Elton's future.

♪

By the time he got back to Britain, and with hardly any time off for frivolity, Elton was back in front of a festival audience, for only the second time in his career so far on 21 June at the Crystal Palace Bowl in South

London. It was where he topped the bill with Yes, Rory Gallagher, Fairport Convention, Hookfoot and Tir Na Nog.

The sessions for the *Madman Across The Water* album started in August 1971 after Elton had completed his tour of the States. Dave Glover remembered: "I felt more confident about doing this album due to the success of *Tumbleweed*. It was rehearsed and recorded in much the same way in that we laid down the basic track and then Gus added the orchestra and other instruments later."

Madman Across The Water was arranged in a similar way to *Elton John*. Buckmaster still didn't have a piano, so he used the tried and tested 'tape recorder and headphone and then put to paper' technique. The title track saw Dudgeon using his skills and desire to push the boundaries by recording his new session guitarist, Davey Johnstone, on the title track, on 14 August 1971, with a reverse reverb on his instrument, creating a unique guitar sound for the time. Johnstone had also been involved in the sessions for 'Holiday Inn' on 9th August, the same day that he joined members of Hookfoot, including Roger Pope and Dave Glover on the iconic 'Tiny Dancer' with ace UK pedal steel player B.J. Cole. He also contributed to 'Rotten Peaches' on 14th August.

♪

By 1968, B.J Cole had met up with Stuart Brown who had recently left Bluesology, and the friendship that developed led to Brown asking Cole to join a new band he was putting together, which later became Cochise, with Mick Grabham, (later lead guitarist with Procol Harum), Rick Wills, (who went on the work with Peter Frampton and the Small Faces), and Willy Wilson, (who later joined Sutherland Brothers and Quiver). "We used to go to DJM studio's to cut demos as at the time DJM was the centre of everything in music and everyone used to go there," recalled Cole. "At DJM, we ran into Reg Dwight. He was just another person working there at the time."

On the back of the demos, Cochise got picked up by Clearwater Productions and signed to Liberty Records, plus a separate publishing deal with Dick James Music. With the charismatic Brown as its front man, they embarked on their first album and tour. Although the band appeared destined for success, Brown decided to leave the group and the music business after the release of the first album and head off for the delights of Crete with his girlfriend.

At the same time, Cole was also in demand for session work through DJM. "I got a call from Steve Brown, who asked me if I would come into Trident to do some work for Elton John that evening. I was met by a whole host of people like Gus Dudgeon, Paul Buckmaster, Elton and Steve Brown. We basically spent all night recording but they didn't know quite how it was going to sound at the start of the session. They had the parts worked out, and we spent the rest of the night putting it together. Elton was quite happy to allow us to take a role in the creative process and, by the end of the session, coming out of the studio in daylight; I was very pleased with the results. It was very well structured, but we were allowed to improvise a great deal. I suppose I was surprised how much of the pedal steel guitar they left in on the final master. It starts at the second verse and stays in for the remainder of the song except for a piece when Davey Johnstone takes over."

This, incidentally, was one of the first sessions Johnstone was involved in with Elton before becoming a permanent member of band. The pedal steel guitar on 'Tiny Dancer' has since become an iconic sound. "I am very proud with what was achieved," smiled Cole. "When I hear the track play during the film, *Almost Famous*, starring Kate Hudson, it brings me out in goose bumps. It's a very emotional feeling."

At the same time that Elton was putting together the *Madman Across The Water* album, things were not going well with Hookfoot. They were finding it hard financially and had to turn to other means to make a living. During the balmy summer of 1971, Pope and Glover were engaged on a building site, Pope driving a dumper truck, and Glover laying main drainage pipes. "I was with Gloves, who was doing the shuttering to make the manhole covers," recalled Pope. "It was hard work, but great fun." Ain't rock 'n' roll glamorous? But then, out of the blue, one early August morning, in the middle of laying the pipes, Pope and Glover received a call from Dick James to go to a studio in London.

"We had been at work since 7am," continued Pope. "We got to London town about 6.30pm and went straight into the studio; we were covered in cement because we didn't have any time to go home and get changed." Pope even had to threaten the site gaffer with death because he wouldn't let them go before clocking off time at first. "So there was Elton all clean and we were covered in cement. He played this number once through and we did it in one take. It was called 'Tiny Dancer'. I got sweaty in the studio doing the sessions and as the cement started to set and I started to get a bit scaly. Elton was laughing his arse off." Pope and Glover left the studio at 3am, having recorded three songs during the sessions, and got back to Andover and went straight back to work on the building site.

"We got paid £36 for the sessions on *Madman Across The Water*, and I got £24 for *Tumbleweed Connection*, which took a couple of days session work."

" 'Tiny Dancer' was written by Bernie for Maxine," said David Larkham. "She did ballet dancing and used to dance at the side of the stage when Elton was playing. She was a very small, petite person and that was Bernie's inspiration for the song."

Alongside the Hookfoot guys, Buckmaster introduced various session musicians for the scored parts of the arrangements for *Madman Across The Water*, which was a superstar collection including bassist Herbie Flowers, guitarist Chris Spedding and Rick Wakeman, then of The Strawbs, who was shortly to join prog rock superstars Yes. Wakeman recalled that David Katz, who was a prominent 'fixer', had been recruited to put together the orchestral-based musicians for the album as he had previously done for the *Elton John* album. "I believe Elton had asked for me to do the organ parts as although he is a tremendously talented and unique piano player, he never enjoyed playing the organ." mused Wakeman.

Wakeman was slated to do two sessions a day, one in the morning and one in the afternoon, on top of his very busy schedule with his own band, the Strawbs. "Much of the writing of the music had been done before the sessions. You can't book an orchestra and ask them to play along with no parts, so we did all of the recording live in Trident Studios, and I remember that the studio was wonderfully crowded. Bernie was at the sessions as he was really involved lyrically, but he mainly dealt with the producer and Elton."

Elton had a great deal of respect for the session musicians having been through the experience himself, and that was returned by the other musicians. The end result was perfect as a consequence. "I was given a written part from the arranger," recalled Wakeman, "the band and the orchestra were as one really, I recall having a bit of freedom to work within the part I was given, but it was always piano-based music and quite rightly so."

Once again, David Larkham was recruited to design the sleeve, and again he credits Bernie as being the inspiration, along with their mutual love of denim. "The front cover was actually my denim jacket that we cut the back off, and I drew all the lettering out in blue biro. Janice did all the embroidery and then Steve's wife Jill did the back cover which was just embroidering the song titles onto denim." Both sides were given to Elton as a present which he turned into a cushion.

Although the album only peaked at a disappointing No. 41 in the British album chart, it had enabled the initial introduction of two prospective new band members in Ray Cooper and Davey Johnstone.

By the end of that year, Elton completed his touring by appearing in concert at Croydon's Fairfield Halls with Marc Bolan's T. Rex. Not surprising really, when you consider he had known Bolan since his Bluesology days and that, according to Quaye, was the reason for his impromptu appearance with Marc and his band on *Top Of The Pops* that Christmas, in which he was seen playing piano on 'Get It On'.

Marc and his wife June had become good friends with Elton due to the introduction made by Tony King, who had been watching his career take off with some pride. King was instrumental in introducing him to some influential musicians of the time: "I am quite a social person and I knew a lot of people who Elton wanted to know. Marc Bolan and Elton became close because they were from the same era and were both very popular at the same time. Artists like Elton, David Bowie and Marc Bolan all came along at the same time so they knew one another, but Elton and Marc hit it off from the word go. I also introduced him to Ringo because I worked at Apple, and he used to come in and see me a lot, and we went out to lunch together. Elton then developed his own friendship with Ringo who invited him to his New Year's Eve parties and other events. I also introduced him to Charlie Watts of the Rolling Stones, who I have been friends with forever, and his wife Shirley. Bolan was very friendly with Ringo, too, so it became just a group of people who got to know each other. Marc was a very busy boy, who made sure he was everywhere. He had a brilliant wife, June, and we were all very close. There was something about her that was special and she looked after Marc when he was getting big."

Marc, David Bowie and Elton were all big names at the same time, and then along came Rod Stewart; it was a seventies gang as opposed to the sixties gang who were the Beatles and the Stones, Cilla Black, Donovan and Dusty Springfield. They were all interested in what each other were doing, and so, quite naturally, they all became friends. Bowie became friends with Mick Jagger and Elton with Ringo, and so on, so everyone was intermingling. They weren't separated by a big age gap, so of course, they could relate to each other.

The following year after Elton had appeared on *Top Of The Pops* with T. Rex, the friendship between Marc, Ringo and Elton went a stage further when all three helped to create Marc's film, *Born To Boogie*, which explored a Marc Bolan and T. Rex Concert at the Empire Pool, Wembley in London, through a series of films and concert video footage together with cameo appearances from Elton and Ringo. The scenes were filmed at the Apple offices in Savile Row in London. Directed by Ringo, the film was premiered in December 1972 at Oscar's Cinema in Brewer Street in London.

Around the same time as *Born To Boogie* went on national release throughout Britain, UNI Records in America was subsumed into the giant MCA label. Soon after, Dick James and Mike Maitland of MCA agreed to extend the contract for current and future Elton John products to be released in the States, until February 1975, for an alleged fee of one million dollars. A bargain if ever there was one.

5

Introducing Shaggis

In the summer of 1966, Noel Murphy was invited to Fontana's studios to record his first album, with The Strawbs. "It turned into a legendary drinking session," recalled Murphy with understatement. Afterwards, Murphy thought they had only done seven or eight numbers, and so he called Fontana a couple of days later, and asked, "When do we finish the album?" Surprised at the question, the producer, Terry Brown, told him the album was a rap. Murphy had caned it so hard that he had no idea that he had laid down fifteen songs!

Back in those days, Murphy was touring almost constantly when he wasn't in the studio. One of those tours took him around Scotland. "I went up to Scotland with my guitar, a bag of golf clubs on one shoulder, and a rucksack full of clothes on the other," recalled Murphy. "I was billed to do a gig in Fife at the Elbow Room, which was a famous folk club in Kirkcaldy." At the gig Murphy was supported by a local folk band called the Fife Reivers. "I made a point of listening to the people who were on with me, and this guy was just astounding. He had long blond hair, and a lovely laconic way about him, with fingers that were about 10 inches long, playing the tenor banjo, or the mandolin, and was just a different class altogether. We had a beer and a chat at half time, and it became clear that we knew various people on the circuit even though he was only 16. He told me he had taught himself by watching other people, but it was clear from watching him, that he added an awful lot to what he had picked up. He was that good." In the second half of Murphy's set, he decided that he was going to invite David Johnstone, as he was known then, up on stage with him, and asked him what he thought. "He said 'Wow', which at the time was one of his favourite expressions. If you told him something he would always say 'Wow', so he got up with me, I didn't tell him what I was going to play, but it was just the most bizarre double act, because it was communication without any chatter."

After the gig, Murphy invited Johnstone to have a drink with him, and asked him what plans he had. "I had no intention of offering him anything, because I was a solo artist and loved doing it myself, and was earning a living playing small and medium sized folk clubs, and packing them out. He was far too good to join me in a double act, but I found him to be the most indecisive person I had ever met. 'Oh I might do this, and then no, I am going to do that'. He was 16 and going to be 17 that May. He said he might even go to Art School, but I told him not to give up the music, and whatever he does, he must keep playing with all sorts of people."

The first album sold well, and as a result Murphy was asked back by Fontana to record a second. "The second LP was recorded in the summer of 1968," continued Murphy, "but they took the precaution, this time, of not allowing me to play with the Strawbs, owing to the vast quantities of alcohol that was consumed previously. I was kept under strict control by the production team, and this time the sessions started at 10a.m. They kept us sane for the whole of the session, and we completed the LP in a day, but I think by 5pm they let us out to the pub for an hour and we all came back laughing and giggling. As a result, we did a very jokey track at the end." The second album was considered to be complete by the production team until Murphy approached them again, a little later, and introduced them to his new friend, David Johnstone.

♫

One evening during September 1968, Murphy was on his way out to a gig with his roadie, when he encountered David Johnstone once more. "I was pulling shut the front door of the flat I had in Goldhawk Road in Shepherd's Bush, and he suddenly appeared at the side of the car, with a rucksack, banjo and a mandolin," remembered Murphy. "Five minutes later, it would have been a different story. He had my number, and my address, but he didn't ring or anything, he just turned up, sheepishly, and I said it was great to see him."

Johnstone moved in with Murphy and the two of them set off gigging together. "I was very fortunate in that I had a flat in Shepherd's Bush that had six rooms, and it cost next to nothing, because I rented it through a friend, so he had somewhere to live." Murphy gave Johnstone a nickname as the seal of approval. "I said to him, I have a wonderful nickname for you, and he said 'Oh yea, wow' and I said, 'Yes, it's Shaggis'. It was because he was from Edinburgh, and he had long blond hair. He nearly died laughing at that, so we became Murph and Shaggis. It was obvious when he spoke, that he had a soft Edinburgh accent, so it wasn't a nasty name it was just a play on words, 'Shaggy hair and Scottish Haggis'."

Although the arrangement between Johnstone and Murphy remained a loose one, they went on to play together on the folk circuit for two and a half years: "I had a great list of gigs at folk clubs and festivals, and it was all close up and personal, so much so, that we used to go back to people's houses to stay after the gig, and we sometimes never got to bed until 5 in the morning, just drinking and playing. Davey was far too talented to hold back, he had a totally free hand to do as many solo spots as he wanted. There were certain numbers that were popular, that we were asked to do, and I would normally start a gig to get the audience relaxed and join in, so I could see for myself, if they were in the mood for singing. Davey and I just busked through most of the gigs we did, and he did his party pieces, whichever way he wanted. One of the gigs we used to play, which is also where David Bowie had a residency, was the White Bear in Hounslow. It's the first time I have ever seen anyone play air banjo. When Davey was doing his solo, people would get excited and clapping, but there was this one person playing air banjo, and it looked hilarious! He sat on my left, on stage and I was standing up, and he would reach up with his right hand, with his banjo on his lap and tune my guitar! It never failed to raise a laugh. Since those days, I have seen some Elton John gigs, and I often thought, with all this excitement going on, why doesn't he let him play 'The Mason's Apron' on the tenor banjo, and let him do his own thing?"

It was while Murphy's second album was in its final stages of production that he decided that he wanted Johnstone to feature on it. "I said to Terry Brown that I wanted to do a bit more with the LP, which is not something I would normally do. He refused, saying that it was good as it was and anyway the production had gone too far and it was due to be released soon. I said okay, but could I pop in next week for a lunchtime pint with him and David Voyde, the engineer? He agreed, and the next week, Davey and I went in to the King And Queen with Terry and David, and it was the first time they had met Davey."

Murphy had orchestrated an impromptu jamming session in the pub, so they took their instruments with them, and after a few drinks started playing. "Davey took out his banjo, and I took out my guitar, and we started playing, and the whole pub stopped. There were people trying to climb over each other to listen to this sound, because Davey's playing was so good. When we finished, the whole pub erupted, they were yelling and stuff like that." Brown immediately grabbed the pub telephone and got in touch with Fontana to secure studio time that afternoon. "We went back to the studio and we did two tracks, each one taking only one take each. One was called 'Flowers Of Edinburgh', and the other 'Rakish Paddy'. They were so impressed with the tracks that they halted production and arranged for Davey to be on the cover photograph, even though he had not featured on the original album." The tracks are the only known recordings of Murphy and the 17-year-old Johnstone playing together.

Despite the success of Murph and Shaggis on the Folk Club circuit, Murphy took advantage of some musical changes happening with the Strawbs, and the duo was soon to become a trio. The Strawbs at the time were changing to become an electric band, and Murphy found them Rick Wakeman, a friend of his who used to play the piano in the White Hart pub in East Acton. The Strawbs had brought in an electric bass player, and were doing a lot of recording. Everybody knew about this except their double bass player Ron Chesterman. "He was at a bit of a loose end, so he used to come and join us," recalled Murphy. "I called Dave Cousins from The Strawbs, and said, 'Look, Ron doesn't know what's going on, and it looks like you are becoming an electric band, so would you mind if Ron joined us?'" Cousins agreed, so Chesterman joined Murph and Shaggis on double bass, even though the gigs were still billed as Noel Murphy.

Now they were a trio they needed a name, and Johnstone was to play a big part in the result, although very much by accident. "I was doing an interview for *Melody Maker* in a pub called the Red Lion off Fleet Street in

London." explained Murphy. "I said that we were going to become a trio, and during the interview, I was asked whether this trio had a name. *Melody Maker* was going to put a headline in a future edition about the formation of this new band, but needed a name to promote it. I was just mulling this over and had no ideas. Davey, who was one of the most indecisive people I have ever met in my life, came up with the name, because he was so indecisive. He loved making porridge at any time of the day or night, so when we went to a restaurant and Davey was asking, 'How strong is this curry?' or 'What's in that curry?', because he could not make his mind up with the waiter. I would say do you do any porridge, would you curry some porridge for him, and so it became a running joke, 'Do you have any porridge vindaloo?' So there we are, standing in the bar at the Red Lion. I asked for a pint of Guinness, and Ron and the journalist wanted a pint of beer. Davey looked up and down at the drinks saying, 'Oh wow, they have this,' or 'Oh wow, they've got that.' This went on for some time, and he couldn't make his mind up, the barman was waiting so I just said to him, 'Do you have any draught porridge?' Davey fell about laughing, and I said to the journalist from *Melody Maker,* that is the name of the band... Draught Porridge. I remember we got a taxi to the local station, and all the way Davey was saying, 'Wow Draught Porridge, wow Draught Porridge'."

So the new trio had a name, and the normal round of touring folk clubs started again. Murphy recalled: "We didn't plan for it to be a long term thing, and it only lasted about five or six months but those who were in the folk scene at the time saw it as an absolutely legendary band." In the meantime, various people in the music business had started hearing a lot about Johnstone. "I remember meeting Rod Stewart one night at the Marquee with Long John Baldry, who had become good mates of mine, as a result of them coming along and performing at my all night sessions at the Cousins [The legendary Les Cousins Folk Club in Greek Street]. The Marquee was a venue where it didn't matter whether you were a folk or a blues man, we all used to go there and we were all mates. John Baldry introduced me to Rod, and we went from the Marquee to the Ship in Wardour Street. During a conversation, I suggested to Rod Stewart that he should listen to Davey, because he had a track on his album that needed a bit of mandolin playing. I believe it was called 'Mandolin Wind'. So Davey started getting some session work, and when you do a good job doing sessions, then someone else gets to hear about you, and you start becoming popular as a session musician."

During the summer of 1970, Johnstone started going out with a girl who he would eventually marry. Murphy believes that Diane preferred other forms of music to his and began to influence Johnstone's career path, wanting him to take his music more seriously and go in a different direction. "I don't blame her for that." laughed Murphy. "What happened in the end was that we had short notice, but he joined a band called Magna Carta, without consulting me about it, but we were not in any formal arrangement, so it didn't really matter. I thought it could have been handled with a little more etiquette by telling me what he was going to do, and saying he would leave in about a month, but he joined Magna Carta without any discussion with me."

Despite being disappointed with the lack of notice, Murphy was sensible enough to realise that Johnstone was destined for bigger and better things. "I was only showing Davey the ropes, and nothing more. He was destined for far better things than I could give him and we both knew that. But I also felt that he was destined for better things than Magna Carta could offer as well. That's why I was delighted that he did session work, so he could work with people other than me, and get the experience and exposure."

Soon after Johnstone married, his wife Diane had a baby son who they called Tam and plans were advanced for him to join Magna Carta. Magna Carta was a typical product of the sixties/seventies cusp, where every street, it seemed, had music clubs catering for all styles of music. "You could walk along a street in any city and see a folk club, then a country club, then a blues club." recalled Chris Simpson, vocalist, guitarist and composer for Magna Carta.

Folk music was huge back then. Pentangle and Fairport Convention had a massive following and Magna Carta, with the combined talents of Chris Simpson, Lyell Tranter and Glen Stuart, who was the *de facto* leader of the band, formed in 1969, looked set to follow in the footsteps of those popular bands.

The first recording deal for Magna Carta came about by chance, and the opportunist approach taken by Simpson: "Danny Thompson [of Pentangle fame], had us a potential deal with A&M in America, but I had already got someone drunk from Phonogram and made him sign a beer mat. I took it in to him the next day and told him we had a legally binding deal, which we hadn't really, but he signed us anyway – and that is how we started with Mercury, which was then part of Phonogram." The eponymously-titled first album sold fairly well, and the band embarked on a series of gigs around the folk clubs of England.

"The first album had the added bonus of Danny Thompson on bass guitar, who, at that time, was a leading light in the business. As a consequence, he introduced Magna Carta to a whole new series of openings that we wouldn't normally have had." Simpson recollected.

The next album, *Seasons*, was arguably, one of the best albums in its class, but it all came about, as most good albums do, by chance and inspiration. "I wrote *Seasons* in one night on a Cornflakes packet in my pad in London." continued Simpson. "We rehearsed it, and made a tape, and took it into the agent and he thought it was amazing." The agent then took the tape to Gus Dudgeon. "I had heard of Gus, in fact I embarrassed him when we first met by asking him whether he had been a lowly tape operator with Mike Vernon at Blue Horizon Records. He was very much a public school boy and a very funny guy." When the agent played him the tape, he reportedly said that it was one of the most charming pieces of music he had heard. "So, we started to routine it all with Gus, and then we made the album. Gus suggested that Tony Visconti would be the best arranger, so we went to see him at his house. This young lad would drop in with his wife and listen to us run through *Seasons* with Tony, and he said how beautiful the music was." The 'young lad' turned out to be David Bowie.

Bowie and Magna Carta forged a brief relationship on the road, and played a few gigs together, including one at the London Palladium, where a disillusioned Bowie told Simpson that he thought he would never have a hit song again after 'Space Oddity', and it was now a millstone around his neck.

The resulting *Seasons* album saw Simpson, Tranter and Stuart joined by

Tony Visconti on electric bass, Danny Thompson on string bass, and the keyboard guy throughout was Rick Wakeman, with Stuart doing the speaking parts.

"We recorded at Trident, and a young man called Reg Dwight was coming in and out to see Gus, who was quite proud that he had done an album called *Elton John* with him," said Simpson. In fact, Simpson got to know Elton quite well, and helped him promote his new album by travelling up and down the Northern line on London's Underground, putting stickers on the carriages and station walls. At the same time Dudgeon was discussing the next Magna Carta single with Simpson and during a general conversation he told him that he was in despair over Elton's career as he really needed a hit single, and didn't know where it was coming from.

It was during the recording of *Seasons* that Magna Carta continued to tour the folk clubs of England, earning £12 a gig, plus petrol, so money was tight. Whilst life on the road was fun, it started to take its toll on the band, particularly Tranter, who was planning to marry his girlfriend. "We were sleeping on floors, and having amazing adventures." recalled Simpson. "Sometimes you ended up sleeping on the floor with someone that you didn't think you went to bed with the night before, and it was, to me, like 'Wow, here we go'. On another occasion I remember staying in a cottage, with a hole in the roof, which was rented from a deep-sea diver. It was in the middle of nowhere, and there was snow and ice everywhere. We had a toilet that was so full that it reached the top and was frozen in a pinnacle. We stayed in the place for two days, and we all slept in the same bed, covered in newspapers, it was so cold. I got up one night to get a drink of water, which was difficult because the sink had at least a week's worth of crockery in it, which was frozen solid, and I got bitten in the bum by a dog who was in a cupboard at the bottom of the stairs, and then kicked by a horse that was in the kitchen that I knew nothing about!"

Magna Carta were down to play the 1970 Cambridge Folk Festival. One of the highlights of the Sunday billing was Noel Murphy and Shaggis. Simpson remembered, "I went and watched them with a hangover as big as the Eiffel Tower, and it was when I saw this guy doing '12th Street Rag' on the mandolin behind his head, I became interested, and was very impressed."

Meanwhile, the pressures of juggling life on the road and trying to get wed were too much for Tranter. The lack of money and his impending nuptials forced him – and guitar players of a sensitive disposition should turn away at this moment – to sell his axe, which was his pride and joy. The rest of the band could see that it was only a matter of time before Tranter left.

During the *Seasons* sessions, the band was playing a song called 'Give Me No Goodbye', which to Dudgeon's ears, sounded like a single. Dudgeon decided to add guitar and he asked Mick Ronson to do it. "He liked the track, and agreed to play on it, but when Gus heard the playback, he decided that while Ronson's work was brilliant, and we all agreed with him, it was too heavy for the track. I said to Gus that there was a young guy who I had seen who would be ideal for this track, and he said, he preferred to use people he knew, especially at this critical stage of the album production. I convinced him that he was good, despite the nickname of Shaggis, and so Gus reluctantly agreed after much persuasion. He didn't have a guitar, so he had to go round trying to borrow one. He turned up at the studio in an antiquated sports jacket, which Gus cast a jaundiced eye over, and he played beautiful slide guitar on 'Give Me No Goodbye'. The tuning was dodgy on the final cut, and I'm surprised that Gus let it go past, but Davey's playing was so intuitive." recalled Simpson.

Johnstone stayed in the studio with Magna Carta, and played on some other tracks on the album, where it was needed. Dudgeon was impressed with what he heard from Johnstone, and clearly made a mental note to use him again on further sessions.

After Tranter had left, the band were one guitarist light. "I went to see Davey, even though I thought he may not be into our scene. I knew that Davey was into the strange, the odd, and the different, and he loved freaks, it was all helped by the dope. So I asked him if he wanted to join Magna because Lyell was leaving and he was very flattered."

The new line up set off on the road and through gigging they got to be a very tight band. "Davey had a big part to play by adding other instruments to his repertoire, including lyre, banjo, mandolin and then sitar. He bought a sitar on a Tuesday, and was ready for a session on the Wednesday, that was how quick he was", laughed Murphy. Having bought a new black Fender Stratocaster, and dressed up in his brushed black velvet suit, like the rest of the band – due to the insistence of the manager, and the embarrassment of the band members – Johnstone and Magna Carta toured the UK and Europe blowing audiences away.

The gigs weren't without their low moments though, and one of those came when Johnstone was electrocuted by his equipment. "We were using an Orange PA system at the time, which had served us well. We were at a gig, and feeling chuffed, because it was going well." said Simpson, "Davey got electrocuted and was blown over backwards, got knocked out, landed on his mandolin and broke the neck of his banjo, so it was an expensive fall. Brian Shepherd, who was then head of A&R at EMI, had taken time out of his day job to go on the road with Magna Carta, which was fortunate as he quickly pulled the plugs out. Davey recovered and, being the professional he is, completed the set and still did his amazing things."

The brilliance of Davey Johnstone was seen at the Royal Albert Hall, when Magna Carta supported the Beach Boys, which was to be one of his final concerts for the band. "We ended the set with Davey playing a banjo solo, and the crowd started to clap a bit as Davey built up speed. He got faster and faster, and just when the crowd thought he couldn't go any further, he flipped the banjo over his head, and continued to play it a breakneck speed. He finished and the crowd went mad, they gave us a standing ovation and as we went off stage they were shouting for more. I thought that's all right, an encore; so we started going back towards the stage. Suddenly, we were not getting any further, and we started to be surrounded by rather big men with black coats. One of them said 'Listen motherfucker, you just set one foot on that stage and I'll bust your ass'." The Beach Boys entourage successfully convinced Simpson that an encore was not necessary, and they quickly disappeared into the dressing room.

The last album before Johnstone left Magna Carta was the 1971 *Songs From Wasties Orchard*, which was named after Johnstone's then home. By this time, Dudgeon had realised what a talent Johnstone possessed and drafted him in to play on *Madman Across The Water*.

Johnstone's decision to leave Magna Carta was made easier by the introduction of a new manager, with whom Simpson was less than happy: "The manager was in my opinion, burying us, and one of the most disastrous days of my life was when Gus decided to call it a day. He didn't like the manager, who he thought was too glitzy, glamorous and showbizzy and didn't understand the part a producer played. He regularly asked why we needed a producer." When the manager and Dudgeon met for what was possibly the last time, he had tried to cut his fee down, which was unfortunate timing as Dudgeon had just seen the million album sales for Elton John, and didn't really need Magna Carta and its distractions. "I got a call from Gus, who said he had thought about it long and hard, and concluded that he was just too busy with Elton to really contemplate another album with Magna Carta. I was probably considered by Gus as a little bit difficult myself at the time, as he hadn't realised how 'Reg obsessive' he had become. He would regularly take breaks from recording *Wasties Orchard* to deal with a radio or a television interview about Elton John, and would regularly be interrupted by Elton's people coming in and out of the studio, asking him things. So I said to Gus, that it was a bit disruptive and he should concentrate on what we were doing. He couldn't see it at the time, but he did years later."

Meanwhile back with Elton John at DJM: "There was talk about bringing in a guitarist to augment the three piece of Elton, Dee and Nigel, partly because it was difficult to reproduce the songs that were now being introduced to the repertoire," recalled Stuart Epps. "Caleb was tied up with Hookfoot, and so Gus suggested Davey Johnstone, as he had been working with him on the Magna Carta albums, and he had already done some session work for Dudgeon and Elton on the *Madman Across The Water* album."

Simpson got a call from Davey, who said that he had been offered a place in Elton's band, and he had been up all night worrying about whether to take it. He recalled, "I was stuck for words. I knew the time had come where I was facing the same problem that Noel had faced. I said to Davey that I thought it was a pretty good piece of news, and he said he would miss me, and I said the same back."

Epps remembers the first gig that Davey played, which was at the

Royal Festival Hall on 5 February 1972. "He didn't have an electric guitar, and we all thought that it wasn't a particularly great gig because we were so used to a three piece." Murray and Olsson were not exactly thrilled with the idea either as they had developed a close relationship both personally and musically as a three piece. "There was a different atmosphere during the second Elton John tour, as Elton, Dee and Nigel were such a close unit and Davey was the outsider. It took a while to sort itself out, but Davey's playing got better and better, he sorted his sound out, and they became a great band", remembers Epps.

"Dee and Nigel felt a bit down by the decision to bring Davey in because they had done so well and had conquered America and the World," recalled Anett Murray wife of the Elton John's bassist the late Dee Murray. "They felt that they were suddenly not good enough anymore; Dee tried to take a positive view and looked forward to playing with another band member who was a guitarist. It wasn't that they didn't respect Davey, but the thing that disappointed Dee and Nigel the most was that during the early years they were a trio and they felt like members of a group, much the same as they had been in The Mirage, Spencer Davis and Plastic Penny. They were close like a family and felt they should have been included in the decision to bring in another guitar player. It was not like that though. Just before the third tour the news came out that they had a new guitar player and that was that. They were upset because they felt they were left out. Davey felt that there were icy vibes at the first rehearsal but it was not really directed at Davey it was just at the way it all came about. Davey didn't play electric guitar up until that point so that was odd to Dee and Nigel as well but he picked it up quickly and Davey was such a nice guy that it didn't take long for him to be accepted and Davey and Dee became like brothers." Davey and his wife Diana lived close to the Murray's and so it was natural that they became very good friends."

Dee Murray was born in Gillingham, Kent in England on 3 April 1946, into a conservative, Methodist family. He and his brother regularly attended Methodist Church with their parents, where the boys would sing in the choir. Music wasn't that prevalent in the family home though, although Dee did have some piano lessons.

He left school at 16 having moved from Gillingham to the leafy London suburb of Barnet when he was 7 years old. His father found him a job in the parts department of an automobile service station as an assistant and one of the guys who worked with him called Sid was starting a band and was looking for a bass player. At the time there were bands on every street corner and so 'Sid's band' was not unique in that regard. "He asked Dee if he wanted to be a bass player and Dee replied that he would give it a go," recalled Anett Murray. So they went back to Sid's house where he had a bass guitar and according to Anett, "He just figured it out overnight." So at the age of 17 Murray started gigging with Sid's band, also by now known as The Thunderbolts. "The boys could never quite get used to not calling it Sid's band," laughed Anett. For three years the band had some success playing weddings and bar mitzvahs, covering songs mainly by Cliff Richard and the Shadows, in the evenings after work and weekends whilst Dee continued with his day job at the garage.

The professional turning point for Dee came when he met the Hynes Brothers; Dave, Pete and Pat who, along with the guitarist Ray Glynn, were having some impact in the local music scene with a band called The Mirage. "The Mirage guys were still playing the same sort of gigs as Sid's Band but they were better and more popular," recalled Anett. "So when Pete Hynes asked Dee to join he said he would." Not long after joining the band, Dee was laid off from his job at the garage. Having been issued with an ultimatum from his parents that unless he came up with some money he would have to leave home, Dee moved in with drummer Dave Hynes and turned professional.

The Mirage played long club engagements mainly in Germany and Europe, and released several less than successful singles on the Philips label. In 1968 they were signed by Larry Page, owner of Page One Records, and released a single called 'Mystery Lady' that received a lot of airplay on BBC radio but didn't really bother the chart positions. Although the band enjoyed a healthy number of gigs, Dee still felt the band wasn't really going anywhere. As luck would have it he was at the Page One Records Offices, which were alongside the Offices of the iconic entrepreneur publisher Dick James, where most of the musicians of the sixties went. Lucky because it was the hang out of many musicians who were either looking for songs written by DJM signed songwriters or waiting to record in the up and coming studios managed by Dick's son Steven. Dee was playing on sessions working with the likes of Spencer Davis who was always on the lookout for new band members for his Group. Seeing Dee and Dave Hynes he asked them to join. This was a huge step for Hynes and Dee but the downside was that it broke up The Mirage.

Having established himself in the new Spencer Davis line up with David Hynes, Spencer Davis, and Ray Fenwick, Murray set off on a long tour with the band to America. Two months into it, it was clear to Spencer Davis that Hynes and Murray were getting homesick and so not wanting to lose his two new dynamic members he suggested that they should bring their partners over to the States for Christmas. "Spencer had this great idea that Dee and I should get married," laughed Anett. So the following Friday, 3 January 1969, when there was a break in the touring schedule, they did.

"At the time the band were playing Detroit," recalled Anett. "If we wanted to get married we had to stay in the same place for a week because we had to have blood tests as part of the arrangements, but we could never stay in the same place long enough, so we drove across the border to Canada where Dee had a relative. The Registry Office was closing when we got there but we managed to get married. Spencer was a great businessman and had connections and so when we got back to Detroit the Four Tops were playing at The Rooster Tail Club; Spencer knew them so we had a little party there and the Four Tops played for us. It was the best wedding ever. Ron (Hynes) and me stayed for two weeks and then went home; but the tour continued for two further months."

Even though Dee had a great job with Spencer Davis, money was still tight although by now it was at least regular and Anett had to return to the UK to the one room apartment in Muswell Hill, London where the newlyweds lived, above the landlord. "We had to share the house and bathroom with other tenants," laughed Anett. "I don't know how they put up with us because even when Dee was not on tour or in the studio he was always playing his bass. He always complained that he needed to keep his calluses and his fingers going so he was playing along loudly to records for hours, but the other tenants didn't complain and were wonderful."

Being a prolific touring band The Spencer Davis Group embarked on a tour of Europe before going into the studio to record the album *Funky*. The band were asked to go out on an even longer tour of the States but this time it would be without drummer Dave Hynes. "Dee loved the touring and had a real blast" remembered Anett, "but Dave hated it and wanted to be back with his family in the UK."

Reverting to his tried and tested model, Spencer Davis went back to Dick James Studios where he saw another Page One recording band who had just finished touring with their hit 'Everything I Am' and were in the DJM studios rehearsing with a young drummer called Nigel Olsson. Davis liked what he saw and in August 1969 he asked Nigel to join the band as a replacement for Dave Hynes. Dee and Nigel already knew each other from the days at DJM and Page One Records and quickly got down to rehearsing with guitarist Ray Fenwick and Spencer Davis and off they went on another marathon tour of the States, which was to turn out to be the last for the band. Fenwick and Davis had some 'issues' and so by the time Dee had returned to the UK in December 1969 the band were no more and Dee was left without work.

Dee recorded a solo album with Ray Fenwick and things were looking up but nothing came of it. He and Anett went back to living off her wages in the little apartment in Muswell Hill. Dee kept searching for his next big break at Dick James offices and then one day he went back to Anett and said he thought he had found something at last. "He had met up with a piano player called Reginald Dwight and he suggested to me that I came and met him," recalled Anett. "I went along to DJM and watched them record a demo and I met Reg and his then girlfriend Linda Woodrow with her little dog under her arm." Elton had been recording a new album called *Elton John* with the full backing of Dick James, the up and coming new producer Gus Dudgeon and arranger Paul Buckmaster who were fresh from their success with David Bowie and 'Space Oddity'. Although Reg had been working with the DJM studio band Hookfoot for most of his earlier material he was now looking for a band to tour the UK to promote the new album. Dee and Nigel too readily agreed. In 1970 they played some gigs across the UK and then in Paris. "But it was very dicey," recalled Anett. "I went to one gig in Piccadilly Circus in London and they opened up for Santana which was a real mismatch. They were booed off the stage and it was horrible. They went to Paris and when Dee came home he said it was bad and they didn't like it." In some places they went down really well so in general the reaction of the audience was very mixed. "There was a lot of pressure on Dee because he had to make up for them not having a guitar player," Anett remembered, "He was the only musician on the stage who was standing up and Dee wasn't used to being the focus of attention. He even used to sit down and play because he just didn't know what to do with himself."

Despite the mixed reaction from the audience on that first tour Elton's manager, Ray Williams, managed to convince Dick James to fund a short promotional tour to America which was to start at The Troubadour Club in Santa Monica, Los Angeles. By this time the Head of Universal Records (UNI) Russ Regan, was a big fan of the *Elton John* album but even he was surprised and somewhat nervous when he found out that Elton was in a three-piece band and they were promoting this heavily orchestrated piece of work. He needn't have worried though because the three-piece were an amazing success.

During that short promotional tour and in the absence of the now common mobile phone and Internet communication contact between Anett and Dee was limited if not non-existent and it was putting a strain on their marriage. Anett, living an ordinary life on her own in the small communal house in Muswell Hill, and Dee enjoying the rock and roll lifestyle on tour in the States. When Elton and Co came back from the American tour they were, not surprisingly, excited about the reaction they had got from the American audiences who just couldn't get enough of this new star. With sales of the *Elton John* album flying out of the American record shops, Elton, Dee and Nigel and the entourage set off planning the next tour of the States. Realising the pressure the success was having on the Murray's marriage, Dee agreed with Elton that Anett should tour with them and she stayed by Dee's side throughout his long and successful career with the Elton John Band. Before the heady days of glam rock and feather boas, Dee, Nigel and Elton toured America again but life was pretty basic. "Dee would be driving the rental car from gig to gig with me in the front and Elton and Nigel, passengers in the back seat," laughed Anett. "Bob Stacey, the tour manager, was in the van following behind us with the kit." As they got more successful they employed a road manager who, amongst many things, took over the driving seat with Elton now in the front passenger seat with Nigel, Dee and Anett snuggled tightly in the back. "It was so basic and adventurous," laughed Anett. "There were a couple of times that were reminiscent of the Blues Brothers when we showed up to a gig that looked like it was unsuitable for an Elton John show and we would just drive off and not do the gig."

♫

The Château in France marked the first time that Dee and Nigel had recorded an album with Elton and much like most of the albums before and since it was a scene of collaboration where Bernie would produce the lyrics and Elton would create the melody with the band members adding their influence through their respective instruments. The harmonies that Dee, Nigel and Davey added to the *Honky Chateau* album were synonymous with the Elton John sound and the blend of voices were so natural that they needed very little rehearsal.

As fame started taking over Elton's life there was a gradual separation of Elton from the band. There were fun times though and a lot of banter but this became less and less as fame came along more and more for Elton. Dee was famous for complaining and always complained about something whether it was about his room or the food, but the one thing that he complained about the most was that he wanted to be in a band; a member of a group. "He didn't want to be a backup musician and gradually that is what was what was happening to them," remembered Anett. "They were just hired hands and this started just after Davey joined." Money was also a big issue. "When Davey joined, Nigel and Dee were told that they were having a cut in wages because they now had a new member who needed to be paid; they didn't like that because not only had they not been consulted on a new guitar player, they then had to take a cut in money. Nigel decided to take this up with John Reid after a gig in Minneapolis-St Paul to ask for a raise. When he came back he said it went really bad. There were never any negotiations it was like a dictatorship and they had to accept it or leave. This approach really did cement in the mind of Dee that he was just a hired hand even though they had contributed so much to the success of the Elton John Project."

6

The Death of Reg

1972 kicked off with the death of Reg and the birth of Elton John. On 7 January, Reginald Kenneth Dwight officially became Elton Hercules John by deed poll, following the application he made on 8 December 1971 to change his name. It was duly announced in the *London Gazette* four days after his solicitors had confirmed his new name.

Steve Brown remembered it well: "Reg came to me one day and said I think I'm going to change my name. He was always Reg and everyone called him Reg and at some point he just said listen I really want to be called Elton, which I really struggled with and even his mother had to call him Elton. Anyway I said I would set up an appointment for him so he could legally change his name. We went to the lawyer's office for Dick James in Piccadilly and he completed all the paperwork and recapped the details. He asked Reg if he wanted to change his name to Elton John; Elton said yes; the lawyer then said well do you want a middle name. Reg said well what do you mean by a middle name and the lawyer said well do you just want to be Elton John and Reg said well I hadn't thought of that. I'll call myself Hercules. So literally on the spot in the Solicitors office on that day he became Elton Hercules John."

Reg Dwight was no more and Elton John was now the main man, which caused much consternation with his closest friends and colleagues at DJM. Up to that point any newcomers would start by calling him Elton and when they thought they knew him well enough, they would start calling him Reg. Not anymore. Elton announced to the staff at DJM that he would no longer answer to Reg.

Chrissie Cremore remembered: "We just couldn't bring ourselves to call him Elton because he was Reg. So we just didn't call him anything for a while." Even his mother Sheila had to call him Elton. "I found it difficult at the time so I asked him if he could wait awhile so I could get used to it, and so for a time, I didn't call him anything, and then one day I just said 'Elton' out of the blue and I was surprised when I did," remembered Tony King. "He became Elton with a little bit of Reg in there somewhere, but what he created was a character and had become it, which was brilliant."

Changing his name permanently came about as a result of an embarrassing incident of the 'Don't You Know Who I Am?' variety. "I was out shopping with him one Saturday," explained Reid. "We were in Fortnum & Mason, and Reg was wearing his full Elton John rig. We went to the antiques department to look at the music boxes, and when he had chosen the ones he wanted he went to the sales assistant to pay by cheque, but the lady assistant wouldn't take it because it said Reginald Kenneth Dwight and not Elton John."

By this point, Elton John was known by most people in Britain, as his music had reached the masses but the assistant hadn't heard of Reg Dwight, although she knew and recognised him as Elton John. "I could see he was getting angry. His face changed and he got grumpy and then this guy walked past and asked whether there was anything wrong and could he help? So I took him to one side and told him what had happened, and so he told the assistant to accept the cheque," said Reid. The assistant quickly did as she was told, probably in a state of trepidation as she had been confronted not only by the famous Elton John, but also by the owner of Fortnum & Mason!

Armed with his purchases, Reg and Reid left the store but it wasn't the end of the saga. Still angry about the situation, though not to his credit, with the hapless assistant, Reg decided to take matters into his own hands. "When we left the store, Reg said to me, 'Fuck this, I'm going to change my name' and that is what he did." Reid continued, "The next week he took action with his solicitors and changed his name to Elton Hercules John."

When he told his mother, all she said was 'What's all this about? Only you could name yourself after Steptoe's horse.' [*Steptoe & Son* was a popular TV comedy about a couple of rag and bone men who had a horse called Hercules] Despite the mild rebuke, she was the only person to accept the change easily, unlike his colleagues and fellow musicians.

"An edict went out saying that he would only answer to the name Elton John; we all had difficulty with this, even me. You just couldn't say it, so there were all kinds of nicknames given to him; Elt, Herc, but EJ became the easiest. The only person to this day who calls him Reg is Ringo Starr, which irritates the life out of him. Marc Bolan also refused to call him Elton and when he was told otherwise all he would say was 'Don't be silly, dear, you're Reg", laughed Tony King.

♪

On the music front, things were not quite so dramatic. *Honky Chateau* would be the next album which, following the advice of his accountants, was recorded at the Château d'Hérouville in France, a so called 'castle' located just outside of Paris. It was owned by the French film composer Michel Magne, who had purchased the building in 1962, the same year that he was nominated for an Oscar for *Gigot*. He converted part of the castle into a residential recording studio after a fire devastated the left wing in 1969. It would later become jinxed though with legal and financial problems when Magne attempted to sell it in 1984. Eventually the studio was closed in the summer of 1985; exactly one year after Magne had committed suicide.

For the making of the album, which was Davey Johnstone's full debut as Elton's newest band member, Dudgeon found the studio after attempts by Epps to use the Rolling Stones' mobile recording equipment had failed. As well as having all the right equipment for Dudgeon to weave his magic, it had to have all the facilities for the band and the ever-growing entourage to live in for the duration of the album's production. It was still some years before other studios, such as Richard Branson's Manor studio in Oxfordshire, were to introduce living quarters for artists and crews, so for Elton and Bernie, Maxine and the entire entourage, the place was perfect. It also marked the first time they would all be living together while they created and recorded an album.

The Château had plenty of bedrooms to accommodate everyone, a swimming pool and a games room where Elton would demonstrate his competitive streak. "I loved table tennis and would often play Elton, but if I was ever winning I would suddenly feel Elton's frustration and I often let him win rather than get him upset," laughed Epps. Well, that's his story and he's sticking to it!

"It was not always plain sailing though, especially living with people you work with and I do remember a few arguments between Elton and Sheila, Gus's wife," recalled Epps. "She could really wind Elton up, and she would often challenge what Elton said by saying, 'Don't be so fucking stupid' in her broad Brazilian accent, which would have Elton raging and leaving the table." Understandably so too - he was the host, after all. Dudgeon would often end up being the peacemaker by diffusing the situation; not that he was always successful.

As had happened before, some of the lyrics for the album had been written before they went into the studio, but the musical arrangements hadn't. They would be created in the commissary of the château or the studio itself. It was just one of many changes Dudgeon would make during the production, and one can only imagine how the form of a song and songs would change with both melody and lyric. Certainly the change of lyric aspect was why Bernie was now such an important and integral part of the band and needed to be there - a case of 'Is there a lyricist in the house?'

To help with the sessions, Elton took some albums with him, so everyone could listen to them for inspiration. Jazz violin wizard Jean-Luc Ponty was surprised how eclectic his musical tastes were. In striving to find new sounds, Elton had contacted Ponty who he had first heard on one of the many albums in his vast collection. Frank Zappa had produced and arranged Ponty's album called *King Kong*, which was an album of Zappa's own music, in Los Angeles in 1969. Elton was particularly taken with the sound produced by the electric violin that Ponty was playing. "He found out that I was in town, while he was recording *Honky Chateau* near Paris, and he had someone track me down to ask me to come to the studio and play on a couple of songs." remembered Ponty.

One of the tracks Ponty played on was 'Mellow'. "It was a beautiful song, very inspiring to play on. I forget who suggested I plug my violin into the Hammond Organ, but I agreed and it worked great. I had tried this before with Eddy Louis, who was a great organ player, and he knew how the organ should sound. I think I handled it really well by using a few violinistic expressions such as sliding notes that cannot be played on an organ, mixed with a more typical organ phrasing." The result was a hybrid sound that was revolutionary at the time, because it was before the days of midi instruments, which can now be plugged into synthesisers or samplers, and can make a violin sound like anything but a violin. "I thought Ken (Scott) did some great engineering on that song," Ponty recalled.

John Reid was also impressed with Ponty, and attempted to sign him to the newly formed Rocket Records, but at the time Reid made his offer Ponty was signed to another label.

The lead single from the album, released in April 1972, was 'Rocket Man,' which became an instant hit on both sides of the Atlantic. It reached No.2 in Britain and No. 6 in America. Tony Taupin remembers how the first few lines of the song were thought up while Bernie was driving around the lanes of Lincolnshire near his home. "He was going round this bend when the first line came to him and he didn't have pen or paper to write it down, so he raced home as fast he could."

By the time the album came out, two months after the single in June 1972, Elton was one of the world's biggest selling artists, and the packaging on his records was given star treatment. For *Honky Chateau*, Michael Ross joined DJM as the Art Director, to help share the load with David Larkham. Ross was based in London and Larkham in Los Angeles, where he was now living with his wife. "Michael did the artwork, and I got the photograph together through Ed Caraeff," explained Larkham. "The concept of the gatefold sleeve came about as we [Caraeff and Larkham], wanted to do something different. We printed the picture onto canvas paper and sent the shots to England where Steve Brown and Ross looked at it and loved it. They tweaked the cardboard flap a bit, and opted to print a canvas style picture, glued separately onto the front. It was so different from the run-of-the-mill album covers at the time."

With a second, less successful, single 'Honky Cat' released in the same month as the long player, the album ended up spending 23 weeks in the British chart peaking at No. 2 and becoming his most successful charting album since *Tumbleweed Connection* eighteen months earlier.

♫

The 1970s was a time for affluent rock stars to open their wallets and decamp to the countryside to live like latter day lords of the manor. Elton and Reid duly left the bright lights of London, but plumped for the more conventional stockbroker belt charms of Virginia Water, Surrey which many entertainment personalities from the world of music, film and sport called home.

One of those entertainment personalities was film maker, actor and photographer, Bryan Forbes, who became one of Elton's most trusted allies and personal advisors. "I had a bookshop in Virginia Water for about thirty-four years," said Forbes. "I was there one day when a young man came in who I had never seen before, but he had purple hair and green sideburns and he bought £200 worth of books, so of course, he was very welcome in my small shop."

No prizes for guessing who that young man was, of course. "It was a guy called Elton John who had just moved to Virginia Water; to a house he named Hercules [after his new middle name], but I was unaware of his name at this point," recalled Forbes. "I'd never heard of him before, and nor had I heard his music, but we got chatting. I was the president of the National Youth Theatre and that night there was an Elton John concert to raise money for it at the Shaw Theatre on 20 February 1972. When he went on the stage I realised it was the boy I'd met at the shop, who I had now found out was Elton John." Elton was supported by his friend from the days of the house in Hampstead, Linda Lewis who by now was making a name for herself in the Folk scene.

Forbes went backstage after the gig, and said how awful of him for not knowing who was in the shop earlier that day. "He had not mentioned he was performing that night. I asked him if I could take him out to dinner as a thank you, as it happened we had invited Princess Margaret to the show to help raise more money, so we all went to a restaurant in

Hampstead and that was the beginning of a friendship for us all." It was also Elton's introduction to the Royal Family and showed just how far Reg Dwight from Pinner had progressed.

The concert itself was successful for both the charity and Elton, but the jury was still out on Davey Johnstone. Some of the entourage considered Elton's latest newcomer was getting in the way. "Davey wasn't really an electric guitar player and he didn't even own an electric guitar," recalled Stuart Epps. "Elton had bought a Les Paul guitar at Manny's Music Store in New York, fully intending to learn to play himself, but he gave it to Davey instead. I remember not being too impressed with Davey in the band to start with; he hadn't really got his sound together at that point. I don't think Dee and Nigel were very happy either, as they were quite content with the line up the way it was." Time was to prove the doubters wrong, of course. Davey refutes that he wasn't an electric guitar player or that he didn't own an electric guitar though so it could be a question of memory playing tricks again.

The Forbes clan were to become almost like a surrogate family for Elton. Although his career was on a steep upwards curve, he still wasn't a household name. "He was very unsure of himself," confirmed Forbes. "He used to come into the house and ask me why I had so many books and I explained that having spent 25 years in the same house you do accumulate a lot of stuff. He then asked how he could do the same. He always said that I taught him taste, which I don't think I did, but I guided him towards things and protected him because he suddenly had money. He had this yearning to buy Magritte paintings and there were some in a Bond Street gallery that he wanted. I told him not to go in himself because they'd take him to the cleaners, so I went on his behalf. I pointed to a painting and asked how much - it was £78,000. I asked how much the other one was and he told me it was £47,000. I then asked him what he would sell both for in cash. So, in shock, the gallery manager went into a back room with a pencil and piece of paper, and came back with an offer. 'The £78,000 you can have for £52,000 and the £47,000 for £33,000' and I agreed. So, I gave him Elton's cheque and told him it wouldn't bounce and off I went with the paintings."

"We spent holidays together, as well. He took a house in Malibu one year, and we all stayed there for about five weeks, all sorts of music people would call in - people like Alice Cooper, who, interestingly enough, was nothing like his stage persona."

Elton's friendship with Forbes started at the time when his career was taking off and the record company was really making an effort to ingratiate themselves. "I recall that his American record label asked Elton if he wanted a Cadillac, and Elton rather cleverly said I don't want a Cadillac, but what I'd like is for us all to go down to Tower Records and help ourselves to a few records and they agreed. Elton and his entourage all piled into cars and went to Tower Records on Sunset Boulevard and came back with about $75,000 worth of records. We came out of the store as well with a lot of records and cassettes. We had so much luggage after the five weeks holiday that Elton had to hire a Pan American 707 aircraft to take us home. But the most amazing thing was the fully-grown lion and trainer (with a gun) he had arranged to greet me on my birthday in the courtyard. And all because I was a Leo!" laughed Forbes.

Elton's life was now becoming entwined with that of the Forbes family: Bryan, wife Nanette Newman, and daughters Sarah and Emma. Forbes recalled that it gave them a new lease of life. "Nanette and I were middle-aged and it changed our lives at the time, because I became a bit of a hippy and grew my hair a bit longer and, whenever we went out, Elton would babysit for us. I remember when *Deep Throat* was in the cinema and Elton wanted to see it, but he was babysitting Emma... so he took her with him. Apparently the man in the box office said 'You can't bring that child in here', and Elton replied: 'How dare you, it's not a child, it's a midget, a 45-year-old midget'. Full of apologies the box office clerk let them in. Emma of course went to sleep as she didn't know what it was about anyway."

In return for an insight into the world of music, Forbes introduced Elton to his film world and to the likes of Groucho Marx and Katherine Hepburn. "Groucho took a great shine to us all," continued Forbes. "We used to go to his home and see old films which he starred in." Another friend of Forbes' was Katherine Hepburn who was invited to Elton's home one day only to find there was an animal, (some say it was a frog), in the swimming pool. Hepburn said: 'Look at that, get it out', and Elton said, 'Oh, no I couldn't possibly do that', so she dived in and rescued the animal," smiled Forbes.

♪

The start of 1972 saw Elton on the road in the UK with his new guitarist and reports sent back to the girls in the DJM offices from Elton were that Davey was settling in well. But not every gig went off smoothly. Elton was playing a gig on 24 February 1972 at Watford Town Hall, with Linda Lewis as support. The Police received a bomb threat at the venue and the organiser was left to whisper in Elton's ear in the middle of a song with the crowd going wild, that he had to leave the stage whilst they evacuated the place.

By the Spring of 1972 the band were back on tour in North America promoting the new album *Honky Chateau* prior to its release and were supported by one of Ray Williams new found groups: Family. The guitarist of Family was none other than Jim Cregan who by now was the husband of Linda Lewis. Linda had known Cregan since he had played session guitar on her album *Lark*; but she remembered him back in the days of his first band, Blossom Toes: an English psychedelic band. "It was very organic stuff coming from the instruments and voices," remembered Lewis.

But not all gigs on the tour went according to plan for the support band. "I went out to visit Jim as I was now his wife. They were playing this massive gig in Anaheim and I remember getting there and they were all panicking because the equipment had not turned up from the last gig warming up for Elton. Elton saw me and said 'you can sing and play the guitar'." The band agreed with him and Linda was eventually persuaded to pick up her guitar at short notice and play in front of an arena audience for the first time without any rehearsal time. "They convinced me to play by saying you have already played in small clubs just pretend you are doing the same thing. I went on stage and something just kicked in; you just get absorbed in the music and what you are doing." In fact Linda went down amazing well with the American crowd and when Warner Brothers heard they arranged a tour for Linda and also arranged more gigs with her supporting Elton. Jim Cregan agreed, "Linda Lewis was now my wife and she came out to visit me on the tour; she knew Elton from a couple of gigs she'd done back in the UK and from his frequent visits to her at the house in Hampstead Heath, London, England". All the time Family toured with Elton they never had an encore. "When our gear failed to turn up Elton asked Linda to play as he knew she had done it before and she agreed and actually received two encores!" laughed Cregan. Backstage the rest of Family laughingly asked Cregan to tell his wife to go home. "A little girl with a guitar blew us off the stage."

Sure enough when Elton returned to the UK for a short tour in the summer, Linda was the main support but when he returned to the USA for his autumn tour he was back with Family. Family's set was well received by the crowd. In December 1972, Billboard reviewed the bands live album *Live At The Music Hall* from a gig recorded at the Music Hall in Boston, Massachusetts on September 28, 1972, and reported that. *'With anything less than such an overwhelming headliner, Family could have walked off with the show.'*

While Jim Cregan was in Blossom Toes, he and the other band members were very familiar with some other guys who lived in the same road and were in a band called Family. "We were a progressive rock band like Family so we had a lot in common," remembered Cregan, "we regularly went to each other's houses; getting stoned and taking acid because we didn't get into the pubs and clubs very much at that time."

When Family needed a bass player Cregan was on hand to help and approached John Wetton, who was a close friend and indeed, he and his girlfriend used to babysit his sister's child. "He was a great bass player and he was looking for a band to join after turning down a chance to join Robert Fripp and King Crimson so I introduced him to the guys in Family". Wetton stayed with Family for a couple of years until the middle of 1972 and was then approached by Fripp again to join a revamped King Crimson, and this time Wetton accepted. "After John left John 'Charlie' Witney, (a founder member of Family and its lead guitarist), who was one of my drinking buddies, approached me and said that they were looking for a bass player again: I reminded him that it was me that introduced John to the band and I would try my best to find someone else. To my surprise Charlie asked me to be the bassist; in fact he didn't just ask, he insisted, and despite my initial resistance - because I was a guitarist not a bass player- I agreed; after all I was promised a brand new bass guitar.

Family were a force to be reckoned with as a live band even though their music was deemed to be complicated and progressive to some. The likes of Jimi Hendrix however felt intimidated by their presence and allegedly refused to appear after them at festivals such was their reputation. Family had some impact on the British record buying public but had yet to break the US market, but was 1972 to be their year? Family were asked to tour North America with Elton John in late 1972 and according to Cregan, it turned out to be a most extraordinary time. "Elton was a bit of a Family fan and so I guess it was fun to have us on tour," laughed Cregan. "It was certainly an honour and pleasure for us." In fact both Elton and Bernie wanted Family to be on tour with them. Bernie was on tour with Elton all the time and the relationship that Bernie and Cregan developed during that tour led to a collaboration much later when Cregan went to work with Rod Stewart in Los Angeles and then formed a band with Bernie called Farm Dogs.

It was a very intensive tour travelling wise and they didn't have a private plane like Elton had on future tours. Nor did they travel in a tour bus which was the normal mode of transport for rock bands during the seventies. They travelled by scheduled airlines which invariably meant travelling with other passengers at awful times of the day. "If we had to get somewhere that needed a connecting flight then sometimes we had three plane rides to get us to a venue by 4.00pm for a sound check; it was brutal in terms of scheduling but it worked", explained Cregan. However Elton was always the one to lighten the journey between aircraft and Cregan remembers one time when Elton was in good form. "As the tour went on we all got crazier and crazier, 'tour crazy' we called it; I remember going to catch the plane, it wasn't that busy and so there weren't many people around, Elton was wearing a pink fur coat and was dancing down the jet way singing 'I feel Happy, Oh so Happy, I feel Happy and Witty and GAY in a loud voice'. Of course everyone in the business knew Elton was gay but at the time it was unacceptable in public life to admit to it, and it could cause havoc with record and ticket sales if anyone found out so it was a music business secret. We all fell about laughing."

Cregan's song writing in Family was limited by Roger Chapman and John Charlie Whitney who were already the established song writers for the band. "As a writer I couldn't really get a look in" amused Cregan. "I wrote 'Check Out' with them which was a bit rockier than Family were used to but as a writer I just wasn't needed." It was a bit like George Harrison trying to get a song on a Beatles record; even though he was a good and prolific writer in his own right, he was limited to one or two songs on an album because Lennon and McCartney were the recognised writers. As a result Cregan left the band after two years and went in search of an outlet for his songs but turning some lucrative offers down along the way. "I was offered a job to join Bad Company as the bass player when they first started in 1973. I said to Mick Ralphs at the time that I was grateful for the offer and I was sure it would be a great band but I don't want to do it."

Another offer that came along was one that Cregan could not resist even though it was not the song writing gig he was looking forward. However in accepting the gig he went on to bigger and better things. "I got an offer to sit in with Cockney Rebel after the original band had broken up and Steve Harley was forming a new band." Cregan was asked to sit in on a gig at Reading Festival as the Rebels guitarist but having received the call on the Thursday he was expected to learn all the numbers by the following Saturday when Cockney Rebel were due to appear. "I spent the rest of the week writing out the lyrics and chords on sheets of paper. This is when I learnt a valuable lesson that I now share with all young musicians who are about to play outdoors: don't forget to bring a lot of clothes pegs so you can keep the lyrics and notes together on the stand." On the third number all of Cregan's cue sheets and notes just blew across the stage which made it an incredibly difficult gig. "I did okay though," joked Cregan. As a career move it was only going to be temporary for Cregan as he was still looking for that lucrative song writing deal. Even so he found that working with Steve Harley and the rest of the band was more than interesting musically. Unsurprisingly given whom he was sharing the stage and studio with, the arrangement was to be short-lived. "There was Duncan McKay who later left and went to 10cc when I went to Rod Stewart; George Ford joined The Shadows for a while and then he gave up and went to Canada; Stewart Elliott went off and played with Eric Clapton."

Cockney Rebel were asked to support The Kinks at the Roxy Club in Los Angeles and during their 'off days' they would play their own gigs anywhere they could. During one of those gigs the opportunity for Cregan came in the form of Rod Stewart. "Rod and Britt Ekland came down to see us." remembered Cregan. "We were having a big hit in the UK at the time with 'Come Up and See Me Make Me Smile'; Rod would go and see any hot band that was coming through and was always interested in what others were doing. He saw me at the gig and liked what I was doing and so he got one of his managers to call up and asked if I wanted join."

But it was not plain sailing for Cregan, in fact he had to wait three months before anything really happened and then it was down to his wife Linda Lewis. "I waited three months and heard nothing so I thought the offer had gone away; by some weird coincidence I went to LA with Linda who was recording some tracks with Cat Stevens and, as he knew me, he asked me to join in on some tracks. I finished my sessions and was at a loose end so I thought I would see what was going on with Rod. I called him and the lovely Britt Ekland answered. She eventually put Rod on the phone and he told me to come down to rehearsals the next day, so I did and I was asked if I wanted to join his band there and then."

For Cregan this must have been a dream come true, not only was he going to be the guitarist with Rod Stewart, who by this point in time was a major star on both sides of the Atlantic but he was actually going to write songs with him. Cregan received tour receipts, appeared in all the videos and, like all his band mates, were far more than session musicians. "Rod had not really been a main artist before so he wanted to recreate the same vibe and spirit as he had with The Faces and he actively encouraged it. He wanted it to be fun and witty. Song writing just started with me going up to Rod's house with my guitar and both of us playing around and seeing what we could find". In all Cregan wrote about 33 songs with Rod Stewart as either the lyricist or composer or both. When there was ever a difficulty in them putting a song together then Cregan would call up his friends Bernie Taupin and Steve Harley to lend a hand. "It was all so easy going," remembers Cregan, "I can remember that it was same working with Bernie when I was with the Farm Dogs. There was one occasion when I said to Bernie look the way it's going musically we don't have enough lyrics, so he told me to wait a minute and went off to the kitchen. About half an hour later he came back with another six lines of lyric, which was just what we wanted. He was also so un-precious about his lyrics; quite often you get a lyric which is excellent but just doesn't work for the circumstances. At times like that Bernie was happy to just leave it to one side and use it again at a later stage."

As with Elton John, Bernie was a prolific lyric writer for Farm Dogs. "When I was working with Bernie our best writing day was two and a half songs, which for me was unbelievably quick. He would arrive with a handful of lyrics, say ten pages, and I would sift through them and take out one that I liked either because of the title or something else and read through it. Because of the way Bernie writes the lines it seems to suggest what the tempo, melody and feel of the song is going to be. It's almost inherent in the lyric, so it makes it terribly easy to write the song because the words would fall right; the vowels would be right and the lyrics just sang" explained Cregan. "That's why poetry and lyric writing are so different; it's all in the vowels. I did hear from somewhere that when the Gershwins wrote together, George would give Ira the music but he would also sing the vowels that were needed in the lyric at a certain point for the melody to work properly. Ira would try to make the lyric sound that way; that is when poetry moves to lyric. In lyric writing you can get a great word for a song which describes the sentiment exactly but you have to throw it away because it just doesn't sing and a good lyricist will accept this as part of the process."

Linda remembers Elton being very generous and he always invited her and Jim and the rest of Family to dinner and entertainment after a show. "Elton hired a whole cinema and he wanted the film *Beyond the Valley of the Dolls* but they put *Valley of the Dolls* on. "Elton and John Reid were, quite rightly, furious with the cinema owner," remembered Linda. "John Reid was ready to tear the whole cinema down." Cregan agreed, "Support bands were often seen as little more than an irritant to the main groups and were treated quite poorly by the headline acts, but not so for Family.

For us it was a pleasure and we were always welcome to join Elton and his entourage in all that they were doing," explained Cregan. "If he threw a party we were all invited especially at Thanksgiving."

There were times during the tour though that Linda felt Elton struck a sad figure amongst all the glitter and glam of his costumes and entourage: "I remember him during this flamboyant period and asking him to let me wear his stage costume, which was so heavy but he loved all that. Although he was a lot more outgoing I always thought he was a bit sad because at that stage he knew he was gay and we all knew as well but he hadn't come out."

♪

During the tour Elton had another new temporary member to his band – 'Legs' Larry Smith, who was drummer with the Bonzo Dog Do Da Band – who made a star appearance every night tap dancing on the track 'I Think I'm Going To Kill Myself'.

"It used to really tire him out tap dancing," says Epps. "He would come off stage in a real state." But that wasn't the only appearance Smith made during the performance. Elton and Larry had worked out a strange routine for the middle of the show. "The tour manager, Marvin, would come on stage wearing a tuxedo and he would sit at the piano and mime while a tape of 'Singing In The Rain' was being played. Elton and Larry then came on stage wearing long raincoats singing the song."

It helped that Smith had a trunk full of props in his dressing room that he would use to excellent effect on stage, including magic wands that fired tissue paper. Elton and Smith would have one of these in their pocket and during the song would fire them into the audience. Bernie's wife, Maxine would then come on stage and sprinkle glitter everywhere.

Throughout the 1970s, Elton's flamboyance would become more exaggerated, and the more attention he received, on stage and off, the more he wanted to push the boundaries. "With Elton, he would latch onto something, like a little bit of flamboyance, and then it would grow bigger," explained Reid. "He was influenced by Marc Bolan, who he was very friendly with at the time, and David Bowie – although he would never own up to it – and so, he always had an eye on what they were doing, and he considered that was the playing field that he was on." If anything, Elton was very switched on to the whole marketing thing, and he picked up very quickly on the reactions of people to what he was doing, and the effect it had on them. The result was that he had a permanent need to push the envelope.

According to Steve Brown the flamboyant stage of Elton's career was influenced in part by the fact that he was liberated by firstly the emergence of his success and secondly because he had established he was gay. "Before I left to go to the farm Elton wasn't into drugs; he may have smoked a few joints but he was not into cocaine and that sort of thing. In fact some years after I'd left and gone to live on the farm he sent me a card saying that if I had still been around he would have not got into the heavy drugs. At the time I took the comment as he was blaming me for introducing him to these drugs but I later realised I was wrong and he meant that I would have guided him away from that path. He craved the flamboyant lifestyle and he used to say that his father was very strict and he had to have his hair cut short and wear sensible clothes and he reacted against that by wearing the flamboyant clothes. It was not something I encouraged. He started off by buying some stage clothes from a designer called Mr Freedom which were mainly jumpsuits which were unusual at the time but then it progressed from that getting more and more extravagant. In hindsight he probably went too far and I certainly know that Bernie felt that way. Bernie took his lyrics very seriously and there was this guy going on stage playing in a Donald Duck outfit. Bernie felt it took away some of the seriousness of the lyrics."

"I used to have terrible rows with him about it," continued Reid. "For instance, when we were at the Water Gardens, he would go to a hairdressers called Smile every week, and he would come back with different coloured hair. I told him if he carried on doing it, he would lose his hair. He did the same with his eyebrows, one pink, one green; one shaved, both shaved. I told him I refused to go out with him, but it was him having fun really."

And as if to prove Reid's point, he was constantly asked by the media why he chose the extravagant stage persona, and his response was to blame his father for his restricted upbringing. Indeed, Elton took the flashy to the max and by the time he got to the gig at the Hollywood Bowl to promote *Goodbye Yellow Brick Road*, one year later, he was simply outrageous.

It was down to Michael Ross and David Larkham to design both the set and billboards for the Hollywood Bowl concert in 1973. "Elton wanted an extravaganza, so I came up with the idea of a series of pianos spelling his name," recalled Larkham. "With the help of Universal Studios, we came up with the theme of having lots of lookalikes being announced by [porn star] Linda Lovelace." This was probably as a result of Elton's recent visit to the cinema to see *Deep Throat*. As Elton reached the pianos in an outrageous feathered costume, and enormous platform shoes, the piano started opening.

"There was glitter everywhere and white doves that didn't want to fly out, so we were shooing them out to make it work. After that, he started jumping around the stage in drag dressed as Tina Turner and I just wanted to kill him," laughed Reid. "Steve Brown hated it the most, and Bernie disliked it as well. In fact, Steve decided to leave because he couldn't take it anymore. He was a brown rice and moccasins sort of chap and he blamed me for the direction Elton went off in because of our relationship. To a degree I encouraged the showmanship bit, but I had nothing to do with the costumes, that was all him. He would find someone to make things for him, and he would just surprise everyone with it. Freddie Mercury was exactly the same."

Following *Honky Chateau*, and the obligatory tour, *Don't Shoot Me, I'm Only The Piano Player* was another album which had its sleeve designed by the Larkham/Ross partnership. Ross was busy in London creating the inside cover and parts of the inner sleeve, while the outer section was done on the Universal Studio film lot by Larkham. Elton had come up with the album title, the inspiration for which came from a party in LA with some leading film and music celebrities, and a French film.

"Being based in LA, Elton, Bernie and I would often socialise together, when he was over from Britain," recalled Larkham. "We would go to Groucho Marx' house, where Marvin Hamlisch would play piano and Groucho and Elton would sing, and Bruce Johnstone from the Beach Boys would play the piano and harmonise on some songs, and it was magical. It was when Groucho jokingly pointed his index fingers at Elton, as if holding a pair of six-shooters, that made Elton put up his hands and say, 'Don't shoot me, I'm only the piano player' so naming the album." The line had actually come from a 1960 French film Elton might have seen at the time, called *Shoot the Piano Player*, a French crime drama directed by Francois Truffaut and starring the singer and actor Charles Aznavour, hence the cinema connection in Larkham's mind when it came to designing the sleeve.

"Elton was unavailable for a photo shoot, and he also hated having his picture taken," continued Larkham, "so once again, Ed Caraeff was called in to take the front cover shot, which was to show a young couple outside a cinema box-office paying for their tickets to go in and see a fictional movie called *Don't Shoot Me, I'm Only The Piano Player*, starring Elton John. As the shot also included a Cadillac parked outside the cinema entrance, they found both the Caddy and an appropriate film set on the Universal backlot that was ideal." Larkham hid behind the car with a smoke machine to create the right atmosphere, and his assistant looked busy behind the cash desk. "I put together the outer packaging and a lot of the photographs, which were then sent over to England where Michael put it all together."

The album was recorded at the chateau in France using the same format of recording as the previous album but, by this time, with Davey Johnstone now firmly settled in the band as one of the boys. 'Crocodile Rock' an homage to the 1950s, was the first single to be released off the album in November 1972. It struck gold, hitting the top spot on the American Billboard charts. The second single, 'Daniel', considered the strongest of the album cuts could only make it to No. 2 in the States. Not that it mattered; Elton and John Reid had bigger fish to fry.

7

The Rocket Years
and DJM

It was soon after the early success of Elton John that the singer along with Bernie, Steve Brown, Gus Dudgeon and John Reid started talking about forming their own record company. Dudgeon had already produced a solo album with Davey Johnstone, titled *Smiling Face,* which he didn't want released by DJM, and so an alternative option was to start their own record label.

In many ways, it wasn't that surprising. Steve Brown was finding it difficult working for Dick James and remaining loyal to Elton, especially as talks were already underway about forming a new label. Indeed, Brown did leave DJM and join in with the new venture, which was to become Rocket Records. "I didn't think the formation of Rocket was actually discussed, it came about from a combination of naivety and altruism," said Reid. "DJM was great, but the label was run all wrong and the idea to form Rocket came principally from Gus and Steve, and then Elton and Bernie, and finally me. It was all conjured up overnight, after a recording session."

"Elton asked me if I would go with them" recalled Brown. I wasn't really sure because Dick had been good to me. He had given me 1% of Elton's record sales even though I wasn't the Producer, which has earned me a lot of money ever since. I never had any problems with Dick and he told me he recognised what I had done with Elton since I had been with DJM and he rewarded me for it. I don't think any other publisher would have invested the amount of money that Dick invested in an unknown artist to make the *Elton John* album; yes he could afford to do it because of the amount of money he had made from The Beatles but he didn't need to do it. It was for sales of his records up to *Goodbye Yellow Brick Road* and even now every quarter a cheque drops through the post. Elton said he was going and Gus was joining him with Bernie and John and eventually I said fine I'll come as well and we formed Rocket. But that decision was my downfall and was why I left the business."

According to Reid they all knew that Elton would be out of his recording contract soon: "We also knew he would be leaving DJM altogether, so it was just an idea for a while. There was never any real consideration that Elton would stay at DJM, and his leaving was inevitable because everyone felt that his career was going to be huge. I don't believe there was ever really any thoughts in Stephen or Dick James' minds either that DJM would keep him – they had made hay while the sun shone and as a result did very well."

The words 'very well' show Reid to be a master of understatement as by 1973, Elton had provided them with five gold albums and $1m record sales. Add to that the significant success of Northern Songs and the Beatles' catalogue in America and you can see why DJM scooped the Queen's Award for Export.

"What we are offering is undivided love and devotion, a fucking good royalty for the artist, and a company that works its bollocks off." This was how Elton described the intentions of the new label to the press during the launch of the Rocket Record Company in the UK. Elton had seen incredible success in his own career, and held strong views about the record business. He was desperate to change it, so that the artist received more of kudos and cash. Having set up offices in London's Wardour Street, John Reid had signed his first artist: Kiki Dee who had worked with Reid at Tamla Motown. Longdancer are often cited as the first official signing by the Label featuring David A Stewart who would later go on to form The Tourists with Annie Lennox and then the very popular hitmakers The Eurythmics. However the purists argue it was actually Davey Johnstone, whose album *Smiling Face* was the catalyst for Dudgeon to want to form a Label rather than release it on DJM.

The announcement to the US music business was somewhat more

subdued. He announced to the readers of the LA Times in October 1972 that he was forming his own record label and during the interview with Robert Hilburn he made the following statement: "The only thing that depresses me is the business side of things. There are too many accountants in the record business, too many people who don't know anything about music but make a fortune from it. That's why I'm starting my own label. It'll be called Rocket Records and there are five of us involved – me, Bernie, my manager John Reid, Gus Dudgeon and Steve Brown. We all know something about music. I won't have anyone working for us who doesn't understand music."

By 10 July 1973 the Label was up and running and launched to the unsuspecting music business. David Larkham was asked to design the logo for the new label and recalled: "Rather than an actual rocket, Elton wanted a train, though not in the vein of Stephenson's Rocket, so the image was based loosely on the Reverend Awdry trains in his *Thomas The Tank Engine* books." Larkham designed it so that it would curve around the centre of a vinyl single.

Rocket was formed on the basis that Elton, Bernie and Reid would each find an artist, whom Gus Dudgeon would produce, whilst Steve Brown would run the label. Reid would also supervise the artist management side of the label and Tony King would run label administration as General Manager. The whole idea of Rocket was to emulate the Apple label which the Beatles had set up in 1968 and many of the other Independent labels that had been established at the start of the seventies. Apple was initially intended as a creative vehicle for the Beatles, plus a selection of other artists that included Mary Hopkin, James Taylor, Badfinger and Billy Preston; then by the mid-1970s it had become dominated with releases by the former Beatles as solo artists. Among the principal players at Apple was Tony King, which made him an ideal choice to work for Rocket.

Having poached the best that DJM had to offer in the form of some key staff, much to the displeasure of the James gang, and by adding Tony King to the mix, Elton believed he had the right team for his new label. But, with hindsight, Reid believed that the label was a bad idea. "It was exciting, but artists shouldn't run labels and Elton considered it his label."

Brown was in no doubt who was doing all the leg work for this new venture: "When Rocket settled down, Elton was preoccupied with his own career and John [Reid] was also preoccupied with Elton's career. Bernie was the lyricist and had no interest in the business side and Gus was not only producing Elton but several other artists as well. So a lot of the stuff was down to me. I found myself managing 3 or 4 acts and being the head of the record company and all that it entailed; record sleeves, promotion, whatever, to the point where I really burnt myself out. I was working 24 hours a day, eating and breathing the job and at one point I called them all in and said 'listen, I can't do this anymore. So I left and went to my farm in Kent for about 10 years and left the music business completely. Me and Stuart Epps were doing all the leg work. There was no falling out and no disagreement in any way I just felt it was time to take a break and I was right. We had a good time together and we used to socialise all the time. If someone was in the recording studio or recording an album we would all go over and watch and then go out in the evening and the next night someone would be doing a gig so we would all go and watch. It was a lifestyle rather than a job. It was seven days a week."

Not that any of Elton's records would be released on the label initially. He was still signed to DJM, so it was left to Kiki Dee to launch the first Rocket release. "I had known Kiki for some time from my days at Motown and loved her voice," recalled Reid. "In the narrow range of artists that I knew at the time, Kiki was the only one who was available and could sing. She had a fantastic voice, but her biggest problem was her drive. I can't put my finger on it, but she just didn't have that last push. She sang like an angel, a bird, all day, but she lacked that killer instinct."

At the time of signing, Kiki's career had stalled, and she had gone back to Bradford and being Pauline Matthews again, having given up with the music business. "I asked her to sign, and she accepted over dinner," remembered Reid.

Her acceptance led to a short, but successful, revitalisation of her career at Rocket, and at the same time, provided the label with their first hit. "I first met John Reid when I was recording for Tamla Motown and he was the label manager," remembered Kiki. "By 1972, I was at a loose end as my career at Tamla was not a success. I gave John a call and asked him what I should do. He told me he was managing Elton John, and he was starting a label. He invited me to his place in the Water Gardens with Elton for dinner, and we discussed what I wanted to do and my thoughts on joining the label. I remember that Sheila, Elton's mother, was there and so was Neil Diamond. I made a fool of myself by trying to open a cabinet and smashing the glasses. Elton thought it was hilarious and so we hit it off straight away. He was a shy man but someone I could really relate to."

The first distributors for Rocket were Island Records who had similar values to the founders of Rocket and supported the concept of artists running the label for the benefit of the artists. The first hit in 1973 was 'Amoureuse' by Kiki Dee. Other artists soon followed, like Longdancer, Mike Silver, Maldwyn Pope and Blue amongst others. However, despite the enthusiasm and commitment, the label failed to repeat the success of its first release.

"The launch of Rocket followed another Steve Brown esoteric idea to have it in an idyllic village hall setting," remembered Reid. "The unsuspecting village hall in the Cotswolds turned out to be in Moreton-in-Marsh. The week before the launch, I was browsing in an art gallery in St James' when I saw a painting by LS Lowry of the very village hall that the party was to take place in, and so I bought it and gave it to Elton."

Elton subsequently sold it in the Sotheby's auction of his belongings in 2003, which included contents from his Holland Park home and fetched over £800,000. At the time, he said he was selling some of his personal artefacts to create more room for his collection of contemporary art which includes many works of art by young British artists such as Sam Taylor-Wood and Tracey Emin.

The Rocket charabanc boarded a train from London's King's Cross station that was very liberally stocked with champagne. "I got pissed on the train going up there, and all I can remember was running up and down saying there's a disco at the back," said Tony King. When they reached the destination they were met by a brass band and they all marched behind it - with Elton John leading the way - to a small village hall for a meal, more bubbly and live entertainment in the shape of new Rocket signings Kiki

Dee, Maldwyn Pope and Longdancer. Then it was back on the train to King's Cross where the party continued until the booze ran out.

Elton played a big part in recording and promoting the artists on the label. With Clive Franks he co-produced Kiki Dee's first album *Loving And Free* for the label in 1973, which saw a welcome return for BJ Cole and Roger Pope to the Elton John fold at Rocket and even ended up with Elton lending his own talent and band to the album. "He got me writing and I played him some stuff, and he liked it," recalled Dee. "It was a special album for me, and I was also playing and recording with musicians of my own age so we had a lot in common. This album made me find out who I really was as an artist. Once we had the hit 'Amoureuse' things started to change, and I started to lose the experimental things I was doing before. If I had taken more control of my career at that point then I may have had less commercial success, but I would have been doing what I wanted."

The recording of the album also proved to be a good experience for Dee. "Elton and I would routine the songs first with him on the piano and me singing and then we would get together with the rest of the band and record. We would put together a loose arrangement and then it was down to the musicians and the creative process. All the musicians were very quick at picking up the mood of the songs. Elton and I hit it off very well and he respected me as a singer. He liked my songs and I felt very comfortable with him as he always saw what I was doing as being a creative thing rather than a commercial product."

Kiki Dee made her first live appearance as a Rocket artist at the Bottom Line in New York on 12 June 1974 to an invited audience of 500, which set a club 'one night stand' record. Elton was there to support her, taking some time away from the Caribou Ranch in Colorado where he was recording *Captain Fantastic And The Brown Dirt Cowboy*.

Roger Pope became a session player at Rocket, and was prominent on many artist recordings during the formative years of the label, including those with Kiki Dee. And he would eventually become the drummer in her band. Pope himself recalled that it was a fun place to work. "Elton used to find women's names for everyone and he called himself Elsie. Everyone at Dick James was called Sid so he was either Elsie or Sid. Elton couldn't get a name for me though, but one day Elton, Tony King and David Nutter were just looking at me so I asked them what they were looking at. They asked me what my mother's name was, and I told them it was Hilda. They all fell about laughing and from that day on they called me Hilda."

Kiki Dee agreed with Pope that it was indeed a good laugh there. What she liked most about it was how she was accepted into the Rocket family and what cemented her acceptance she says was her nickname: Stanley, after the footballer Stanley Matthews. Well, her real surname is Matthews after all.

Elton put his heart and soul into Rocket, and even went on the road to support the Rocket artists; in particular he plugged Neil Sedaka's records and worked on him with the song 'Bad Blood', contributing backing vocals. Rocket also helped rekindle the career of Cliff Richard. "I worked with Cliff on the single 'Devil Woman'," recounted Tony King. "I am particularly proud of it, especially as Cliff has remarked on a television programme how he regarded the song as one of his best." Elton went out to promote the song as well.

It was King who also found 'Amoureuse' for Kiki Dee, which was to become her and Rocket's first major hit. Elton's first hit as a producer and would lead to a very successful collaboration with Gary Osborne, who wrote the English lyrics for the song and recounted: "I had written four songs for a French female singer [Véronique Sanson]. She was a sort of French Joni Mitchell who had just broken into the business and was big in France - a beautiful voice and lovely writer. It all started when Warner Brothers wanted her to do some of the songs in English, to see if they could break her in English speaking territories, and needed a lyricist to take on the task."

For some reason they told her they could get Paul McCartney, which was clearly never going to happen as she was a complete unknown. "So, she was coming over to meet McCartney and Warner were beginning to panic as they didn't even have a lyricist, let alone McCartney, but she had to meet somebody." remembered Osborne. "The Warner people knew that I spoke French, but I was not a big writer then and I was struggling, mainly doing jingles at the time but I was making money doing it. I had translated and re-written a few French songs into English for Serge Gainsbourg. Martin Wyatt, who went on to look after Christine McVie and Justin Hayward, was at that time Head of A&R for Warner and asked me to get them out of a hole and meet this girl. I said you must be joking, what a complete disappointment for this young kid when she was expecting Paul McCartney and got me. Anyway I agreed."

They gave Osborne the album to listen to overnight. There was a particularly short track that he used to show what he could do: "I thought, well it's 58 seconds, I can write that, and so I wrote the lyric for that track. It almost translated, so I moved it to English by part translation and part adaptation. When I met her, she was slightly taken aback because I wasn't Paul McCartney, but after I apologised and gave her the 58 second lyric I had prepared, and told her that if I was to do the lyrics this is what I would do for her. She loved it and asked me to do as many as I could as she was recording in a week's time. I decided that I could probably do two but they wanted four, so they could record an EP. I had a partner called Paul Vigrass and we did lyrics together. I told him I would do two complete lyrics if he could start another two for me to finish. Paul agreed. I couldn't decide which two to do, so I decided to listen to the album. I was living with a fashion model in Belsize Park. She was so beautiful, but her only flaw was that she would only listen to Bob Dylan. It was quite incredible, as I had never met anyone who would only listen to just one artist but if you put anything else on except Bob Dylan she just hated it. So I'm playing this album and listening to it and 'Amoureuse' comes on. She came into the room and said 'Er... what's that?' and I replied 'It's one of those songs I have been asked to write and I don't know which one to do. This was Friday night and on Saturday we split up after two years and so, on Sunday, I was heartbroken. I had discovered that she had been unfaithful to me and it was close to home, but two days previously I had not expected to be single and now on Sunday I had to do some writing for recording next Saturday. So I chose the one she hated."

This was, of course 'Amoureuse' which Osborne had written the English lyrics for, with Sanson's original melody. "The record came out and did nothing," continued Osborne. "It was played a lot on the *Kid Jensen*

Show on Radio Luxembourg, and he liked the French version. But now he had the chance to play the English version for his English listeners, but he was pretty much the only person to play it."

Tony King heard it on Luxembourg and got a copy, and played it to Elton, who thought it was a beautiful song that was just right for Kiki who he was just about to record. At the same time Polly Brown, who was the singer with Pickettywitch, recorded it as a solo single. "The same day both of these records came through my letterbox; I was a struggling writer and all of a sudden I had two people covering my song," laughed Osborne. "Kiki Dee had been around for some time, but never had a hit, whereas Polly Brown had just had a couple of big hits, but had now gone solo. So I am figuring that Polly's has got the biggest chance, but I had been in the business long enough at the time to realise that it could be that nothing would happen with either of them."

In fact, Brown's version sunk without trace, and Kiki's bubbled up the charts for about fourteen weeks and finally sold 250,000 copies. "While it was going up the charts, there was a reception for it that I went to. I had known Elton vaguely as someone to nod to, and I used to see him at the Cromwellian. We got chatting at the reception and, of course, we now had something in common because we had this song that was starting to take off, and it was my first hit; Kiki's first hit; Rocket's first hit and he was really excited. Later when we had hits like 'Little Jeannie and Blue Eyes', he would get excited about them, but he had been much more excited about 'Amoureuse'. It was more exciting for him to have produced something as a hit, and then be able to give it to Kiki as a gift."

A lot of money had been poured into Rocket, and finally they had a hit. It created a bond between Elton and Gary which was to prove significant in the years to come.

8

The Yellow Brick Road To Excess

The next album 1973's *Goodbye Yellow Brick Road*, was originally planned to be recorded in Kingston, Jamaica, where the Rolling Stones had recorded *Goats Head Soup*. This idea was abandoned and it was back to the chateau in France.

David Larkham recalled there was a lot of hanging about in Jamaica: "The Dolby machinery wasn't right, and the band and the entourage had to wait for parts to be flown in from England. Heaven knows how the Stones managed to record such a good album in such primitive surroundings. In many ways, the studio was like going back to the early days of DJM. Jamaica was a third world music industry, and the locals weren't used to music business types. The hotel we all stayed in was owned by the Chris Blackwell family and so in this enclave, us white guys were okay, but when we were driving out through the streets, in an oldish VW Wagon, we had to be looked after by minders because people didn't take too kindly to strangers being driven about."

Most of the songs that finally featured on the released album were actually written in Jamaica, but some were penned when they decided to move to the château. Elton and Bernie were going through a purple patch and had enough material to fill two albums; so it was decided to release it as a double. The songs that were produced for Jamaica were in rough form, and the rhythm section and strings had not been completed yet. "Elton isn't a great one for sitting around the hotel pool and, partly to alleviate his boredom and partly to give me an idea of the music, one day after breakfast he and I went off to the recording studio, where I sat in the corner and he played piano and sang me the songs that he had written so far for *Goodbye Yellow Brick Road*. The album didn't have a title at the time but it was the best concert I have ever been to. Other than that, Elton, Bernie, all the musicians, management, technicians plus partners - we all killed time during the day, before eating dinner together at a long communal table in the evening," recalled Larkham.

Del Newman, who had previously worked with Elton as a session arranger for Warlock Music and Joe Boyd, was drafted in to replace Paul Buckmaster. "I had never heard of Elton John at the time of the Warlock sessions and it was not until the *Elton John* album came out that I got to hear about it, and only then because I knew Buckmaster was such a good arranger and cellist. He didn't overdo it, and he was the right man for the job. I only got the gig because I was told he was unwell." Buckmaster denies that he was unwell. In fact, he was working abroad at the time and was not available due to prior commitments.

Newman claimed that Buckmaster had already completed a couple of sessions for the album and didn't finish the job, but because studio time was expensive they couldn't wait for Buckmaster, so Dudgeon called orchestral booker Dick Katz who recommended Del Newman. After accepting the gig, he was invited to meet with Elton and the band.

"They were recording at the château in France, so they suggested I go over and meet the band and hang out with everyone, and see what was going on," Newman reminisced. "I was out there for three or four days and all we did was sit around, talk about what they were doing, and share ideas and views on how it should be done. I was like a fly on the wall, agreeing and disagreeing without saying anything."

Newman soon found out that it was how Elton, Bernie and the band worked, as they had known each other for such a long time. It was all part of the shared creative process that has been a theme running through Elton's career. "Elton asked me what I thought and would I do it." said Newman. "I was really pleased that he asked me as I'm often taken for granted, and it was assumed, by some artists, that I would do it, so it was courteous that he asked. I thought it was a great project and so, I agreed. In those days I relied on cassette tapes. Elton told me which tracks he wanted me to be involved in, which was a sort of big deal for me because Gus was involved. He had a chat with me and explained what Elton wanted. He then sent me the material, which was a rough mix without orchestra and just consisted of piano and vocals on a cassette. Then I was left alone for about a week which was how I preferred it, while I composed the arrangements. I tried to follow the vocals, as I wanted to be part of the band, rather than working against the vocals. When my arrangements were complete I went to the studio, with my sheet music, to meet the orchestra that had been chosen by Katz."

"It was a big orchestra, because it was for Elton John," continued Newman. "The first thing I had to do was to check that all the music was okay, because in those days you didn't have computers, so you gave the work to copyists; some were good and others not so good and they could make mistakes. I ran through the arrangements with the orchestra and once I was happy with it, the arrangements were recorded by Dudgeon. Elton was thrilled with the end product; my arrangements were accepted by Dudgeon without question. At the launch party, Elton was so pleased with the album that he gave me a big kiss on the lips."

Ross and Larkham went back to LA with all the song titles before the songs were recorded, so they were ahead of the game with the album cover. "We started illustrating a feature for each of the songs," recalled Larkham. "When it became nearer to the deadline, I was told by John Reid, who was in LA at the time, to get all of the material together and fly that afternoon first class, to London. I did, and found myself drawing all the way." By the time Larkham had arrived in London, he had no time to do the illustration for the cover.

"We wanted to tie the cover design in with the illustrations on the inside covers and Steve Brown had found an illustrator to work with, Ian Beck. We got him into Rocket Records, looked at his portfolio and between him, me and Steve Brown we came up with a concept which illustrated Elton stepping into a poster, partly styled on a Bowie drawing Beck had in his portfolio, plus a few other ideas. Also included in the final front illustration was a tiny bit of the previous album cover *Don't Shoot Me I'm Only The Piano Player* partly hidden behind a torn corner of the poster. I based myself with the Browns and completed my drawings for the inside cover.

Steve Brown was responsible for choosing the running order of the songs on the album, "Elton used to entrust the running order of his albums to me as he was too close to them. I remember considering the running order for *Goodbye Yellow Brick Road* and spending hours and hours trying different orders until we found a running order that I was happy with" laughed Brown.

"Because it was a double album, we decided on a triple panel and so I did a tracing of how each drawing would fit" recalled Larkham. "I didn't have the song sequence at this stage, so I had to rely on David Costa, who had taken over from Michael as the art director for Rocket, to complete it. I left the layouts for David to finish, and instructions how the outside cover should work, and left for LA. By the time I had got on the plane, I had completed all of the drawings - with a couple for David Costa to complete, (Costa brought in Mike Scutt to finish the work) - all in a weekend, having only had about two hours sleep. I woke up when I got to LA, not realising we had detoured to Calgary in Canada to deal with someone who had a heart attack on the plane."

As expected, the album went to No.1 just four weeks after it was released in October 1973 and, to this day, is regarded by many as Elton's best work. It also helped that it created a string of hit singles, most notably 'Candle In The Wind'. "But that," said Gary Osborne, "came as a bit of a surprise to Elton, who didn't know that the metaphor had been taken from the title of a book written by Russian author Aleksander Solzhenitsyn in the 1950s."

"I'm not criticising Bernie, and good on him for taking it and standing it as the image that encapsulated the life of Marilyn Monroe," explained Osborne, "but it was only when I was in a bookshop with Elton that he discovered the truth about it. The book was in front of us and I asked, 'Have you seen this?' And he says, 'Bloody hell, it's not named after my song is it?' And that's when I told him, 'No, it was written in 1957.' He seemed a bit taken aback and said Bernie had never told him."

♫

Prior to the release of the *Goodbye Yellow Brick Road* album, Elton embarked on a tour of North America in the second half of 1973 which was, to some anyway, to show Elton at his flamboyant best, at the now famous performance at the Hollywood Bowl in Los Angeles on 7th September. Elton teamed up with a popular band from the UK who were having some success in the US called Sutherland Brothers and Quiver.

Although Brothers Iain and Gavin Sutherland were the main songwriters in both The Sutherland Brothers Band and then Sutherland Brothers and Quiver it was Iain who started the ball rolling being the eldest. "He'd had a school band since he was 15 and was writing stuff with the keyboard player." recalled Gavin. It was probably down to the influence created by The Beatles and Lennon and McCartney that caused them to start writing. "We just thought it was what you did as musicians, write songs; you don't just sing other peoples songs you write your own". The boys were living in Stoke-On-Trent in the Midlands area of the UK and were unaware of the thriving London music business and the existence of the Tin Pan Alley songwriters from Denmark Street in London's West End, who were producing song after song for the world of music publishing and for well-known artists like Tom Jones, Cilla Black, Petula Clark, Lulu and Englebert Humperdinck.

When The Beatles came along it demonstrated to the Tin Pan Alley scene that actually there were songwriters who could write hit songs that they could sing and play them themselves. The start of the seventies saw the emergence of the singer/songwriter as a force to be reckoned with; they had all drawn their influence from Lennon and McCartney of The Beatles and Jagger and Richards from the Rolling Stones. The Sutherland Brothers therefore knew no different.

Both Gavin and Iain were composing little ditties as schoolboys. Gavin first learnt three chords on his acoustic guitar and joined his brother's band. "I wasn't bothering with a fourth chord, it just wasn't necessary," laughed Gavin, "the rest of our creative writing was established after a long build up process and reflected our surroundings; but it was always the old three chord trick disguised in different ways. I am not an arrangements guy; I didn't go for the progressive rock thing as I wouldn't remember what I had written let alone be able to play it if I did. I wrote simple songs. Why put yourself through all that? It's like sitting an exam.

I'd much prefer to get a groove going and let everyone have a blow."

The guys started producing songs using two part harmonies with both boys playing acoustic guitars in a folky sort of way. "We would huddle around the small record player and listen to Everly Brothers songs and try to work out how to sing and play them." Ironically the Everlys would later cover one of Iain songs 'Arms of Mary', (a song taken from the 1975 album - and the first the band released on the CBS label - *Reach for the Sky*), which was a major hit in the UK in May 1976 reaching number 5 in the UK charts, but could only make 81 in the Billboard Hot 100 in America. "I remember we got a call from The Everlys' people who said that they wanted to cover the song; we agreed and when we heard it we were so thrilled, they had copied almost identically the harmonies and phrasing and had kept faithful to the sound."The Everlys released the song as a track on the 1986 album *Born Yesterday*.

Realising that he wanted to be a musician Gavin left school at 16 and joined his brother Iain's band, New Generation, and started scraping a living playing the ballrooms and clubs around the north west of England. The band became popular in the soul clubs even though their roots were certainly not in soul music. Due to the limited or non-existent scope for them to further their careers in the ballrooms and Club circuit, the Brothers decided to move to London. "It is fair to say that outside of London there were few, if any, outlets to make music." recalled Gavin, "Most of the recording studios were in London.There may have been one or two starting to emerge outside like The Manor but if you wanted to make a demo record or get the music business interested in what you were doing then you had to be in London. It was William Leyland who got us our first record deal when our band New Generation was signed with Spark, a little record company owned by Southern Music Publishing in Denmark Street, London's Tin Pan Alley." Leyland was an entrepreneur and small-time agent, who ran a show-biz empire called the LE Agency based in a wooden 'shed' in Hindley in Lancashire, England and he also had a club called the The Pink Elephant, in Aspull in Lancashire "Leyland would describe it as one of the north of England's hottest night spots," amused Sutherland. "We played there a few times, usually when we were doing a double at The Nevada Ballroom in Bolton or what was soon to

Dee Murray enjoys a welcome break with his band mates in The Mirage (1968) (Courtesy of Anett Murray)

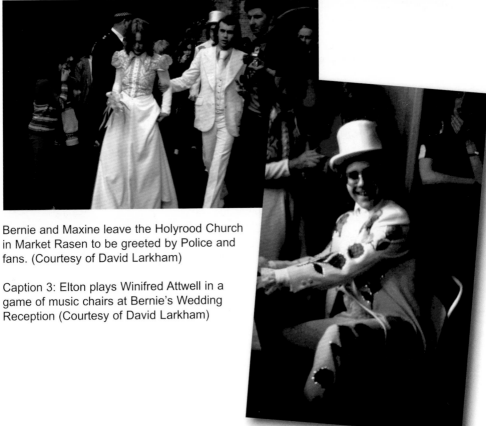

Bernie and Maxine leave the Holyrood Church in Market Rasen to be greeted by Police and fans. (Courtesy of David Larkham)

Caption 3: Elton plays Winifred Attwell in a game of music chairs at Bernie's Wedding Reception (Courtesy of David Larkham)

Handstands on the piano: Elton live in 1971 *(Courtesy of Stuart Epps)* and inset, in mid song at the Friars, Watford Town Hall on 24th February 1972 before giving up his seat to Police. *(Courtesy of Mike O'Connor, Friars Aylesbury)*

Inspector O'Connor who announced a bomb scare and evacuated the venue.

Below: On his return to the stage Elton gets the crowd on its feet again and continues his set. *(Courtesy of Mike O'Connor – Friars Aylesbury)*

Larking around in Hawaii; on tour in 1974 *(Courtesy of Roger Pope)*

Left: On stage at Oakland Coliseum, 9th September 1973
(Courtesy of Dan Cuny)

Below: The Troubadour, Los Angeles. The time: November 30th 1973. Elton had played Manchester, England the previous day (no wonder John Reid looks jet-lagged). From left - John Lennon, Elton John, Tony King (in the foreground - Lennon's PA at the time), David Larkham, John Reid, Janis Larkham, and Pete Brown (assistant manager).
(Courtesy of David Larkham)

Davey with Kiki Dee during a break between gigs in 1974. Kiki was supporting Elton on his North American tour.
(Courtesy of Roger Pope)

Ray Cooper relaxing on his balcony prior to a gig in Hawaii in 1974.
(Courtesy of Roger Pope)

Nigel Olsson salutes
the crowd on stage.
*(Courtesy of
Lynden Song)*

Dee and Davey in perfect
harmony on stage during the
1974 North American tour.
(Courtesy of Lynden Song)

.

Below: 'This One's for You';
Elton on stage during the North
American tour complete with his
trademark feathers.
(Courtesy of Lynden Song)

Left: On the way to rehearsals
in Amsterdam 1975.
A rare shot of Jeff 'Skunk' Baxter
with Kenny Passarelli.
(Courtesy of Roger Pope)

John Reid in Amsterdam 1975.
He managed Elton for 28 years, and also
managed Queen for three years during
that period.
He was hugely instrumental in
helping to establish Elton's career.
(Courtesy of Roger Pope)

Below: Elton camping it up
backstage at Dodger.
(Courtesy of Roger Pope)

Elton enjoying a joke with Ringo Starr and Kenny
Passarelli on the way to rehearsals in Amsterdam.
Even after Elton had officially changed his name, Ringo
continued to call him Reg. *(Courtesy of Roger Pope)*

Above: Lyricist Gary Osborne with Kiki Dee in 1974 backstage at Hyde Park.
(Courtesy of Gary Osborne)

Below: Elton relaxing on the piano with his band China at Shepperton Studios in 1978 prior to his gig at Wembley Empire Pool in aid of the Goaldiggers Charity.
(Steve Emberton)

Above: Obligingly signing an autograph at Brighton for a charity football match.
(Steve Emberton)

Below: With Watford Town manager Graham Taylor (left),
plus a couple of *Penthouse* models, and model professionals for good measure!
(Steve Emberton)

Elton at the Rainbow Theatre, London in 1977 doing what he does best: Entertaining audiences around the world with his songs, singing and wonderful piano playing.
(Steve Emberton)

become, the Mecca of Northern Soul in the UK, the notorious Wigan Casino."

Southern Music was a pretty formal set up; typical of the Tin Pan Alley publishing houses of the late sixties, with writers working more or less nine to five in little rooms around the building. John Carter, (formerly Shakespeare) and Ken Lewis, (formerly Hawker) were the main songwriters working at Southern at the time, who were responsible for a whole bunch of pop hits like 'Funny How Love Can Be', 'Beach Baby', 'Can't You Hear My Heartbeat', and 'Lets Go To San Francisco' and formed bands using names like The Ivy League and The Flowerpot Men, as an outlet for their songs. One of the songwriters' early bands was called The Southerners who boasted a young Jimmy Page as their guitarist for a brief period and who later became a founder member and lead guitarist for the iconic Led Zeppelin.

Being able to work in Southern's recording studio was a blast for the Sutherland brothers, even if it was a pokey little room in the basement of the London HQ. It was during a basement session that the band was introduced to Wayne Bardell, one of Southern Music Publishers' Pluggers. Bardell's job was to take new releases to the BBC and to try to schmooze up some interest, get some air play or maybe even a TV spot for the bands working at Southern. A year or so later, Bardell left Southern to work for The Beatles at Apple. "We didn't know it then, but he was eventually going to manage The Sutherland Brothers and help us get a deal with Island Records and to introduce us to a band called Quiver." recalled Gavin.

Meanwhile New Generation released a single on Southern's record label Spark called 'Smokie Blues Away', which was a minor hit in the UK, and the brothers got jobs to tide themselves over financially whilst they looked for another outlet for their music. "We had a couple of record companies show an initial interest in what we were doing but nothing really happened until Muff Winwood, who was at Island Records, called us and said that he liked what we were doing and could we come in and meet him," recalled Gavin.

By this time the band line up had changed and the resultant combo were renamed the Sutherland Brothers Band. "We were given some time in the studio with Muff producing us and he played the songs to Chris Blackwell. Chris agreed to take a chance and signed us. There was never any discussion about money; as far as we were concerned it was all about the music, we just wanted to get our songs out to people and the fact that we were doing that through a great record label with a recording contract was a dream come true to us." In Gavin's view it was the same approach that Island took with all of its artists. "Yes Island was a business but it was not all about the money; they were prepared to take a chance if they liked the music and that was mostly what it was all about."

Island Records, although established by Chris Blackwell in 1959, was the most established and arguably the most successful independent label during the seventies and had built a reputation of building its music repertoire around its artists. It was the blueprint that other labels would follow later during the decade as the music business changed from Tin Pan Alley publishers, sheet music and hustling songwriters to singer/songwriters, records, producers, disc jockeys and the all-important record charts. "We learnt so much from Muff, we were very green when we came to London and he taught us a lot about the business." explained Gavin. "The great thing about Island was that it was small and compact and everyone loved their music. They were very discerning about the music."

At Island the brothers were now mixing with some fantastic bands and artists like Free, Traffic, Cat Stevens, Bob Marley and the like and the guys in the bands would all hang around the Island offices together talking about all sorts of things not just music; "Mostly football actually!" laughed Gavin, "Muff used to encourage the interaction between the bands and we used to learn a great amount from each other just jamming and talking about what we were doing and what inspired us and we all played on each other recordings". They released a first single in 1972 called 'The Pie' which had limited success and the brothers toured as the Sutherland Brothers Band. "We had a better class of gig when we were with Island." remembered Gavin. From 1971 they were touring with the likes of fellow Island artist Cat Stevens, in their own right and then they found themselves supporting David Bowie on his Ziggy Stardust tour in 1972.

The Brothers began writing for a new album, later called *Lifeboat*, which was recorded and produced by Muff Winwood at Island's studios in Basing Street, London in the latter part of 1972. This new venture was the start of a new relationship between two bands as well as the skills of arranger and conductor Martyn Ford and his orchestra to create a new sound for the Band. "I remember we had some great people playing on that album like Steve Winwood (Traffic) and Dave Mattacks (Fairport Convention). It was like Team Island." joked Gavin, "Martyn did some great strings on it and I remember one song that Martyn had produced some very intense string arrangements for that we felt didn't really suit the song that we set out to make; Iain decided to rewrite the words to verbalise the string arrangement that Martyn had done which is not normally the right way round but it is what we wanted to do." It was rumoured that Tony Blair, the former British Prime Minister, was one of the backing vocalists on the original version of 'Sailing', as he was in a band at the time and Muff Winwood needed some backing vocalists and he happened to be around with his band at the time, how true that is remains a mystery.

By the time the *Lifeboat* album was planned the Brothers decided it was time to consider their future as a live band as well as a recording band. Wayne Bardell took the initiative and persuaded the brothers to go to a gig by Quiver. Quiver had also built up a respectful following as a live act and had toured with The Who and been the first band on the bill at the new Rainbow Theatre, which had previously been known as the Finsbury Astoria and was a well know cinema owned by Rank, as well as a prime venue for acts since the 1930's. Rank sold the cinema in September 1971 and it was reopened on 4th November with The Who and Quiver. Liking what they heard, it resulted in the Brothers teaming up with Tim Renwick on guitar, (who was the founder member with Cal Batchelor and would later be the mainstay guitarist on Elton John's 'comeback' album *A Single Man* in 1978), Bruce Thomas on bass, Willie Wilson on drums and latterly Peter Wood on keyboards. In the press release prior to a major tour with Elton John in 1973 Iain Sutherland summed up his opinion of the marriage of the two bands: "Now we can write what we want, we can write anything and know that we've got the scope to cope with it. We've got a strong line-up and we feel that the six of us can handle anything we want to do."

An album was released in the UK under the banner of Sutherland Brothers Band and in the USA as Sutherland Brothers and Quiver and a single '(I Don't Want to Love You But) You Got Me Anyway' was simultaneously release in both Countries in 1973 in advance of a UK tour followed by a 42 date, Summer/Fall Arena tour of North America supporting Elton John.

Rod Stewart's girlfriend at the time, Britt Ekland, had been listening to the *Lifeboat* album and told Rod he should listen to what the Sutherland Brothers and Quiver were doing; he did and liked what he heard.

The band set off on a UK tour during which the highlight was at the newly opened (1971) Shaw Theatre in Euston Road in London's North side on 25 March 1973. Not only was it a landmark gig for the new band but it also made its mark on the song writing careers of the Brothers. "We were doing a gig at the Shaw Theatre when, in the middle of a number, I noticed a row of 5 people with spiky hair at the front." joked Gavin, "I thought fucking hell that's Rod Stewart and The Faces." They all met up backstage and had a drink and a chat. "After that I went off with Rod to a studio where he was doing a demo with Long John Baldry and I was invited to play some bottle neck guitar; something happened between Rod and Baldry, they fell out or something and it all fizzled out. I put my guitar in the case and fucked off and never heard any more about it!"

After the backstage meeting at the Shaw Theatre, Sutherland Brothers and Quiver were asked to support Rod and The Faces on half a dozen gigs around the UK. In fact Gavin Sutherland had a brief spell as a member of The Faces when during a gig in Manchester in early August 1973, he replaced Faces' drummer Kenney Jones, who had fallen ill and played on the tracks 'Maggie May', and 'Twisting the Night Away'. "It was a brilliant night for me but not so good for Kenney!" laughed Gavin.

As well as lead singer of Rod Stewart and The Faces it was clear that Rod was focussing on his solo career and his new album, which was in its infancy: "During the tour, Rod asked us for some songs for a solo album that he was doing (which later became *Atlantic Crossing*) and so we got together and knocked up a few songs that we thought were Rod type of songs." recalled Gavin. "We went up to Morgan studios and did some demos with him there because it was a studio he liked as it was relaxed and had a bar. We did about two or three demos with him and then he went off to the States to record the album at Muscle Shoals Sound in Alabama." The album was released in August 1975 and reached number 1 on the UK charts and number 9 on the Billboard charts in America.

A couple of months after the album was recorded Gavin got a call from a representative from Warner Brothers who said that they had a test pressing of the album and did he want to come and hear it. "They asked me if I wanted to know what song Rod had chosen from the Sutherland Brothers catalogue of songs and I said 'No let's just drop the needle on and listen to what happened'. I called Willie Wilson and we got in a cab and went down to Warner."

Gavin and Willy were in for a big surprise; the needle dropped onto the track and the song began to play but it was not a song that had a familiar start. "The song started and to us it had a strange beginning. Willy and I were looking at each other thinking what the fucking hell is this!" laughed Gavin, "We expected it to be one of the tunes that we had written specifically for him".

It was of course 'Sailing', a single released to accompany the Sutherland Brothers album *Lifeboat* in 1972, which was a song that Gavin thought was the least likely to become a Rod Stewart song. "Our version was a very simple arrangement and was reflective of our roots in Northern Scotland with Presbyterian hymns and religion and all that," recalled Gavin. "We weren't deliberately trying to write something that was hymnal but it sort of came out that way, in much the same way as a lot of the songs on that album. They were sort of fisherman's hymns; that was our background. It was a million miles away from 'Maggie May' though," joked Gavin.

It was Warner in England who wanted it released as a single and the decision, it is rumoured, was met with scepticism from Stewart, but Warner were right and it reached number 1 in the UK in September 1975 and remained there for 4 weeks.

Through the contacts Muff Winwood had with John Reid and Elton John, Sutherland Brothers and Quiver were offered a supporting slot on Elton John's tour to promote his album *Goodbye Yellow Brick Road* in the second half of 1973; the tour would take in large arenas across the US over a 9 week, 42 date period. "We were in the studio at Island's Basing Street HQ when the phone rang and somebody wanted a word with our manager, Wayne Bardell," recalled Gavin. "It was John Reid wanting to know if we could open for Elton on his upcoming tour of the States. Ten weeks of serious coast to coast stadium action with the biggest band around at that time. Wow! It would mean cancelling a gig at Cromer Town Hall, but, hey, you have to make sacrifices sometimes if you want to get on in life!" joked Gavin. "None of us had been 'over there' before and it was something all young rock n' rollers dreamed about. We knew Elton was big in the States but didn't realise just how big. The venues were huge, 50,000 some nights, even more on others."

Apparently Muff Winwood was in contact with Elton and he had heard the band's demo songs; no doubt Rod Stewart, who was a close friend of Elton, had said some positive words about the Brothers as well. Elton really liked the demos and so he asked Muff if the band wanted to join him; "We were thrilled," laughed Gavin.

The 1973 tour took the band to some iconic venues from the Hollywood Bowl to Madison Square Garden and all stops in between. "We were having a ball; Miami, St Louis, New Orleans, Chicago, San Francisco, everywhere we went the tour was the talk of the town and our records were picking up air play on stations here, there and everywhere." enthused Gavin. "It really was amazing; we were even treated to a week in Hawaii. We played a show at the University in Honolulu but our visit to the Islands was more of a much needed, mid tour break for everybody. By the time we got around to doing Seattle up in the North West corner, our single 'You Got Me Anyway' was at number six in the local chart. Elton's was a couple of places below us, but we still had to go on first. That's showbiz!" laughed Gavin.

Elton played the Hollywood Bowl where his flamboyance reached its peak: "Elton was dressed in a white feathered suit and big platform shoes and as he reached the bottom of a long staircase the lids of cardboard pianos were opened spelling Elton's name and these doves were supposed to fly out but they were petrified. I remember one just ambled across the stage to the wings," chuckled Gavin.

One of the gigs that went down in history on the tour took place in Boston, Massachusetts on 25 September 1973. It was reportedly the first gig that Stevie Wonder had played since his serious and life threatening car crash seven weeks earlier on 6th August. Wonder suffered serious head injuries when the vehicle he was travelling in collided with a truck carrying timber. Having spent a day in a coma, Wonder started his long journey to recovery and was eventually released from Rowan Memorial Hospital in South Carolina on 20 August. A month later he was on stage as a guest of Elton John at his gig at Boston Gardens.

In front of a 15,000 strong crowd, Elton started to announce Stevie Wonder to the unsuspecting crowd, but before he had chance to finish saying the name the crowd began to roar and Elton's voice was lost. Wonder settled down to his electric piano and they played 'Honky Tonk Woman' followed by 'Superstition' and then finished with a final burst of 'Honky Tonk Woman' before Wonder was escorted off stage to even more roars and applause.

Gavin Sutherland remembered the gig well as it caused quite a giggle in the dressing room after Wonder had left the stage. Gavin took up the story: "Stevie was up for it and with a loan of our Wurlitzer piano, joined Elton near the end of his set to a massive, hysterical welcome from the crowd. He gets led across stage and sits down at the piano and bangs straight into 'Superstition', to rapturous applause. Paulo one of our star road crew notices from the side of the stage that one of the piano legs isn't screwed in properly and it's starting to work its way loose. So he crawls across the stage and under the piano to hold the leg in place. Stevie, quite oblivious to Paulo's presence, starts to get right into it and starts kicking out time on what he thought was a stage monitor or something but was actually Paulo's back. He must have booted him about a hundred times but Paulo, the hero of the moment, hung on in there till the tune was finished. After the show Paulo walked into the dressing room, visibly shaken, with the classic line, 'Getting a public kicking is pretty horrendous, but if it's from somebody like Stevie Wonder, well, you don't mind so much!'"

After the gig Elton John was interviewed about the performance with Wonder by the Boston Globe Correspondent Ernie Santosuosso for a gig review published on 28th September: "I was on the plane in New York this afternoon," said Elton in the dressing-room after the concert, "and one of the guys came up to me. 'We've got a cocktail organist I want you to meet back here,' he said. I wasn't really interested in meeting him but I was finally persuaded. It seems Sharon Lawrence of our public relations staff knows Stevie well so she concocted this plan whereby they hid him on the plane. It was really a trip finding him seated at the organ. I invited him to make the flight with us to Boston. He's such a marvellous musician."

During one of the other gigs on the tour Gavin Sutherland remembered another incident that shows Elton at his professional best, although it could have ended in disaster. "Elton was seated at his piano and we were watching from the wings," remembered Gavin. "The band was in full flow and suddenly a bottle or a can came hurtling onto the stage from the crowd and hit Elton on the back of the head. We all looked in horror. Elton stopped playing and stopped the band. He stood up and rubbed the back of his head a couple of times and then launched himself into a rendition of 'Saturday Night's Alright (for Fighting)'. We were all in awe, not only did he carry on but he had the foresight to play a very relevant song and now had the crowd at a higher level, they were roaring."

Elton was really good to the Brothers and the rest of the band during the tour and whenever he could he would pop his head around the door of their dressing room and wish them luck. "He was very generous guy and set the standard to how we treated the support artists when we became a headline band," recalled Gavin.

By 1974 the Sutherland Brothers and Quiver had released a couple of albums and singles and gone through some line-up changes, but the biggest change saw the band move from Island to CBS. "It was all amicable," explained Gavin, "we just decided that we wanted to try our luck somewhere else when our contract expired. We didn't have a label waiting in the wings for us but we were playing at somewhere like the Roundhouse in London a few weeks after we had left Island. There was an

A&R guy from CBS at the gig watching someone else and he came in to see us after the gig and realising we didn't have a record deal he signed us up."

It was not long after the Band signed for CBS that Muff Winwood also left Island and became the Head of A&R for CBS, the dream team was re-united but in a more corporate setting. "CBS was similar to Island in that they had people who tried to put music first but on a much bigger scale but it was definitely less personal," explained Gavin. "There was no real hanging around with the other artists in the building and having access to whoever we wanted. We were now part of a corporate music business, where you had to be in a certain place at a certain time in a formal meeting." According to Gavin CBS had a bit more of a callous attitude about success; if a band wasn't selling as many records as they wanted then they would be released from their artist contract. At Island the guys were used to hanging around with other artists and having a more social time. At CBS it was more like working for a living. "It didn't really matter what it was but if it was selling it was okay." remembered Gavin, "With Island we were doing specialist shows like the *Old Grey Whistle Test* but with CBS they would do that as well but they would try anything to get on television. It could be a television show in Singapore at 4.00am in the morning and they would get us on it. It's kind of not always what you want to do but it became a living, things changed and it did start to become more manufactured."

Although 'Arms of Mary' was the bands biggest hit the B side on the South African release called 'Something's Burning', a song written by Gavin Sutherland, caused quite a lot of controversy, "We were at CBS offices and someone from the Gramophone Company of South Africa turned up," remembered Gavin. "At the time they had a black chart and a white chart. 'Something's Burning' had a lyrical content that the local black stations in the Townships had picked up which the people could relate to." In fact the song was so popular that it reached number one in the black charts of South Africa. "I believe it was the only time a white band had reached number 1 in the black chart." enthused Gavin. "That was for me, a magical thing as I had written it and it had embarrassed the record company into having to communicate with the black community."

9

Hey Hey Johnny

In the liner notes to the 1995 CD re-release, Elton described the follow-up album to *Goodbye Yellow Brick Road* as being quickly recorded in January 1974. They had only about nine days to get everything laid down, as he and the band were under enormous pressure to finish the album and then head off to a tour of Japan.

All the same, and despite the short amount of time he had been given to complete the album, Elton and crew headed off to record it in the luxury of a ranch in Colorado called Caribou in Nederland, hence the title of the album, *Caribou*. The ranch was owned by James Guercio producer of the band, Chicago. "All the band and entourage had different log cabins around the grounds, and we all had ranch style meals for the time we were out there, and always ate together," recalled Larkham. "Recording started in the afternoons and went on into the night. The next day, they listened to playbacks to see if they wanted to keep the songs, do a re-make or scrap them altogether. As usual, the album cover was something on my mind more than anything else. For this one, I was inspired by the mountains that surrounded Colorado and, because I liked the artist Maxfield Parrish, I painted the backdrop in his style. Once again, Elton was reluctant to have his photo taken and was being moody, so we sent him a Polaroid photograph of the backdrop with me in front of it so he could see how it was going to work, asking him if he would do the same. What happened was that he and Bernie came up eventually and a few beers later he did the photo. The inner cover shot was taken as Elton was getting into his car. He had thick glasses on at the time and we tinted the frames to make them pink. He was quite taken by the photograph and the pink tinting; so much so, that he was tempted, for a time, to change the album's title to something like *Ol' Pink Eyes Is Back*."

♪

John Carsello was the Caribou Ranch Manager from its opening in 1972 following its purchase by the famed band Chicago's manager and producer Jim Guercio, until its closure and sale in June 2014. Kenny Passarelli, who worked as a bass player for the likes of Barnstorm, Joe Walsh and, later, Elton John at the Ranch described Carsello as 'the glue that held the recording part of the Ranch together'; without the communication John had with the artists and the studio the Ranch would not have existed long.

The Ranch first opened with Joe Walsh who was well known at the time for his work with The James Gang and his new band Barnstorm. "Of course we had Chicago recording at the Ranch all the time but also had Rick Derringer and Edgar Winter's White Trash in there very early on", recalled Carsello. According to Carsello the Ranch received a call from Guercio's office in Los Angeles, who was dealing with the management of the Ranch: "We were told that Elton John was interested in coming to record at the studio – now we had Chicago and they were a mega act at the time but we worked with them every day almost so when we heard that Elton wanted to see it we were just blown away." Elton had finished his album *Goodbye Yellow Brick Road* and was coming to the end of his tour to promote the album. At the time his contract with Dick James required him to put out two albums a year. Carsello remembered that Elton John was playing in Denver in September 1973 and the plan was to get Elton to come to the Ranch just to have a look round and see if it was what he wanted. "I got a call from Barry Frey who was the promoter for the show as he had heard that we wanted Elton to come and see the Ranch, so he invited us to the show and we went backstage. We set things up for when Elton had his next day off, (which was around the beginning of September 1973). On the day he came we met him and his entourage at the airport. He had borrowed a plane being used by Bob Dylan; a Boeing 727 jet, which was a horrible dark brown colour but it was fully equipped with a bar and a private bedroom. Elton and the entourage were whisked away in limousines to the beautiful and serene countryside of Nederland, high in the Rockies to spend a glorious afternoon at the Ranch. We got there at about 1.00pm where the staff had prepared hamburgers for Elton and his entourage for lunch; Davey, Dee, Nigel and Clive Franks were in awe of the place and its surroundings."

Rick Derringer had just finished recording his album *All American Boy*, which was due for release in October 1973. Clive Franks and Elton were in the studio checking it out whilst a play back of Derringer's 'Rock and Roll Hoochie Koo' was blasting from the studio speakers. Elton loved it and asked Carsello whether it had been recorded at Caribou and when he found out it had he was impressed with the sound quality. The only drawback of that tour was the Olive Console they were using in the Studio. Carsello remembered: "We had an Olive console (board) in the studio which was a board of the future. It was the first one to use modules but it was making a noise and there were maintenance troubles." They loved the studio and the surroundings and Elton made his mind up right there and then he wanted to record his next album at Caribou Ranch. "He didn't book it right there and then but when they did he said he wanted a different board and changing a board is no mean thing; but we did it for him. Tearing out the Olive board wasn't that bad but replacing it with a Neve, which was the board he had stipulated, was difficult; even finding one was hard enough. In the end we found one through Abbey Road in London through George Martin when they were replacing theirs. We flew it in on a 727 from Europe in a box and it came into New York and then flown down to the studio and we got it installed in one day and so Elton booked the place. Elton also stipulated that we had to buy Tannoy speakers which we hadn't heard of so we flew those in from Europe as well." No expense spared for Elton obviously.

It was early January when Elton got into Denver with his band and Clive Franks after the tour along with producer Gus Dudgeon and his wife Sheila. "We sent trucks down to pick up the equipment and Elton came up to start recording. He had some of the material written already but the way I saw it he was hanging out for a day or two waiting for Bernie to send lyrics, (Bernie would join them later when he had finished the writing and make subtle changes), and Elton would then put everything down right there and then in the studio. Songs like 'The Bitch is Back' and 'Don't Let the Sun Go Down on Me' were all recorded very soon after being written in the studio. My office was next to where Elton was writing the tunes because we had grand pianos in his cabin and I could hear him screaming around writing songs. The album wasn't done live but Elton was very fast when he recorded. By comparison when Supertramp came they took a year to complete an album. Gus and Clive worked on the Neve and the band recorded the album in a week and a half and in two weeks it was recorded and mixed apart from a couple of overdubs. They didn't have a title for it at the time and I didn't find out until I got a copy that they called it *Caribou*. I said to Jim when I found out 'Oh man we are really on the map now'."

The Ranch never had downtime and the engineers were so good they could build and fix anything. "We had futuristic things for music video and just about anything; they even ran movies to the cabins. VCR wasn't available but the engineers had buried coaxial cable to all the cabins so they could play movies through the studio. It was just as well that the engineers were very good because Gus and Elton demanded high quality and so the team just gelled. If something needed to be changed or fixed it was fixed straight away; if they wanted any special equipment it was flown in the same day. The studio was just right every day and engineers made sure that the machines were aligned 24 hours a day so if Elton and the band or Gus and Clive wanted to use it they could. We had three pianos set up for Elton so he had a choice; we had a Bosendorfer with extra 8 octave keys on the keyboard making it 97 keys instead of 88 on a standard piano; we had a 'rock and roll' piano bought from Studio B at CBS records that was used by everyone from The Benny Goodman Orchestra to Bessie Smith and used on classic songs like 'Bridge Over Troubled Water' by Simon and Garfunkel. Elton used that one a lot," laughed Carsello. "We had to build a special facility over the piano so we could mic it properly to isolate the sound so as to make it perfect so you couldn't hear anything else through the U87 microphones." Elton had access to a 1910 mahogany Steinway that CBS was going to throw away but Jim Guercio told them to give him the piano and saved it from the refuse dump. "It had been used by nearly everybody who ever recorded at CBS including Simon and

Garfunkel. Elton didn't use the Bosendorfer, it was more of a concert grand piano, but he used the mahogany Steinway a lot and 'Don't Let the Sun Go Down on Me' was recorded on it along with most of the ballads on the album. The rockier sounds were recorded on the 'rock and roll' piano, such as songs like 'The Bitch Is Back'."

As far as vocals went it was 'hit and miss' as to how well the vocals sounded as vocal chords are challenged at 8000 feet up above sea level. "Elton had some problems with that, not everyone can sing that high up. I remember being in the studio with Gus when Elton was recording his vocals and Elton saying, 'I gotta get this on the first or second take because my voice gets tired up here'."

In their spare time Elton and the entourage had a good time, Elton would play football and when he wanted to relax he would go to his cabin where the bed of former President of the United States Grover Cleveland was and he loved it. "We took Elton snowmobiling with his band; now we are talking deep snow, thirty feet deep in places and if you stopped you started sinking. I remember I was at the rear and Elton was at the front with the band and the studio guys not far behind except Nigel who was just in front of me. He was slowing down and started sinking. Now anyone who has been snowmobiling knows that it's hard and tiring, you have to stand up and on top of that you are at 11000 feet above sea level so there is little air. So Nigel was lying on his snow mobile with his legs sticking out and he said 'Just go on, leave me here', and I said 'you gotta go on, you'll die here'; it was a lot of fun." Elton was never far away from his beloved tennis. "I remember him coming into my office in his bathrobe and asking if they had tennis courts in Boulder that he could book so I arranged the courts for him and told them to keep the people away from him. In the end we would book four courts so he wasn't bothered by anyone else," laughed Carsello. Although Elton appeared to crave anonymity from time to time he could never resist the shock factor of Elton John being seen out in public. "He came into the office one day and said that he wanted to go to Boulder and be incognito so no one knew him and asked where he could go. I told him to go to the Hill, which is the University part of the Town so he went and shopped there. The next day in the local newspaper there was a picture of Elton with a headline *Elton*

John on the Hill; the picture was of Elton walking along the Street wearing a red fox fur coat and his zapper glasses. So much for incognito!"

Sometimes the high jinks got too much and it tried the patience of the Ranch Manager. "I was told I was the only person to dare to scream at Gus Dudgeon," laughed Carsello, "Gus was travelling along the dirt road to the Ranch at about 60mph like a maniac in one of Jim's soft top Blazers; now these vehicles are souped-up with very large dirt track tyres. Ray was staying in a cabin by the road where Gus was driving; there was dust everywhere and Ray's baby and Davey's son Tam were playing around the area by the cabins and the road. I called Gus's cabin on the phone and I screamed at him; I said 'I don't give a fuck who you are; you don't drive like that here, you are going to kill a kid, yourself or somebody else.' He just said 'okay, okay', and hung up the phone. When I calmed down I thought I was going to hear more about this and sure enough Gus came over to my office and I thought the worst. He said 'John I just want to say how sorry I am.' I apologised that I had shouted at him and he just said he was wrong and I was right to shout at him." Although Dudgeon was a perfectionist in the studio and highly strung as a professional producer he wasn't afraid of genuine criticism and as famous as he was he could take it and apologise.

♫

It was during the *Caribou* sessions that John Reid first realised that Elton had started using drugs, although Reid claims that Elton would never take drugs on stage. "I think all the band were doing drugs in about 1973/1974, and I believe Elton started to have a little bit of gear at the time, before I was working with him," recalled Gary Osborne about the previously abstemious singer. "He was always very good on it and the drinking came about because coke is very morish, and you need something to keep you level if you're doing a lot of it. One of the best days of my life was when I decided I was not going to do coke anymore, but I don't deny that it was great fun at the time."

"It was a huge surprise to me when he said he was an alcoholic, because I'd very rarely seen him drunk. The coke keeps taking you up and the booze keeps bringing you back down, so that you pretty much just stay level. To spend that much money, and that much energy, and that much time, just to trying stay level: what the hell were we thinking? We did have some fantastic times though, but I would not recommend it to anybody. However, to deny that the period was fun is to deny a whole slab of your life, which is silly. With coke, you don't go to sleep and you don't eat, you just drink, and on an empty stomach at that. All you keep thinking is I must have some more coke and by the way, I'll have another drink, so you never think you have a drink problem."

♪

While Elton was busy finishing off the *Caribou* album, and sorting out his private life, over at Rocket, the Kiki Dee Band were taking shape, and getting ready to tour. Gus Dudgeon introduced Kiki to her new drummer, Roger Pope, who had been doing session work for Rocket Records after the demise of Hookfoot.

"I got a phone call from Gus at my flat in Harrow, who said he needed some help with a gig at the studios," remembered Pope. "It was with Kiki, and she was finishing a song called 'I've Got The Music in Me'." But there had been some tension with the drummer, and John Reid had gone into the studio to fire him. Up to that time, Dudgeon had completed the basic track but he needed some more drum work. Not wanting to do the track again, Dudgeon asked Pope to fill in. "I sat on the kit and I just accented the drum beat and I left all the original drummer's fills in and Gus was really pleased. It took me about three minutes and I was paid thirty quid!" laughed Pope.

Dudgeon could see that Pope was getting on well with Kiki and the rest of the band, so soon after consulting with her, Pope was asked to complete the album, which he eagerly accepted. "I asked Gus how many numbers were left, and he said they had only done one song, so I thought that that was okay, because Gus worked on a track a day and that was two weeks work."

After a week, John Reid asked Pope if he wanted to be in Kiki's band for a tour of the States, supporting Elton. Pope accepted. "He put me on a wage, after paying me for my sessions, and I was in the band." They completed the album followed by a short tour of England and then some promotional gigs in Europe, which gave them the chance to get familiar playing with each other. "The first thing I did after completing the album was a festival in Nice, and then we did a TV show in Monte Carlo in a small studio with three cameras and a drum kit, with no spurs to keep the bass drum still. We did it at nine in the morning and we were miming, which I hate, and the bass drum kept rolling and only stopped when it hit the tom-tom!"

Pope toured with Kiki Dee for about eighteen months, which included two tours with Elton, beginning with some dates in 1974. "We did a big tour supporting Elton, which was great because we only needed to do forty-five minutes. All the guys in the band were good players and it was a good snappy outfit."

After the success of the *Caribou* album, which was another to top the charts the world over, Elton returned to California to prepare for the *Captain Fantastic And The Brown Dirt Cowboy* album, which was to be followed by a tour of North America, Hawaii, Japan, Australia, and then the rest of the world.

But then Elton received a call from Tony King. "I went to LA initially to work with Ringo [Starr] on his first album, for which both Elton and John Lennon had written material as they wanted to help him have a career after the Beatles, especially as Lennon and McCartney were already enjoying their own successes as solo artists. So when Ringo came to record his album, everybody wanted to help him out. He was such a loveable warm character, so it wasn't surprising to me that Lennon and Elton were writing a couple of songs each for the project. This was probably because Ringo asked Elton: Ringo was never backward in coming forward. He was blunt but in a very nice way. Elton wrote 'Snookeroo' for him, which became an album track and a successful single."

"While I was in LA, I was also asked to do a TV advertisement for John Lennon's album *Mind Games*, which I did dressed as the Queen of England, which also appeared, albeit briefly, in the *Imagine* film. It was in September or October 1973 that I was doing this commercial in Hollywood. I told Elton, who was in California at the time, what I was doing with John Lennon, and asked him to come down to the studios to meet him. I had told John that I had invited Elton to the studio to check it was okay and he said he'd like to meet him as he thought Elton was doing some great stuff. After they had finished the commercial, Lennon went back to the studio to continue working with Phil Spector on his *Rock 'n' Roll* album, after which he went to work with Nilsson on the *Pussy Cats* album in LA and then he straightened himself out and went on to work on *Walls And Bridges* in New York. Elton went to watch the *Rock 'n' Roll* sessions, but he wasn't invited to play on any of the tracks on that occasion. During those sessions, I took Elton in and it was a bit fraught. Elton noticed that it was a 'bit hairy in there', and we left having not stayed very long."

"The relationship between Spector and Lennon was to break down after the recording of the album," added King, "and that's when Lennon and Elton struck up a friendship."

Lennon gave King a job with him in New York, which he accepted with enthusiasm as he had always wanted to work and live in the country where James Dean, Marilyn Monroe and Elvis Presley came from. All three were among some of his favourite icons from the music and film industries. But before moving to New York City, King returned home to Britain to prepare himself to move across the Atlantic to work for Lennon.

"It was a difficult year for me as I was re-locating to the US and because I was working for Apple I had to get all four Beatles to agree to it and that wasn't easy; but I managed to get it done." And so, off King went to New York with John Lennon. "I went over with Elton on the SS France with Julian and Cynthia. John was with May Pang at the time, as he had split up with Yoko, and he wanted to spend some time with Julian. Elton said he was going to pay for me to have this fabulous trip on the SS France. There was a great orchestra of school kids on the quayside playing us off with 'Yellow Submarine'. When the ship finally left, it was two or three in the morning and they were all falling asleep."

By this time, Phil Greenfield had been persuaded by John Reid to take the job as Elton's road manager, following the demise of Hookfoot, and was given the responsibility of making sure the SS France left with all the gear needed for the tour and the recording sessions. "We were due to leave from Southampton; it was its last voyage before they sold it off, so they did this whole carnival with a big brass band to play Elton onto the ship. Rick Bateman was looking after Davey's guitars, and I was doing the percussion, looking after Ray and Nigel and also Elton, so I had a lot on my plate." When the party arrived, Greenfield found out that he and the crew were not travelling on the ship but had been booked on a flight to New York instead.

"I had to do all this running around putting the gear on the ship and then I realised we had lost Elton's Fender guitar case with all his glasses in it. It was all pretty hectic and we thought we had made sure everyone had everything and then Elton said, 'Where are my glasses?' I was on the dockside accusing everyone, and checking the trucks, and everything, to find these glasses." Greenfield remembered that when they first reached Southampton they had booked into a hotel because the ship had not then arrived in Port. "This is where it all went wrong, because if the ship had been there, then all the equipment would have gone straight onto it, but was transferred from the dockside in buses, to the hotel." It turned out that one of the road crew had put Elton's glasses under the backseat of the bus and it had driven off. "No-one knew who the bus company was or anything. I was panicking because if Elton had found out he would have gone ballistic."

Although Elton was on the ship, which was ready to leave, he was refusing to go without his glasses. Greenfield continued: "Psychologically he needed his glasses, so I asked someone on the dock gate if they remembered the buses and this guy gave me the name of a bus company. So I rang them up, they checked the bus and found the two guitar cases. I told him not to touch them. I had an old S-Type Jaguar at the time and went over to the bus garage and picked up the cases and went speeding back to the terminal, where they were just pulling away the gang plank. Somehow, I managed to get the cases on the ship and off they went, with Elton happy that he had his glasses."

As soon as they arrived in New York, Elton and his entourage went straight to the hotel, where King and Lennon were also staying, while Greenfield and his crew travelled with the equipment to Caribou Ranch in Colorado. Lennon had arrived at the hotel and had booked a suite on the 57th floor with May Pang. Elton's suite was on a lower floor. King recounts: "John was already there so I called him and told him I had arrived, and he asked me to come up. I told him that I was with Elton in his suite, at the time, and John told me to bring him as well. Lennon was having a lot of fun with Pang because she liked the rock 'n' roll and music lifestyle, so he was back to being a Beatle again. We went up to his room and asked him what he was doing in New York. He said he was finishing an album called *Walls And Bridges* and played it for us. He suggested to Elton that if he liked it, he could perhaps do some work with him on one of the tracks. He was most impressed with the offer.

When Lennon got to 'Whatever Gets You Thru The Night', Elton and King were confident that it was the hit single from the album and persuaded Lennon that was the case. King remembered "I said that it was the one track that Elton would be good on, so John asked Elton what he thought about doing it with him. He, of course, jumped at the chance and with that, they agreed they would go into the studio that evening and give it a try. We went to dinner with the head of MCA Records, Mike Maitland, and other serious heavyweights at MCA and we had a marvellous dinner. Afterwards, we went to the Record Plant to start the session on the tracks. As I remember it, it was laid down pretty quickly. The session went well even though Elton had some difficulty with it to start with because Lennon's phrasing was so unusual. He had a lot of problems with double tracking John's vocal. They also recorded another song, 'Surprise, Surprise Sweet Bird of Paradox' and that was basically the session. When 'Whatever Gets You Thru The Night' came out as a single that's when Elton asked me if I thought John would be up for playing Madison Square Garden with him. I told John about Elton's invite to join him on stage on Thanksgiving Day and said he would be happy to do it if the record got to No.1. Elton agreed. I went to Al Corey, who was at Capitol Records at the time and being a promotions man myself, I told him that if he could squeeze the song up to No. 1, then John Lennon would play Madison Square Garden with Elton. Al was taken with the idea, and most certainly the opportunity to entice Lennon back in front of a live audience, so he got the record to No. 1. It was great for John as the American Government were trying to throw him out at the time. When the single hit No.1, John was asked to give out a Grammy Award, and he asked me what I thought. I said it was a gift of an opportunity, I told him that they could hardly ask him to give out a prestigious award one minute and then throw him out of the country the next. I advised him to do it, and he did."

By the time Elton had completed his recording session with Lennon, he made his way to Colorado where Greenfield had already set everything up in readiness to start recording the next album. He recalled: "The band started to work getting the tracks down and the whole atmosphere was fantastic. It was a fantastic place, they gave us our own horse for the time we were there and it was like a playground." Not that there was much time to relax. All in all, the time off for band and crew only amounted to two days, which was mainly spent in Boulder, the nearest big town.

"Dee, Nigel and their partners decided to go out for the day, and Rick [Roadie] and me decided to do the same." remembered Greenfield. "We all needed a break, because it was getting very intense working in the studio. We ended up hiring a car, and went cruising through Boulder until we reached an intersection, and when I saw the band, I pulled up. We had a brief conversation and arranged to see them back at the ranch. Another vehicle had pulled up close behind us and started to follow me all the way back to the intersection and the road to the ranch. I had a look in the mirror and a cop car pulled up behind me and sat there, and then all hell broke loose. There were cops everywhere. They forced me up onto a grass bank at the side of the road, and the next thing I know, I had this gun pointing at me. I put my hands where they could see them as I knew they were trigger happy. The one thing going through my mind at that moment was how similar this was to when the Beatles' roadie got shot. They got us out of the car, and then they beat me into the back seat and put handcuffs on me. By now poor Rick, despite his size, was beginning to get upset, fearing the worst. I told him to settle down as we hadn't done anything wrong, but there was obviously something that they were not telling us about. I had this gun in the nape of my neck and my head was pushed down into the boot of the car and it was a screaming hot day, and I was getting burned."

After the ordeal, the police said they thought Greenfield and Rick were college kids who got their kicks by stealing cars. The car that they had rented had been stolen, but the rental car firm had not told the police that it had been recovered, so it was still showing up as stolen on police records.

"I was trying to tell them, with my face pushed into the car boot, that we were there with Elton John and were working for him, but the police clearly didn't believe me and the situation began to get a lot worse. I was starting to get a bit angry too. I started to get pissed off with the policeman holding me down, as he was hurting me by then. I said 'If you have not got a justifiable reason for doing this, you are in deep shit.' He replied with a 'Yeah yeah, you fucking college kids!' That's when I said, 'But I haven't been to fucking college in my life!' After that they all came scurrying around and I said look, 'All you need to do is look in the glove box and there is a contract signed by me from the rental car company, and you will see the Elton John Management Company is written on it.' So the policemen had a discussion, and while this was going on, the place was in an uproar, there was traffic everywhere and an arsenal of guns. Eventually, the police realised that they may have been wrong, so they escorted the two of us back to the rental car compound to check it out. They told us to stay in the car first, and then they very nearly hung this guy at the rental car company. When I went in there afterwards to get another car this guy was shaking, they had really given him a right going over. The police apologised and they arranged for them to have another car. We were given the best car the rental place had, which was a Mustang."

Back at the ranch there was a big party going on, and word had got around of their ordeal with the police. "Everyone was laughing at us, and then the cops turned up, and we thought 'Oh God, not again', but they gave us a whole case of Jack Daniels to say they were sorry."

The downside for Greenfield was that the recording sessions at Caribou would prove to be his last with the band. "I had this big bust up with John Reid over money. I went into the control room and the band asked me if everything was all right, but they knew it wasn't and that night it was a bit flat. Everyone was telling me not to worry, it was only money, and to just forget about him, it's the band that matters. It was clear that they wanted to create the unique feel like Hookfoot had." And by now, it was what Elton wanted as well.

It was during the sessions at Caribou that Elton invited Lennon, through King, to the ranch where he was recording the *Captain Fantastic* album, thus returning the favour Lennon had given him, by asking Lennon to record with him. Lennon agreed, and the fruits of their labours produced an excellent version of the Beatles' 'Lucy In The Sky With Diamonds' and Lennon's 'One Day At A Time', which was also a personal favourite of Elton's.

Lennon had agreed to visit Elton in Colorado on the way to LA after his lost weekend episodes with Harry Nilsson. During the recording of 'Lucy', Lennon wrote a reggae piece to be inserted in the middle of the song, which was subsequently credited to 'the Reggae guitars of Winston O'Boogie'. The Lennon sessions were the way Elton always recorded, with a base song, and the rest of the band adding their parts during the sessions and recording.

For a time, Lennon became one of the band. They played together with Lennon on guitar, and altered the songs together through a meeting of musical minds. When Dudgeon was satisfied with the rehearsal session, he recorded it. Photographs taken during the sessions at the ranch were subsequently used on the first *Greatest Hits* album. Then after that, there was Madison Square Garden.

"When you get Elton you get them all, he just drew stars to his side." remembered Carsello, "I couldn't believe it when John Lennon and May Pang arrived to record with Elton during the *Captain Fantastic* sessions. I remembered letting them use one of the Ranch Blazers to go to town because John didn't even have his toothpaste or toothbrush with him. He looked so good though, he was so cool. We are here in the middle of the Rockies with John Lennon; it was unbelievable. I remember walking into the studio at about 11:30 at night when they were recording. Gus was at the console with Clive Franks and across in the corner on the little couches that looked a lot like love seats was John Lennon all curled up in the foetal position fast asleep with 'Lucy in the Sky with Diamonds' blaring in the background. The previous morning Lennon had been singing backing vocals with Elton on the track. The next morning I walked into the mess hall at 8am and there was John Lennon sitting at one of the Ranch tables on his own except for the girl doing the cooking. I introduced myself again and asked him if everything was alright and he said how great the place was. He had just been reading in *The Denver Post* about the possibility of his green card being revoked over his drug conviction. He said it was beautiful at the Ranch; he loved the space. He used to go horse riding and I even took him to Martins - a rodeo shop in Boulder- to buy cowboy boots with the other guys in the band. He enjoyed the camaraderie of the band and being with May Pang. For me it was surreal being with one of my boyhood hero's from the biggest band in music history, The Beatles."

As Lennon sat at the mess table thinking about the article in the newspaper he looked at Carsello and said "I sure hope they let me stay in this country, it reminds me of home." Lennon had made his home in an apartment in Manhattan New York City.

♫

Following the recording of *Captain Fantastic And The Brown Dirt Cowboy*, Elton was joined by Ray Cooper and the Kiki Dee Band for his extensive tour to promote the *Caribou* album. Although Cooper was asked to stay on permanently on percussion, the tour would turn out to be the last outing for Olsson and Murray until 1980. Everything seemed to be bigger and better than ever before.

Elton chartered the famous Starship plane, which other rock aristocrats also hired to get from A to B in the lap of luxury. With no expense spared, Starship was turned into Elton's own plane with his own livery, as Deep Purple and Led Zeppelin had done, proving that Elton was dining at rock's top table. Everyone flew on Starship, including the Kiki Dee Band and the Muscle Shoals musicians, who were recreating the brass and backing vocals for the heavy brass-influenced sound they had provided on the *Caribou* album. "Starship was a 707 with all the seats taken out and lounge seats put in, a bit like a nightclub," recalled *Melody Maker's* Chris Charlesworth. "It was carpeted, with dining tables, soft dining chairs and a bar area with a bar that was about 6' long."

"At the end of the bar," remembered Charlesworth, "was an electronic keyboard. At various points around the plane were television screens, where you could play videos. It literally had everything you wanted. Behind the bar was a corridor that led to two private rooms, one was full of cushions where people could go and lounge around on the floor, and the other was a bedroom with an ensuite bathroom. There were a couple of stewardesses, chosen for their looks rather than their serving skills, who dispensed food and drinks from the galley, which was just behind the cockpit. I remember Elton was partial to Kentucky Fried Chicken. Wherever he went, his outrageous clothes and spectacles went with him. He had a huge wardrobe in his dressing room because he wore all these spangly outfits. When you opened the cupboard door there would be about 30 pairs of shoes and 209 jackets to choose from, and drawers of spectacles. He was good natured about it all, and he realised that it was all over the top, and he was mocking about it. He thought it was all a big laugh really."

It was much the same for Kiki Dee, who would also support Elton on his 1974 tour. "I was promoting 'I've Got The Music In Me', and I was known as 'Keek', just part of the family. Elton John fans had heard of me from the promotion Elton had given me through Rocket, so I was getting a really good response from them at gigs. We used to travel all over America in Starship. I stayed mainly with Davey and the other band members, Dee and Nigel, but I do remember it being like a real hippy hangout, with vitamins on the bar in packets of ten, and the little stewardess handing out drinks."

To an observer, it was clear that Davey Johnstone and Kiki Dee were getting on well and a relationship was forming. "Yeah, me and Davey got to know each other on tour, and our friendship became something more," admits Dee. One of the highlights for the new couple was when Kiki and Johnstone were sharing a room at the Plaza in New York and John Lennon and May Pang joined them. "We spent the whole night in our hotel room with them. It was a real thrill for us both. John tried to get me to change my stage appearance by encouraging me to wear black leather like Suzi Quatro. Two years later," continued Dee, "Davey would call it day on our relationship. It just ran its course, but we remained friends; it was an important relationship in my life."

One of the highlights during the tour for the Kiki Dee Band was when Elton and his band sang backing vocals from behind the stage, so that the audience couldn't see them. It was clear that Elton was very proud of Kiki, as she was his shining star on Rocket. She was getting rave reviews for her albums, and her singles were shooting up the charts. The reaction she received from the audience, and some prominent music business luminaries, must have taken Elton back to his formative years, and his experiences at the Troubadour. He also spent a lot of time in the wings watching Kiki's band play, but he was also watching something else, Roger Pope's drumming and, in particular, the level of musicianship that was being displayed. He also picked up on the fun they appeared to be having.

It was further enhanced when Caleb Quaye was invited onto the stage during a gig in Chicago, where he was living, and the whole Hookfoot vibe was evident again in the Kiki Dee Band. The creativity and freedom the band showed, led by Pope who was by now, picking up a reputation for being one of the most prolific drummers around, got Elton thinking about his own future and that of his band. He couldn't help but ask himself if a change was needed. Not that he could do much about it at that time. He was in the middle of a tour, and still had an album to finish; an album that would become autobiographical as its content would revisit the story of his and Bernie's formative years.

The culmination of the American tour was two nights at Madison Square Garden, one of which was to fall on Thanksgiving Day, Thursday, 28 November 1974, and was set to become one of Elton's most historic. John Lennon had said he would play the gig with Elton if his single got to No.1 and, as it had, Lennon now had to make good on his promise. All the same, Elton asked the ex-Beatle again, just to be sure. "John asked me what he should do and had he really got to do it." remembered Lennon's then-publicist Tony King. "I told him there was no 'got to' about it, but I reminded him that he already said he would, so he said, 'okay, I'll do it'."

The night before the concert, the band, Lennon and Elton rehearsed at the Record Plant. It was during this rehearsal that reminded King of the same Reg Dwight who had been in the studio all those years before during the Bread And Beer Band sessions; the same person who was in charge. "It was a 'musical in charge' rather than a personal one, as it was his band and his show. John came in and said, 'It's all yours.', and they routined the show and the songs. Elton was the leader of the band, and Lennon was happy for it to be like that. Both Elton and John were strong personalities, but it was just that it was Elton's show. Both John and Elton liked to work very quickly and therefore the rehearsals lasted for about two hours and after that they were ready to go."

According to King, during the journey to the Garden backstage area, Lennon came across as shy and quiet, probably due to the fact that he was about to face the daunting prospect of having to play a live gig for the first time in over two years and at an incredibly high profile venue. The last time he was in front of paying punters was when he and Yoko Ono performed two benefit concerts, with Elephant's Memory and guests, which was staged, coincidentally, at Madison Square Garden, on 30 August 1972.

Before he went on stage for what was to be Lennon's last ever live performance, and which has since been described as one of his best gigs, Lennon was watching the show from the wings. "I was standing at the stairs with John and some others, before he was about to go on, and he was petrified," remembered Stuart Epps. "We couldn't really understand it as this was the guy who had played Shea Stadium in the biggest band in the world. And then when Elton announced him, he turned round, and said to no-one in particular, 'Oh well, here we go, over the hill' as if he was about to go into battle. He said it in the style that only John Lennon could say it, and on he went."

As King noted, "In my career of highlights, of which there are many, I have met some very interesting people and done many interesting things (for instance I was thrown out of the Strand Hotel one night with Phil Spector and The Ronettes, because they were rehearsing in the bedroom and that was a thrill), but to see John Lennon on stage with Elton John at Madison Square Garden was incredible. In fact, there are no words to describe how electric that night was. John had not been on stage for years and, to be honest, if he had still been alive today, he would have agreed with me that he had lost a bit of self-confidence about it, and it was all a bit scary for him. For Elton it was a huge responsibility, because if it had bombed, then Elton would have felt dreadful. But they were unbelievable on stage. They were red hot. I was standing at the side of the stage with May Pang and Elton kept looking over at me and laughing, as if to say, 'What about this, isn't it fantastic?' And when John came off the stage, after the encores, we were due to make a fast exit; John jumped into the back of the car opposite me and said 'That was fucking great', and he was so elated, it was a huge moment for him. The noise from the crowd was amazing, and the wave of appreciation for John was equally amazing; the whole stage was bouncing as they were playing, which made all the limos backstage bounce up and down as if they were dancing. When it came to doing 'I Saw Her Standing There', it was John who said, 'Let's do one of Paul's songs'. He said it so affectionately, and it was chosen with affection. In a way, it was like a sweet message to Paul. They used to bitch with each other, but you could tell that there was still a deep affection there. I thought when John suggested it, what a nice gesture, and John was holding out the hand of friendship to Paul by saying he was doing one of his songs out of respect for him."

During Lennon's appearance, the building was literally vibrating, and the huge PA which was hanging from the roof was swinging up and down; Epps was worried the whole place would collapse. Dudgeon was busy recording the appearance on his mobile recording desk, and everyone backstage was crying with the emotion of the moment. Yoko Ono was in the audience. "We didn't leave straight away, as planned, because Yoko came backstage," recalled King. "Before the gig John had heard that Yoko might be coming and said he wouldn't do it if Yoko was there. I knew that she was going to be there, as I had got her the tickets and had escorted her to her seat eleven rows back. John said that he couldn't sing if Yoko was in the audience, and so Elton looked at me in shock, because he knew she was there as well. At the end of the day, although May was a fun person, spiritually John always belonged to Yoko, and indeed ended up back with her."

Part of that getting back together may have started at the concert, when Yoko turned up at Lennon's dressing room after the show. "I was in his dressing room when there was a knock on the door," recalled Epps. "I opened it to find Yoko standing there. It would have been okay, but John was with May Pang and I didn't know that this was all amicable and that she had actually put the two of them together. I was relieved when John said 'Hi, come in' and it was all okay."

"After the gig there was a party at the hotel," added David Larkham. "Elton had flown me and my wife to New York. We stayed in the Plaza Hotel, but my wife went back to LA because the weather was too cold for her on the East Coast. I stayed to watch the gig and take photographs. The night before, we had gone for a curry, when curry was just becoming popular in New York. And after the after-show party, we all went back to the promoter's apartment with Paul Simon, Elton and Bernie, and the party continued. And of course, as expected, the main topic of conversation was the amazing appearance of John Lennon."

♪

By this time, John Reid was becoming a force to be reckoned with in the world of music business management and to add a further string to his bow would soon become the manager of some of the leading artists of the time. In addition to Elton, he had Kiki Dee, and then he signed Queen in 1975. "Queen became part of the John Reid Management enterprise, much like Elton John, because of David Croker," explained Reid. "He called me up and said, 'Do you know a little band called Queen who are signed to EMI?' At the time, the band was having problems with management, and were looking for someone else. David asked me if I was interested, and my now classic response was, "Can they play live?"

This was possibly the strangest question Croker had heard, given that Queen were renowned, even at that time, for exhilarating stage performances. "I had never seen them and all I'd heard was 'Killer Queen' and 'Seven Seas of Rye', but they actually set up a full rig show at the place where they were recording, just for me."

In fact, there was supposed to be three other people, all potential managers, who should have been there, but Reid was the only one who bothered to turn up. He duly signed a jewel of a group to his management company and, as a result, Freddie Mercury and Elton ended up becoming very close friends. "Freddie, like Elton, would latch on to something, and push it to the limit, while the others in the band, would be going ballistic."

Of course, the bigger and more successful they and Freddie Mercury became the more the other band members accepted Freddie's foibles, to the point where they all dressed up in drag for the hilarious video for 'I Want To Break Free'. Reid recalled how "Elton came into the office and I played him the test pressing of 'Bohemian Rhapsody', and I remember him saying, 'Are you serious? Nobody [radio stations] is going to play that, not in a million years!'. Oh well, you can't be right all the time!"

At the same time that Reid had taken on Queen, Elton was becoming less interested in his personal relationship with John Reid, and really wanted to end it, but he couldn't do it. One of the many strands in Elton's character was his difficulty in delivering bad news to anyone; maybe he was too tender-hearted. On the business front he had others around him, including Reid, who he relied on to take control of awkward tasks. He would make a decision, and if it was likely to affect someone badly, he would ask Reid to do it. You can argue it is a manager's function to do just that, of course.

For Elton though, he couldn't do that when it came to ending his relationship with Reid. He would, according to Reid, drop subtle hints, like playing 'I'm Not In Love' by 10cc whenever Reid was around, in the hope he would get the message, or respond, by asking what was happening. The end finally came when the prospect of the pair moving house into something bigger was raised by Reid. "I had already started looking for bigger houses for the both of us to live in, but Elton suggested that I got an apartment in London on my own, and if he had a room at my apartment, I could have a room in his house." Reid found himself an apartment in posh Montpelier Square, Knightsbridge: the kind of area he had promised himself he would live in when he first came to London nearly ten eventful years earlier.

Elton purchased Woodside in Windsor in early 1976. Amazingly he bought it 'sight unseen', and had sent his mother to view it such was the close relationship he had with her. "He possibly watched a video or viewed it in a brochure, but he told his mother to buy it for £380,000 to

£400,000." said Reid. Fred Farebrother was drafted in to take on all the building work at Woodside, and also at Reid's new apartment in London. His other home, Hercules in Virginia Water, had been sold, and Reid had moved into his apartment. From that moment, Reid and Elton went their separate ways personally but not professionally.

"When he first bought his house in Windsor, we went round to the housewarming and he had this room with all these albums in it; he was a music fanatic," remembered Greenfield. "It was like a record store. He used to have this competition, where he would ask us to name an album, and he would go over a pick it out from his collection."

Although Reid expected his role as Elton's manager to end at the same time that his personal relationship did, he was surprised when Elton wanted him to keep him on to carry on looking after his career. Not surprising, when you consider, that in June 1974, Reid had secured an astonishing deal with MCA for Elton to re-sign in the US for $8 million for seven albums.

It also helped that the pair remained very close, and Reid could still talk to Elton like no-one else could. "Although I knew Elton vaguely in the early days," recounted Osborne, "by the time I knew him well enough, John and him were not an item, and that was about 1975/1976. They seemed to have a very good relationship still though. It was a combative relationship, but a lot of genuine affection between the both of them, and a lot of respect for each other. Elton thought that John was doing a fantastic job for him, and he certainly was. They were always fighting but in a fraternal way. They had huge rows, and they had the kind of row that a manager and artist would not normally have, but then, they had this relationship before which kind of made it okay because they were closer than just manager and artist. They were really close friends."

10

Pinball Wizard

In the same year as he had played on the same stage as John Lennon, Elton started work on his first venture into the celluloid world, when he was asked to play a part in Ken Russell and Robert Stigwood's film *Tommy*. The film was an adaptation of the rock opera album written by Pete Townshend and the Who in 1969 and, according to director Ken Russell, it would probably be regarded as the greatest opera of the twentieth century. In a radio interview during the production of the film, Russell described it as two hours of action without dialogue played out in music and song.

"It was daunting but stimulating, as you had to get the whole dramatic scene over in three minute segments as that was the average length of each song," Russell said at the time. The film took two years in total to make with an eighteen week shooting schedule that introduced rock music to the opera and film industry. The film featured some of the best known rock stars, including Tina Turner as the Acid Queen, Eric Clapton as the Priest, and Elton John as the Pinball Wizard, whose crown is taken by the young deaf, dumb and blind boy called Tommy.

It was reported that Elton was, at first, reluctant to take on the role, but after Russell had turned to David Essex to test record 'Pinball Wizard' in the studio, he eventually agreed, after much persuasion from producer Robert Stigwood, and the promise that he could keep the boots! "There was a fair amount of acting involved, and I had to pull nasty faces and things," said Elton. "It was a very nice way of being introduced into making a movie, because it was Ken Russell who I greatly admire, and yes, it was great to work with Townshend and The Who, and I got to sing one of the best songs in the film, and one of the best rock 'n' roll songs ever written." Most of Elton's scenes were shot in The Kings Theatre in Portsmouth, not far from the village hall that he used to share with Hookfoot whilst rehearsing songs for his *Empty Sky* album.

According to Russell, the actual characters came out once the actors started singing. He later went on to describe the film as about, 'False gods, rock gods, the publicity machine, the media, the hopes and disappointments of the century, and the destructive elements. It was the shedding of Victorian religion and the striving to find a replacement.'

Beryl Vertue was the Executive Producer for the film, which turned out to be a baptism of fire for a relative newcomer to the film industry. She began her career as a secretary to the television scriptwriters Ray Galton and Alan Simpson, as well as personalities such as Spike Milligan and Eric Sykes. She then became their agent and took on stars like Tony Hancock and Frankie Howerd, so she got to know the cream of Britain's comic talent at the time and, during the creation of *Tommy*, she was going to need a sense of humour. With considerable success behind her, Vertue was offered a position with the Robert Stigwood Organisation in 1967, where she eventually became the Deputy Chairman. "It was through Robert that I was introduced to the music business. He was manager of the Bee Gees, Eric Clapton and Cream, and a very clever man."

Indeed, it was Stigwood who had the vision to make Pete Townshend's critically acclaimed rock opera, *Tommy*, previously released as an album in 1969, into a film. "We were new to the film making business so it was quite daring in itself, but Robert was quite a visionary," continued Vertue. "For instance, he was the first to take a record, *Jesus Christ Superstar,* and put it into the theatre, and he did the same with *Evita*. I became involved just before Robert and Pete Townshend were going to make *Tommy* and Robert convinced Ken Russell to direct it. He produced a 'treatment', a form of storyboard, but it didn't have a script because the dialogue was in the songs." Stigwood decided to rely heavily on Vertue as she, at least, had some idea about the film industry, but her previous work was confined to television. "He hadn't made films, and that is where he used my talents, so we kept to Ken's treatment, which was very short, clear, tied the story between the songs and kept to the album. Pete was really good, too, and was involved in helping with the story revisions."

The cast included names from both the film and music worlds. "Robert wanted Elton to play the Pinball Wizard; John Reid was not sure about it to start with but eventually came round to the idea. I don't remember him being auditioned, he just got the role. You had to be able to act but in a musical role, and he was good at singing and playing and was a flamboyant character on stage. I remember him being very enthusiastic about the role, and one day he came to the office to see Russell and me, with a huge case. He showed us about 300 pairs of glasses, and he kept trying them on, and asking us which was the best pair for him to use for the film," laughed Vertue.

Stigwood and Russell really wanted to get Tina Turner for the role of the Acid Queen so they turned to Vertue to try and achieve what they thought was impossible, to persuade Ike Turner to let Tina do it. "My lack of knowledge of musicians was helpful at this point," said Vertue. "Robert told me that he was rather busy, and I would have to go and see her and Ike to see if I could get her to do it, so off I went, quite innocently, not knowing that Ike didn't like her to do anything without him. I made appointments to see them but he kept cancelling at the last minute, but then one day this big black car turned up. We got to this very uninteresting building in downtown LA and I was put into the reception-come-hallway; it was deathly quiet. Eventually Tina turned up and said she really wanted to do the film and asked me to persuade Ike to let her do it. I said I would try my best."

They were both taken through an arched doorway into a large, very dark and gloomy room. "It had crimson hangings on the wall, and settees all around the room. Sitting in a corner in a very relaxed manner was Ike Turner. I prattled on for a while, telling him about the film, and how good Tina would be in it, and then Ike took out a cigarette. To my surprise, Tina, who was sitting next to me, suddenly jumped up and dashed across the room and lit his cigarette for him. At that moment, the penny dropped, and I realised what sort of relationship they had. I could understand afterwards why the others didn't want to meet Ike as they were music people and he wouldn't have liked it; but of course Robert didn't tell me about this. I continued the conversation in a very polite and British way about the film and explained that we would love to have him in it but there just wasn't a suitable part, but there was for Tina. The part was called the Acid Queen and I tried to persuade him to let Tina play it. I assured him we would take good care of Tina during the filming, and during her stay in London. He couldn't really argue with me, as I was being so polite, and terribly English."

When Vertue had finished her audience with Ike Turner, she was politely told that he would think about it. "I said that would be wonderful, and explained that I needed to know the following week, because we were just starting to film. Then Tina and I left the room. We were walking along the corridor, when she suddenly pulled me to the ground. I realised that there were cameras all around us but while we were sitting on the floor out of camera shot, she started asking me whether he would agree to it and telling me how much she really wanted to do it. I kept reassuring her that he would. Sure enough Ike agreed and Tina Turner was one of the leading lights in the film. She came to London on her own, and had a really good time. It was the first thing that Tina Turner had been allowed to do on her own and it was a high profile part. It was likely that *Tommy* got her to realise that she could be successful without Ike."

Having secured a key cast member, Vertue was then tasked with finding the finance to make the film. She was sent off to America to meet with the powers that be at Columbia Pictures who had already shown an interest in investing in the film and, following a convenient change of personnel, Vertue was able to collect 50% of the funding they required to make the film. She then returned to Britain, flushed with success, and to a meeting with Stigwood. "Robert asked me to get the rest of the money. I kept getting these jobs that I'd never done before, but that was the level of trust Robert had in people. So off I went around the world to try and raise the money from the distributors. I didn't know what to ask for, but I used my common sense, and asked for advances against the money, and I always said against fifty percent of the gross, which sounded fair to me, and I liked using gross as it sounded right. The distributors were a little startled by my approach, but it seemed to work. I was doing well until I got to Iceland, where I met a distributor who was a sweet man and wanted to have the film, but said he'd never done anything for gross. I didn't want to do something different for Iceland as I wanted to make sure the deal was the same for everyone, so I had to persuade him to take the same deal. I kept telling him that it had all these famous musicians in it, but he wasn't budging. I found out he had a young son, and I suggested he went and asked him. He came back and said he had talked to his son, and we must have the film with John Elton in it! Of course he got the name wrong, but it was a new concept for the film and music industry to be combined. Some distributors found the whole concept difficult to comprehend, because they had no interest or knowledge of the music business."

Despite Vertue's success, the film still hadn't raised enough money to be completed, and they would soon be starting the shooting schedule. "It was the first and only time during my fifteen year career with Robert that he told me the project was a bit of a nightmare, and I have never heard him say anything like that since."

The making of the film was full of firsts, and one of those was the decision to use a new sound system developed by John Mosely called Quintaphonic sound. "The sound was very difficult to manage," recalled Vertue, "because before it was due to go in the cinemas, this man named John Mosely called us, who had invented something called Quintaphonic sound, and for some extraordinary reason, we thought it was a good idea to use it for *Tommy*; so the sound was a bit of an experiment. The cinemas weren't equipped to do it, so at the last minute, before the film's appearance on screen, the cinema people were all rushing around fiddling with the speakers to get it to work. I remember that a preview of the film was nearly cancelled, and it went down to the last minute before the screening was due to get the equipment to work. I wish we hadn't done it really, but when it worked it was great and something new."

Russell filmed much of the movie on the south coast around Portsmouth, but the opening and closing sequences were shot in the Borrowdale valley of the English Lake District, near Russell's home. As usual, with any pre-production process of a major motion picture, the locations were largely chosen by the location unit manager, and the choice of the south coast locations proved ideal for the holiday camp and pier scenes. The Gaiety Theatre on the Southsea South Parade Pier and Hilsea Lido were used for the Bernie's Holiday Camp ballroom sequence and exterior shots.

Sod's Law dictates that the one day that Vertue wasn't on the set, disaster struck. "I opened up a newspaper the following morning and was shocked to see that the pier had caught fire during filming. It was actually caused by the lights setting fire to the curtains, a complete accident but it all went up very rapidly."

It was 11 June 1974 and, according to Russell, the fire started during the filming of the scene of Ann-Margret and Oliver Reed dancing together during the Bernie's Holiday Camp sequence, and smoke from the fire can be seen drifting in front of the camera in several shots. Russell also used a brief exterior shot of the building fully ablaze during the scenes of the destruction of Tommy's Holiday Camp by his disillusioned followers.

There was speculation at the time that Keith Moon was behind the blaze, but these suggestions were untrue, despite the reputation that preceded him. In fact, Moon had met his soul mate in Oliver Reed when it came to outrageous behaviour. "They were two tearaways together," laughed Vertue. "Reed had a house near Dorking in some fabulous grounds, and they used to race round in these fast cars and were always drunk, but they were always on form for the film." The filming of the *Pinball Wizard* scene was one of the highlights for Vertue who was on the set during filming. "I was in the theatre when they did *Pinball Wizard*, it was teaming with kids. Elton came out in his big boots that were a creation from the imagination of Ken Russell and the designer. He thoroughly enjoyed himself and it was a really big thing in his career. He was doing well in his music career, but it was his first big film part and he loved it. It was a real challenge for him. There was an air of excitement around the theatre when they were doing the song. The smoke blown in from the effects people and the flashing lights created a great psychedelic atmosphere. The song was recorded live for the first take, and then played back for the subsequent takes. When I look back, it was an incredibly brave thing to do as it was so different. It was an exciting time and we were being very progressive; it was a real change in the style of film making, using music and lyrics of songs as dialogue with a very famous cast. The cast all knew the music of *Tommy* from the original album, and so they rated both the music and Pete Townshend as well. But especially they all rated Ken Russell and they all wanted to make the film with him and Robert."

A cast album was produced by Pete Townshend, featuring the new version of 'Pinball Wizard' performed by Elton, which utilised the arranging skills of Martyn Ford, who not only contributed to the arrangements, but would also later work with Elton on the albums *Blue Moves* and *A Single Man*.

"Pete Townshend called me up and said he wanted some strings on the soundtrack of *Tommy*." recalled Ford. "I was told to report to The Who's Ramport Studios in Battersea, which, in my opinion, was one of the best studios around, and I recorded some of my best work there. When I got there, Pete said he wanted to put some strings on 'Pinball Wizard', and then he asked me to do the arrangements for Uncle Ernie's Holiday Camp song with Keith Moon. They had hired the Stones mobile and recorded it at the Leicester Square Odeon on the Wurlitzer. I got to sit in the studio all day with Ken Russell, who was very professional and knew exactly what he wanted, much the same as Pete did, and they were both very focussed throughout."

Ford started his musical career playing the French horn. He had a burning desire to be a professional musician and enrolled in the Royal Academy of Music as a mature student: "In my last year at the Academy, I had met a conductor, who became a good friend, and that's when I decided I wanted to create my own orchestra. I went to the Principals of all the main music colleges, and asked if they would put forward their best musicians, as I was going to put on a concert at the Royal Albert Hall. I was playing in about seven orchestras and I got to know a lot of the musicians. I had developed this gut instinct as to who I wanted to select. I hired the Albert Hall, and put on this concert with an unbelievably talented set of musicians." It received enormous critical acclaim in the broadsheets, but the venue was empty of an audience, because Ford couldn't afford to publicise it. For Ford, though, it was a huge stepping stone.

Ford also kept up his own instrument by playing in theatre, in particular, in the original run of *Jesus Christ Superstar* and *Showboat,* and also with Cleo Lane *In The Strand*, as a session horn player.

Through a new-found friend, the DJ Dave Cash, Ford was introduced to Johnny Nash, and was also asked to arrange a new song titled, 'I Can See Clearly Now'. He thought it was the kind of material that was destined to be a huge hit. It was. Despite the success Ford wasn't credited for his arrangements and to make matters worse, his fee of thirty-five pounds was rejected by the record company as being too expensive. In the end, he settled for thirty pounds.

Both Nash and Ford were upset at the attitude of the record company, so Nash made amends during the recording of his album, and credited him. After that, Ford's career rocketed and his orchestra and arrangements were in demand.

"I was very influenced by Paul Buckmaster's arrangements and especially the work he had done on the *Elton John* album. It was during my last year at the Academy, when I was out buying jeans, that I heard this amazing piece of music in the shop. The combination of rock and orchestral arrangements was amazing, and it was the music I really wanted to do. Two years later, I met Paul while he was working on *Madman Across The Water* and we became close friends, and through him I started getting more work," recalled Ford.

Indeed, it was through Buckmaster that Ford got involved with Elton John. "Paul asked me to conduct his arrangements for *Blue Moves*, after Elton had asked him to come and salvage the project, which was not going as well as his previous albums." Ford readily agreed, as he was not only a friend of Buckmaster, but a fan of his arrangements, and had based his own career on what Buckmaster had done up to that time.

After that, Ford went onto work extensively with Phil Collins, especially on the *Hello, I Must Be Going!* album, which included the smash hit 'You Can't Hurry Love' which he arranged and orchestrated. One of the first televised performances of the song after it became a hit was on the Terry Wogan show. Ford conducted his orchestra live on the show with Collins. In echoes of the Johnny Nash disappointment, Ford was again uncredited for his arrangements on the hit single much to his and Collins' annoyance.

For the *Tommy* film soundtrack, Elton re-recorded 'Pinball Wizard' which was released by MCA in the US in 1975 and in Britain the following year. To promote the combined release of the film and single, Bally designed and produced a pinball machine, showing Elton in full pinball costume. It was combined with a summer radio promotion campaign to support the sale of the new *Captain Fantastic* four-player game. The campaign ran for four months to coincide with Elton's tour of the US and to further promote his back catalogue. It all came to a glorious conclusion at KHJ Radio in Los Angeles. Things, it seemed, could not be better.

11

Desperate Changes

Dick and Stephen James always realised that at the end of the recording and publishing contracts Elton would leave DJM. The publishing contract expired in 1973 and Elton duly set up his own publishing company called Big Pig Music, but with DJM publishing everything up to *Goodbye Yellow Brick Road*. The recording contract lasted until 1975, although as a gesture of good will, Elton agreed that DJM could release two *Greatest Hits* albums.

For the second release, he even agreed to give DJM permission to use a couple of Rocket tracks to make it the definitive *Greatest Hits*. "There was obviously a lot of goodwill in the relationship right up to 1978 when we released *Greatest Hits 2* and everything appeared, on the surface, to be positive," remembered Stephen James.

Following the end of the recording contract with DJM, Reid struck an amazing deal worth $8m with MCA in the USA and Elton moved to Rocket Records in the UK. But the move away from DJM, also prompted Elton to reconsider his musical direction and his thoughts turned back to the days of touring with the Kiki Dee Band. He decided he wanted a change and to do that he needed a new band line-up.

Reid was asked to tell Dee Murray and Nigel Olsson that Elton was going to replace them. "Mainly because he wanted a different sound, a meatier sound, a harder sound. He had four solid years with Dee, Nigel and Davey, and he had got musical fatigue, so he looked around for someone he knew," recalled Reid. However Anett Murray recalled that it was Elton that told Dee of his dismissal and this seems to match what Gus Dudgeon has reported in interview when he claimed that he was in the room when Elton told Murray and Olsson on the telephone. "It was very rare that you would get someone new, although we did audition James Newton Howard and David Foster (who we offered the gig before James), but David turned it down." said Reid.

♫

Whilst Elton had moved on and was in the process of forming his new 'supergroup' the effect the change had on Dee Murray was devastating. Anett Murray takes up the story: "In between tours, Dee discovered a passion for scuba diving and so after every tour we wouldn't go straight home we would go scuba diving; after the 1974 tour we went home and then to Barbados. Towards the end of the holiday there was a phone call and Dee was asked to come to the phone and speak to Elton. When he finished he told me that he had been fired because Elton wanted to change the band. He was quite baffled and he didn't know why. He kept asking what he had done. It was not that the 1974 tour was a flop but Dee never did get an explanation. It was always emphasised that if they didn't like it they could go. The possibility that they would get fired was always there if they said the wrong thing. Apparently before Elton had finally decided to fire Dee and Nigel he had visited Davey and asked him what he thought of the idea. Davey was non-committal so Elton was in two minds about doing it but he did and Dee was devastated. He was crushed. He never really found out why he was fired, even when he re-joined for the 1980 Elton John tour. Dee was capable of playing whatever Elton wanted to play and in whatever style he wanted so he couldn't understand it when he criticised the way the band was playing in the press."

After Dee was fired the couple came back to England from Barbados only to be told by their accountant that because of the high tax rates in the UK it would be better if they moved to America. One ray of sunshine emerged though when Anett announced she was pregnant. The couple packed up and moved to Los Angeles and stayed in a hotel suite at first, sorting out some immigration problems which meant they had to move to Canada for a while. During that time they just toured around sightseeing until Dee met David Foster, a prominent Canadian keyboard player and later record producer, and they discussed a possible solo album. Despite auditioning songwriters and musicians Dee didn't really have the heart to do it as he was still unhappy about losing his job with Elton; he felt like a nomad and his wife was pregnant. The couple returned to California and bought a house. Nigel Olsson followed across to California in the autumn 1975 closely followed by Davey who was still in the band but he moved closeby the Murrays in December 1975. Anett gave birth in December 1975. In early 1976 Nigel and Dee were asked to record with Billy Joel in New York and Dee was suddenly excited again. Kiki Dee was promoting her album *Loving and Free* and Dee played in her band and toured with her for a while. "He tried hard to find work but found it difficult; yes he played a lot of sessions with the likes of Alice Cooper and other artists but it was short lived and he became very depressed," recalled Anett. "He felt he wasn't getting any sessions because he was being labelled as Elton John's bass player. Dee couldn't read music so he tried to learn but he couldn't do it, he just wanted to close his eyes and play." Dee was finally asked to re-join Elton in 1980 and he was invigorated again but it was short lived and Elton only used him for one tour. Dee turned to Nashville to look for work and sessions. That was the beginning of the downward spiral and Dee Murray died in Nashville on 15 January 1992.

Anett explained: "After he was fired in 1975 Dee was highly strung and not always in good health. He would sit out in the sun by the pool drinking as he was in a lot of pain. Alcohol and sun were not a good combination. Dee went for a medical for his insurance and was told to have investigations into a spot that he had on his back. He didn't take much notice but when he went to Nashville he had to have another medical. By that time he had developed full blown skin cancer. I remember it well. He called me and he was crying and he said they had only given him 4 years to live. He was 34 at the time. By this time he didn't have medical insurance and instead of returning to the UK he went for unconventional treatment; plus the fact the Dee didn't want to lose his hair. Dee was injected with small doses of smallpox vaccination. During the tour with Elton in 1984 you can see the marks on Dee's arms where he had the injections. He had surgery to remove parts of his back but his lymph nodes were affected too. He went into remission until 1991. He called me up and told me he had cancer in his lungs and it was everywhere. Within 4 months of that call Dee died. In all that time I was worried about plane crashes and never thought Dee would die of cancer. Dee never knew how much he was loved by the Elton John fans; he never considered himself Dee Murray the star; he was always a friend to anyone who chatted to him."

♪

According to Stuart Epps, "Elton always wanted to make things bigger and better. He wanted a supergroup, and nothing would stop him, even if it meant firing someone he had known for a long time, but to him it wasn't firing it was just change. That's why he has survived, because he doesn't keep to the same formula. Nigel and Dee were devastated, but these things happen." Absolutely… if David Bowie hadn't broken up the Spiders From Mars we can only speculate what direction his career would have taken, for better or worse, but constant reinvention seems to be part of his game plan to stay fresh.

Roger Pope was also surprised, but for a different reason. "We [the Kiki Dee Band] went on *Top Of The Pops*, and everything went well. I got a telephone call at 9.30 the next morning, it was Elton. He told me that he was disbanding the Kiki Dee Band, and I was now out of work. I told him he was a fucking arsehole, but he laughed, and said 'Don't worry. I want to put a new band together and you're the only one I want in it at the moment. Can you come into the office later and have a chat to see who else we want in it.' Of course I agreed."

Stuart Epps was also told the news. As he was working closely with the Kiki Dee Band, Reid had to tell him that the band was no more. "I accepted it at the time, but looking back it was a great shame, the tour couldn't have been better, and her album had hit the US charts, and 'I've Got the Music In Me' was doing really well. It wasn't a good idea to question John's decisions, and so we reluctantly accepted it." Making matters worse was the news that Steve Brown by now, had left Rocket, allegedly because of differences with Reid, claiming he'd just had enough of the whole business.

Pope, on the other hand, was on top of the world. He went into the Rocket Records office, about an hour after being told he was in the new Elton John Band and Elton was jumping up and down, he was so excited. "He said he wanted to express himself a bit more and boogie so he was looking for a kick-ass band. He kept throwing up names but I didn't know many of them. We were like little kids in John Reid's office. Reid pulled out a 25-year-old bottle of Johnnie Walker whisky, and we did some coke. He was so fired up, but in a positive way. He had made his decision, and he was now actually doing it. I was the mainstay of the band, because I saw him every night on the last Kiki Dee tour. He used to sing backstage with Davey, Dee and Nigel without anyone seeing them, and he used to watch me all the time. They all wanted to be up there with us. There were some nights that we went down better than Elton. He told me he wanted a drummer like me, they made me an offer and I took it and John drew up the contract. I was put on a good retainer, so I was available to Elton at anytime, but I was allowed to get paid for other session work. The same applied to the rest of the band although I don't know who got paid what."

It was like Elton had been on a train that he couldn't get off, and it had now arrived at a station and it was the right one. He already had an idea who he wanted in the band by the time Pope had reached his office. "I hadn't heard of James Newton Howard, so I asked Elton, who replied that he was working with Melissa Manchester, which didn't really mean a lot to me either, but obviously Elton, being a keyboard player, knew all about him. He turned out to be a wonderful keyboard player and master of the synthesisers."

Another signed up was Jeff 'Skunk' Baxter, ex-Doobie Brother and Steely Dan. Pope continued: "I couldn't work that one out but I didn't care. He [Elton] liked Kenny Passarelli because he considered him a good driving bass player; he had a really good rock groove and 'Rocky Mountain Way' that Passarelli wrote with Joe Walsh was a real classic." So, that was the bass role sorted.

Another bassist who had been interested in the gig with the new band was Freddy Gandy, who was now working with Rocket as a session musician. "Through DJM and Roger, I got to do sessions at Rocket and I worked well with Roger and Caleb Quaye." explained Gandy. "I did make sounds about joining the Elton John Band instead of Kenny Passarelli, but I was dealing with an organisation which had its own agenda. Elton had already spoken with Joe Walsh, and I think Joe had pushed Kenny's name forward. I also knew that Tony Murray from The Troggs tried to get in. Roger was pushing my name forward but it wasn't to be."

♪

Kenny Passarelli was a classically trained musician who started playing trumpet at the age of six; having been tutored by Byron Jovelitte, who, prior to his selfless work with young local Denver musicians to develop their musical abilities, was the conductor for the US Navy Concert Band and an incredible trumpet player. Passarelli joined a local Denver concert band and progressed rapidly to an Inaugural Band, which was the highest accolade you could get, playing in front of the President at the Inauguration. By the mid-sixties, and because of the British music invasion starting with The Beatles, everyone who was into playing music wanted to be a Beatle and bands started appearing all over the country. "I noticed that no one wanted to play the bass guitar, they all wanted to play drums and guitar but I wanted to play the bass as I thought it was a good instrument so I started playing it with a couple of High School friends and became proficient quickly because of my musical education." In February 1969 he joined a local band called The Beast and had a record deal with ATCO.

By the middle of 1969, Passarelli was making a name for himself as an accomplished young bassist in Denver which led to a golden opportunity for him to meet Steve Stills (later to be known as Stephen Stills). "Somebody who owned a record store told me that Steve Stills was up in the mountains recording and was looking for a bass player to finish a project; I had been recommended and he wanted to meet me." Not someone to be asked twice Passarelli made his way up into the Mountains to a place called Goldhill just above Boulder in Colorado where he met Steve Stills. "I walked into his cabin and he played me the acetate of *Crosby, Stills and Nash,*" the self-titled first album combining the talents of David Crosby, Stephen Stills and Graham Nash.

"I heard Crosby, Stills and Nash for the first time and it was fantastic and it was where I wanted to be." Passarelli and Stills jammed together and Stills liked what the young guy could do so he suggested that he join the band at a festival, which would go down in history as the most historic festival of all time, called Woodstock.

"He gave me the number of his manager, who was David Geffen, and he told me I'd got the gig but speak to David first." Passarelli was beyond elated; he was now working with Steve Stills at the age of 19 and about to play Woodstock in August. "I remember calling David but something sounded odd about it all; I couldn't get hold of David Geffen again so I didn't do the gig. I found out later that Neil Young had got involved and had someone who he wanted on bass. Stephen told me much later that when he had met me that first time he initially thought I was ideal but was persuaded that I was too young; but had he rethought it he would have taken me along for the ride. Anyway we worked again later." That interaction with Stephen Stills was the catalyst to give a young 19 year old the confidence to know that he could do it.

After Passarelli had left College he started playing with the iconic guitarist Tommy Bolin, who formed a jazz fusion band called Energy, right at the start of the fusion craze. Although the band didn't release any material it did create a significant impact in the world of jazz and led Bolin and Passarelli to New York where Bolin eventually joined Billy Cobham's recording band for the making of the album *Spectrum*. Meanwhile Passarelli moved to Vancouver in Canada and started working sessions as a bassist.

Passarelli's first break was to play with Joe Walsh, a gig that he got from his friend and mentor Tommy Bolin. "When I was in Canada, Tommy Bolin called me sometime towards the end of 1970 and told me that a guy called Joe Walsh had moved to Boulder with his wife and child and he had quit his group, The James Gang, and was starting a new band. Tommy had told him about me and said he was going to call me. I was making good money doing television work in Vancouver and was hanging out with David Foster who was doing keyboard sessions and Richard "Cheech" Marin and Tommy Chong, (Cheech and Chong) who were a hilarious stand-up comedy duo and also did films about the counterculture movement. It was just an amazing team at the time, so I wasn't really looking to make a change". David Foster would later become a prominent composer and producer.

Passarelli decided to take a call from Walsh, even if it was just to find out what the deal was and as a result found himself going back to familiar ground and the Rocky Mountains in Colorado where Walsh was now based and forming his own band with drummer Joe Vitale. "I listened to what Joe was doing; he had cut two tracks and he wanted to start a group called Barnstorm. When I heard the tracks, well that was it for me and so I said I would be in the band; it was my first real break into the music business." Bolin died in 1976 following a drugs overdose at the age of 25. "I owe the start of my music career to Tommy" remembered Passarelli.

Barnstorm had a successful couple of years until 1974, during which time Passarelli, Walsh and Vitale combined their song writing talents to write the hit song 'Rocky Mountain Way'. It all came to an end just like most bands when the management decided that one of the members should be a star and persuaded Walsh that he should go solo. "Joe and I were very close, we did the Dan Fogelberg record together called *Souvenirs* in 1974 and by then I had acquired a reputation as a fretless bass player." Walsh had been given an experimental fretless base by Fender and he had given it to Passarelli with strict instructions to learn the instrument. "It took me a year and a half to get it really right and that instrument was part of the reason why Elton John took a real interest in me later on. He had heard my bass work on the Dan Fogelberg record and the Barnstorm stuff and he had also heard some work I had done on Rick Derringer's record *All American Boy*, recorded at Caribou Ranch and liked my fretless bass playing." A lot of the early stuff Passarelli had worked on was recorded at Caribou Ranch and the sound that was created there, according to him, was unbelievable: "That was one of the reasons that Elton decided to come over and record there."

By the time the breakup of Barnstorm came Joe Walsh had separated from his wife and had decided to move to California to find fame and fortune as a solo artist. Passarelli remembered: "I was shocked because we had worked together for two years and had toured over 200 dates a year. We had 'Rocky Mountain Way' as our first hit and things were looking good, but Joe was persuaded by his management that he was a star and it was happening in California. He asked me to go with him; I said yes to start with but decided not to in the end." Instead Passarelli joined Stills in his new band Manassas until 1975.

By this time Joe Walsh was hanging out with the rich and famous in the music business and had met up with Elton John and David Foster in Las Vegas. Elton was looking to change his band and had been telling Walsh about his plans. Walsh and Foster took the opportunity of promoting their old friend Kenny Passarelli; Elton was interested. "I got a call from Joe and he said he had spoken to Elton John who was interested in hiring me. Joe told me that Elton's management was going to call me and they did. Then Elton called and said it would be great to have me on board. The first gig was Wembley Stadium. He said we were going to rehearse for a month in Amsterdam in May 1975 and the gig was in June. I said straight away that I would do it and so I flew to Paris with Elton to listen to a playback of *Captain Fantastic* - the album we were going to play live in its entirety."

♬

Although Johnstone didn't figure in the band to start with and looked set to suffer the same fate as Olsson and Murray, Elton changed his mind even though he now had three guitarists. "I convinced Elton to bring in Caleb Quaye, by telling him he was the greatest guitarist in the world, and an old mate," smiled Pope. "So the band had Baxter, Quaye and Johnstone, all on lead guitar." An amazing *volte face* when you consider the initial touring trio of Nigel, Dee and Elton didn't even have one guitarist to its name.

Quaye was still living in America. "I had the opportunity to get a Green Card, so I went to Chicago and worked with Bill Quakeman in a production company that did jingles. They gave me a lot of session work and an opportunity to work with a lot of blues musicians, so I could get back to my musical roots." recalled Quaye. "I lived there for about nine months, having suffered one winter and decided I had to get out; it was too cold."

Quaye had bumped into Pope when he was on tour with Kiki Dee supporting Elton and by 1975 he was in the Elton John Band. "I got a call from Elton who asked me to join. He invited me to Phoenix, Arizona where he was staying, to meet him and discuss it. He told me he was forming a new band that was an expansion on his old band, so he had more musicians to make the sound funkier. I agreed to do it, but on one condition - that we didn't play 'Crocodile Rock'. Quaye and Pope felt that the song spoilt their street cred and was not the sort of song they wanted to play. He agreed until the last gig at Madison Square Garden when he started playing it. By this time everything had started to go wrong, and it was the last gig before the band was disbanded."

The rehearsals for the new band were held in Amsterdam over a three week period because Elton needed to be out of the UK. The Labour Government was still charging high earners 83% tax, so even though they wanted to stay in Britain, it made financial sense for him to emigrate.

"It was a fabulous time," added Pope, "we stayed in the Hilton where Lennon had previously done his 'bed in' with Yoko. Rehearsals were in a large warehouse by a canal that we all got to by taking a typical Dutch canal boat. To start with we didn't play through the PA, we just listened to each other to get to know how we each played. I didn't know James, (Newton Howard) and I hadn't met Jeff Baxter or Kenny so I didn't know how to play with them. I knew Davey and Caleb from Hookfoot, and the previous Elton tours with Kiki. If you know your craft though, then there is no problem; you can play with anyone. Our rehearsals were simply to get to know each other and for the Wembley gig." This gig was to be the first one for the new band and the launch of the new album, *Captain Fantastic And The Brown Dirt Cowboy.*

Released in May 1975, the album debuted at No.1 on the US Pop Album chart, the first album ever to do so, and stayed there for seven weeks. It was certified Gold on 21 May 1975, then Platinum and triple Platinum on 23 March 1993 by the RIAA. In Canada it also debuted at the top of the RPM national Top Albums chart and only broke a run of what would have been fifteen consecutive weeks at the top by falling one position to No. 2 in the ninth week. In the UK it peaked at No. 2.

The 1970s was the golden age for the concept album and this was Elton and Bernie's first shot at the genre. It offers a fascinating autobiographical glimpse of the struggles Elton [Captain Fantastic] and Taupin [the Brown Dirt Cowboy] had in the early years of their musical careers in London's Tin Pan Alley from 1967 to 1969.

The packaging for the album, designed again by David Larkham, was equally unique. The original vinyl edition included a lyric booklet, curiously beginning with a lyric for 'Dogs In The Kitchen' that was never completed and not on the album's lineup, and another booklet called *Scraps*, which collected snippets of reviews, diary entries and other personal memorabilia of Elton and Bernie during the years chronicled on the album. It also contained a poster of the album's cover. There were also a number of limited edition copies pressed on brown vinyl, pre-dating the craze for coloured records that Jake Riviera was to perfect at Stiff Records.

Elton, Bernie and the previous band of Olsson, Murray, Cooper and Johnstone had laboured harder and longer on this album than perhaps any previous record they had ever done. As opposed to the rather quick, almost factory-like, process of writing and recording an album in a matter of a few days, or at most a couple of weeks as with *Goodbye Yellow Brick Road*. The team spent the better part of a month off the road at Caribou working on the recordings. Gus Dudgeon was also very satisfied with the results. In Elizabeth Rosenthal's *His Songs: The Musical Journey Of Elton John*, an exhaustive detailed accounting of nearly all Elton's recorded work, Gus said that he thought *Captain Fantastic* was the best the band and Elton had ever played, applauded their vocal work and soundly praised Elton and Bernie's song writing. "There's not one song on it that's less than incredible," marvelled Dudgeon.

It was while they were rehearsing in Amsterdam, that various names from the industry would turn up unannounced. "Keith Moon turned up out of the blue with his dog," recalled Quaye. "We had taken a break from rehearsals and were sitting around eating burgers. Keith sat on the drums with his dog sitting next to him and started a drum solo. It was like he was doing a Who gig all of his own. We were all looking at each other, wondering what was going on, and then he just stopped, threw his sticks down and said 'okay, that was fine,' took his dog, and walked off."

On another occasion, Ringo Starr turned up and asked if he could sit in with the band. "One of the songs we were rehearsing was 'Lucy In The Sky With Diamonds', so he asked if he could play it with us," Quaye laughed. "So, we had Ringo on Roger's drums with Ray on percussion and went through the song." Before he started playing he needed a set of sticks, so he turned to Pope, who asked Ringo to go over to his drum case where there were 300 pairs of 'Ringo Starr' brand drum sticks. "It wasn't because it was Ringo Starr, it was because I really liked the weight of the stick, so I gave him a couple of pairs." Starr was then equipped to join the rest of the band on the Beatles classic. "We thought the song sounded great and yes, we were thrilled that we were doing a Beatles song with the Beatles drummer," smiled Pope.

"Afterwards Ringo said that he'd been out of work for a while and would like to play with us; could he come on tour? We stayed up all night, taking drugs, just racking our brains as to what to do. Roger was out of his mind wondering what was going to happen to him as he was now looking at the possibility of losing the gig. But we were thinking, how do you tell the Beatles' drummer that we don't need him - the most famous drummer in the world? There was no question that we wanted Roger, but we stayed up all night trying to figure out how to turn Ringo down," remembered Quaye. It, inevitably, fell to John Reid to break the bad news to Ringo.

The first gig undertaken was as high profile as they come: Wembley Stadium with the Beach Boys, billed as Midsummer Music. Elton decided to headline, and play the entire *Captain Fantastic* album. "I said to Elton that I wasn't sure that playing the entire album was a good idea because no-one in the audience knew the numbers as it hadn't yet been released," remembered Pope. "We were also on after the Beach Boys who were icons. What we should have done was gone on before the Beach Boys, and let them close the evening; we were a very new band playing an album that no one had heard before, track by track, and only Davey had played on it. You could see people leaving because they didn't know the numbers. During the course of playing the set, Elton realised he had made a mistake, but he couldn't do anything about it."

According to Reid: "I went into his [Elton's] room and said, 'Well, that was a fucking disaster, wasn't it?' Then I looked around and there was Billie Jean King and Jimmy Connors, all these tennis players," recalled Reid, "People were streaming out three quarters through his set, and the Beach Boys had stolen the show, because they had the six o'clock slot, and the weather was warm and sunny." Many of the media suggested after the gig that the Beach Boys should have been the headliners, because they were so good, it put Elton's set in the shade. "Elton picked the bill, but he wouldn't support anyone, and had to be the headliner." continued Reid, "The only person who ever went on after Elton was Frank Sinatra at a private charity gig."

"It was a big gig for Elton," said David Larkham, "Elton flew us over from LA and put us up in a hotel. He did the gig and we went back to the hotel for a party with Paul McCartney, Nilsson, Billie Jean and Ringo. It was where Elton took me to one side and asked me what I thought of the gig. I told him I thought it was a bit of a mistake playing the whole of the album. He felt he could ask me to give him an honest opinion, but I don't think it was what he wanted to hear."

Despite the hype around the new band in the music press, Pope wasn't in the slightest bit nervous, even though it was the first gig with one of the biggest artists in front of thousands of people. "I was more worried about meeting the drummer from Rufus, who were also on the bill. He was a great drummer and the thought of meeting him was the only thing that was making me nervous. I saw him coming towards me when I was backstage; when he spotted me he went down on his knees and I asked him what he was doing. He said he was bowing to the best drummer in the world! After that my entire day was made."

For the gig, Elton played with three guitarists but, according to Quaye, it was clear that during the gig 'Skunk' Baxter was the odd man out. "Davey, Roger, Ray [Cooper] and I had worked together on and off for years, and during the early DJM period," said Quaye, "so we were tight together both relationship-wise and musically. He was the odd one out and didn't really fit in. Elton had brought him in because of the great work he was doing with the Doobie Brothers, but we knew that it wouldn't go far and we suspected that at the rehearsals." Quaye was right, and almost as soon as the Wembley gig was over Baxter was out of the band.

During 1975 things weren't going the way Elton had planned them. While he was pleased with his new band, the first gig was a bit of a disaster and the music press was less than complimentary. To make matters worse, Rocket Records wasn't doing too well. The advance that Rocket had received from Island Records for the distribution of new material had dried up, and Elton had lost interest in it (something that would change after he went into semi-retirement a couple of years later) and was not investing any money. None of the artists on the label, with the exception of Kiki Dee, had made any money.

Steve Brown had left, and John Reid apparently wasn't creating happy campers. Gary Osborne recalled how, on one occasion Reid sacked everyone at Rocket. "It was when the offices were in Lancaster Gate near Hyde Park." Osborne continued, "I remember arriving and seeing all the staff out on the street. I turned around and went home, because I didn't want to get involved, but I called Elton and he loved it. He loved stories about John's excesses. In many ways, out of the two of them, John was a bigger prima donna than Elton."

Soon after the disaster of the Wembley gig, Elton and the band went off to the chateau in France to do an album for Davey Johnstone, but the studio had broken down. "We stayed there for about six weeks," recalled Pope. "As we couldn't use the studio, we set the equipment up by the pool and just played. We got wrecked as usual, but no album materialised."

After the album failed to get off the ground for Johnstone, the new band launched into a heavy schedule of recording and touring during which time two albums were produced, *Rock of the Westies* and *Blue Moves*. After both albums had been completed, the touring followed immediately afterwards. Elton was getting exhausted and the cracks were starting to show, especially with his ever increasing dependence on drugs and alcohol, which was fuelled by his desire to do everything to excess.

Rock of the Westies was recorded at the Caribou Ranch in Colorado, its title being a play on West of the Rockies reflecting Elton's love of wordplay. "This was when a lot of industry pressure was beginning to cave in on Elton," recalled Quaye. "I remember we were in the middle of recording, and we heard a helicopter turn up. The recording was interrupted for some attorneys, who had brought some contracts for us to sign for the tour, following the album. But it meant our creative zone was suddenly interrupted. We were saying 'We are recording an album, can't this wait?', but that didn't bother them. It struck me at that point that we all were stuck in the middle of a machine, and it was getting out of control."

"I was fascinated by the ranch, and the stories that related to it being built on an Indian burial ground." recalled Pope. "There were loads of things that went on at night time that were strange, but it only seemed to affect people who were weird, I never had anything bad happen to me. We all had a log cabin each, with open fires, fuelled by logs that they cut and brought round every day."

Kenny Passarelli agreed that Caribou was an excellent place to record the album. "It was like a second home for me as I had already cut two records with Joe Walsh as well as two Stephen Stills records, so when all the lads turned up it was a hell of a time. Roger and his then wife Vickie were really at home there and he was clearly a fan of the countryside and open spaces."

Pope and Quaye flew to Denver with their respective spouses. "When we arrived, there was no-one there to meet us, and we didn't have a number or an address," continued Pope. "I knew it was near a place called Nederland. Caleb was bitching and moaning, and we were all tired. We had been on a flight for hours, so I got a taxi and we went to Boulder. I went into a bar, and all the people in there were looking at me. I asked them if they liked Elton John and I got a muted, positive reply from some of them. I asked them if they had heard of the *Caribou* album, and that I was looking for the Caribou Ranch where it was made. Someone said it was near Nederland, which I already knew, so we got a taxi to Nederland. When we arrived, I went into another bar whilst everyone else stayed in the taxi. Someone in the bar knew where Caribou was so he gave me directions and we found it. When we arrived, there was this great big gate and an intercom." Having convinced the managers of the Ranch that Quaye and Pope were musicians with Elton, they were admitted to the sprawling 33,000 acres of ranch land in the Rockies. It was two miles along a dirt track before the tired band members and their wives reached the ranch itself, but when they finally got there it was, said Pope: "A beautiful place to be. The rest of the band were there, and all primed up, but it didn't take me long to catch up." And according to Pope, there was always plenty of coke and stuff available for the band during the sessions.

All the same nobody, it seemed to Pope, had a clue what they doing when they arrived. "I think Elton might have had the basis of one or two songs because Bernie had written the lyrics, but basically everyone was just sitting around doing it. It was completed quickly and the music was written by Elton in collaboration with the band."

Elton wanted everyone in the band to be part of the music-making process. "One of the reasons he put this new band together was to get away from the 'Yes-men' that had previously surrounded him. Above all, he wanted people to say 'Try this' and 'Do that', which is what we all did. He used to say he was the worst musician in the band, but he really wasn't, he was a fantastic singer, and a bloody good pianist and an all-round great guy."

The band rehearsed for the first week. "I sat and turned the pages while Elton wrote the songs at Caribou. The other guys added their own interpretation and it was all written spontaneously," remembered Passarelli. "We then recorded the album and every one of those tracks was a first or second take. Roger was the best time keeper in the business, he never sped up or slowed down he was like a metronome. Then you added Ray Cooper to it and it was amazing. We were funkier than Dee and Nigel so it was our sound by the time we got to the tour; it was our sound playing the older songs. The album wasn't received as well as Elton's previous albums and some of the critics butchered *Rock of the Westies* but it still had hits like 'Island Girl' and excellent tracks like 'I Feel Like a Bullet (In The Gun Of Robert Ford)'. Another great track was 'Yell Help'; it was amazing the way Roger changed the track around. I'll never forget when he did it in the studio - we all looked at each other and said 'What was that? It's unbelievable!' He changed the beat around. I remember him just doing it without any apparent thought." According to Passarelli Gus Dudgeon didn't appreciate what he was doing and preferred Dee Murray's playing. "I remember that all the guys were basically recorded live and the only overdubs were on my bass track." I hated Gus for doing that but I also had a deep respect for his skills as a producer, when I came on the scene I was used to playing with Joe Walsh and Stephen Stills so I could cut a record together with them and I can overdub but Gus just couldn't get a sound on my fretless bass."

"For Elton, it had just got a bit too much of the same old thing recently, and that's why he needed a total change. Much of his inspiration to change things had come from the Kiki Dee Band, which was a little opening act who went on and did a 45 minute set that was absolutely superb and the energy in it was very high and that is what he wanted," insisted Pope.

Quaye agreed with that summation. "The recording process started with Elton who had written some songs to Bernie's lyrics and they were working on them at Caribou. We all lived in log cabins. Elton had a piano in his; we would get together in his cabin and he would play us the songs and we stood around and would get ideas for our various parts. Roger might be banging on a sofa to get his part. Davey and I would have had an acoustic guitar each with us, and we would start to flesh out some ideas of what our parts would be. Then once we had an idea of what the song was, James would scratch out some chords, and then we would go into the studio and start to record it. A lot of it was done live in the studio, with very few overdubs. For instance, my guitar solo on 'Street Kids' was recorded live, both at the beginning and the middle break." On *Rock of the Westies* and for the next *Blue Moves* album Quaye claims that "Certain of us were credited against certain songs because we added something, or suggested something when we were putting the song together in Elton's cabin." This was another good example of Elton's collaborative way of working and generosity of spirit towards fellow musicians, of course.

The album took four weeks to record and, usually, they were averaging one track per day. "We were in no hurry," remembered Pope. "If there was nothing for us to do musically, then Caleb and me would go out horse riding and exploring the beautiful countryside."

"Yes," recounted Quaye, "we had a great time on the ranch. It was a fully operational ranch, with horses and cattle, rivers and streams." On one occasion, Elton and the band took a helicopter ride to Denver to see the Rolling Stones play. "They knew we were coming, so we landed behind the stage but the Rolling Stones were not that pleased about it," laughed Pope. "Gus and me went up high beside the stage to watch. Gus had a video camera, so he was recording it and someone started to give us a hard time. The Stones got Elton on stage, but they treated him like shit; they were belittling him, even though, by this time, he was bigger than they were. We were supposed to go backstage and meet them all, but they would only let Elton in, which we were pretty annoyed about. We were his band, after all."

According to Pope, making music was easy if you knew what you were doing: "We'd just go to Elton's wooden chalet everyday and everyone would sit around and be writing and chipping in and making changes and additions. It became a bit like going to work to do any job. We didn't have a set timetable, but we got locked into a pattern. Playing and learning the material wasn't difficult, but the problems came from where the artists' heads were at. That was the hardest bit, as we felt like we were treading on egg shells with Elton, because he was the famous one, and it was frustrating at times."

It was during the collective writing process that the band used to stay up drinking and taking stuff and, according to Pope, it got out of hand. By this time, drugs and booze were part of the rock star territory. "The hard drugs really started during the *Captain Fantastic* period. Elton was really going for it at that time, especially when we were in Amsterdam. After *Captain Fantastic*, we were at the highest point in Elton's career, and the drugs were part of that territory," recalled Quaye.

Dudgeon considered Pope his favourite drummer, using him on a lot of sessions during his Rocket years. "Roger Pope had such a natural drum sound and I remember one comment that was made in America by a studio engineer who said 'Man, you can record this guy in a toilet'." "He had such a good sound," agreed Freddy Gandy, "it just sounded right. It would normally take days to get a drum sound right, but with Roger, he would just set up in the corner and play, and that was it usually, in one or two takes. When Roger and I worked with Gus at Rocket it was already an established arrangement and working together was a dream. He used to get a bit fussy about the bass sounds sometimes but we used to stop, do something else, go back to it and it would be fine then."

When it came to recording the album, Pope was given a high profile on some of the songs, like 'Billy Bones And The White Bird', 'Street Kids' and Roger's personal favourite, 'Grow Some Funk of Your Own'. To all intents and purposes, the sessions for *Rock of the Westies* went pretty smoothly and better still, Elton was happy with the results. "He wanted to do an album that was different, he wanted to boogie and party and that's what he got. There were some songs like 'I Feel Like A Bullet (In the Gun Of Robert Ford)' and 'Island Girl', which went back to his previous style, but those songs were influenced more by the lyrics Elton was given by Bernie. Overall, Bernie's lyrics and Elton's interpretation of them was fantastic. It's not Elton, it's not his soul he's pouring out in the songs, it's his interpretation of his friend's lyrics, but the two of them together were brilliant!" enthused Pope.

According to John Carsello the new Elton John Band worked hard and partied just as hard but it was a different vibe all round. Instead of recording the separate parts the band did most of the recording live. "They went everywhere together even outside the Ranch. Davey, Roger and Kenny would go to a bar called The Pioneer Inn and would play with anyone in town. Roger Pope was one of the nicest and sweetest of people and boy could he play the drums; his backbeat was second to none. Ray was the sweetest though, he would come and chat with me when he could and even bought me a bikers jacket and sent it over from London when he found out I was into British road bikes. James Newton was the wizard on the synthesiser and, of course, we knew Kenny Passarelli as he had been a regular at The Ranch. I remember we went to a bar called Shannon's and we were drinking Mimosas; I hadn't had one before; one of the Roadies got so drunk he went outside and got in someone else's car thinking it was ours and went to sleep. We were looking for him everywhere. It was 2 am and we thought he must have got a lift back to the Ranch so we went. The next morning we got a call from Boulder County Sheriff's Department to say that the Roadie was in the Boulder jail so we went down and got him out. He hadn't done anything wrong but we later found out that the driver hadn't seen him in the back seat and he was just as drunk as the Roadie was but he had side-swiped 5 cars and got arrested and the Roadie was arrested along with him!"

"I remember once we used Jim's motor home. Me, some guys from the Ranch and Elton went out in the mobile and got to this place called the Red Barn. Elton didn't want to eat dinner at the Ranch so he asked whether there was anywhere to eat in Boulder. He said 'I want a hamburger or something.' The studio was booked out to Elton for $1000 a day including food and we provided trays of food well into the night in case they were recording. On this occasion though Elton didn't like the thought of having roast duck, which was on the menu that night. You see we had a new girl making the food and she didn't really know what to do with it so she cut it up like a chicken with wings and legs. Elton didn't like that so he came into me and laughed and said, 'They are serving up rubber duck in there can we go out and eat somewhere?' So we drove down the canyon in this mobile home and we pulled into the Red Barn, which is like McDonalds. Elton had his apple glasses on with diamonds on the stems, a white t-shirt and white corduroy pants; we were deciding who should go and get the food when Elton insisted that he did it. So he wrote down everyone's order and he went in and we were all watching intently to see what happened. At first it all looked fine and then, all of a sudden, he got noticed and he was getting mobbed and everyone was asking for his autograph. He was enjoying himself signing autographs and then he came out and back to the mobile with a big bag of food. He used to do it to freak people out and get a reaction."

Stevie Wonder was invited to the Ranch for the weekend as Elton's guest, much the same as Lennon did a few months previously, but it was more for the high jinks than the collaboration with Elton and the band musically. Carsello seems to recall that they may have jammed together a few times but didn't actually record anything together. One event did stick out in his mind though and still makes him laugh today. "Jim Guercio had these Jeeps and they were all decked out like the military had them; almost replicas. We had everything on them except a machine gun on the back. Stevie was in a Jeep with Jimmy and Larry Fitzgerald who was Chicago's manager at the time and Stevie was behind the wheel, they had a stick or something and they were working the steering wheel so it looked like Stevie was driving. They drove by the studio and everyone is just staring and not wanting to believe what they were seeing but Stevie was playing along and doing a good impression of a driver. Bernie was waiting to be picked up from his cabin 'Running Bear'. Stevie turns up and Bernie really thought he was driving! We had some great times at the Ranch but when it was time to work we managed to create great sounds and produce some amazing albums." Arguably Elton's best albums came from the Caribou period but he was never to record there again.

12

I Split, You Split, We All Split

For Bernie, though, things on the home front were not going well. Maxine had hooked up with Kenny Passarelli and while Bernie was with the rest of the band in Caribou, Maxine went her own Rocky Mountain Way to Colorado with Passarelli. Although the rest of the band were well aware of what was happening, nothing was ever said, and Elton continued to use Passarelli as his bassist for the remainder of the album sessions.

With hindsight, the other band members could not understand why Passarelli was still around, but clearly Elton was capable of separating business from personal as David Larkham recalled: "It seemed no-one was talking directly about it. I did have an opportunity to draw Elton on it, but only by diplomatically saying 'What do you think of Kenny?' and his reply was along the lines of 'Kenny is a fucking great bass player and (looking me in the eyes) I'm not changing this line-up for anything'."

Larkham had noticed the cracks were starting to appear in Bernie's marriage for a while. "I could sense in Jamaica, when we were waiting to record *Goodbye Yellow Brick Road*, that things were not right. Bernie certainly wasn't very happy and that was really the beginning of the end that led to them splitting up." Things seemed to get worse when Elton decided to bring in Passarelli who Maxine some said, was pretty much instantly attracted to.

But, according to David Larkham, it wasn't quite that simple. "In the early years of their marriage, particularly when based in England, they seemed to be very much a couple who went everywhere and did everything together. Elton's increasing success in the States meant that more and more time was spent in America - on the road, radio and press promotion and so on.

With Bernie and Maxine being very much part of the on the road entourage, it eventually made sense for them to move to Los Angeles. I get the impression that possibly Maxine might have been a bit homesick and was probably very glad to be back in her old stomping grounds, socialising with old friends and enjoying a lifestyle funded through her husband's success. When you talk to those around Elton and Bernie, the impression is that, probably out of respect for Bernie, no one would ever say anything directly about Maxine. Whatever occurred between them in those times, Maxine always remained with Bernie until she met Kenny Passarelli."

Quaye remembered, "By the time we recorded *Rock of the Westies* at Caribou, the relationship between Maxine and Bernie was more or less over. She had, by then, started a relationship with Kenny." Pope also noticed it, not with the *Westies* album but when they were recording *Blue Moves*. "I first found out about Kenny and Maxine when we were in the studio. I remember one occasion when Kenny had disappeared and I had absolutely no idea what was going on. I was saying to the rest of the band 'Where the fuck is Kenny?' and they told me that he had been going out with Raquel Welch, and he had gone off to see her. The way that the guys had said it made me think that something was not quite right, but it was a well-kept secret."

Bernie and Maxine's split was followed soon after by David Larkham parting from his wife, which is sad when you consider that the two couples met at the same time during the Troubadour days. "I sent Janice a one way ticket to England and we got married in Wandsworth Town Hall Registry Office, where I had two best men in Elton and Bernie. John Reid was also there with an amazing checked suit. We had a flat in Putney and we all went back there for a reception. The weather was not to my wife's liking and like Bernie, I had a hankering to live in California, so very soon after I moved over to the American West Coast with £20 in my pocket and gradually started to get work over there with Norman Winter, who was

Elton's US publicist."

In a further mirroring of their lives, after the marriage separations, David moved in with Bernie and shared his house for a while. "Then Bernie found a new girlfriend," said Larkham, "and as he had to be out of the States for a while, he went down to Acapulco and I stayed in his house. He would call me up to tell me what films to record and what his plans were."

The next Christmas Bernie rented a villa from the LaGuardia family, a relative of the ex Mayor of New York. Since it was Christmas, he invited Larkham to join him. "I remember he wanted a turkey so he paid for two first class seats, one for me and the other for the turkey! It was 90° and the villa came with a cook and a gardener, but I still had to take this turkey and other stuff he wanted with me. When the gardener caught us running around the grounds spraying artificial snow out of aerosol cans on the cactuses, and in the swimming pool, he must have thought we were mad. We had our Christmas dinner on the patio in our swimwear. It was totally bizarre."

Bernie also returned to the drinking binges that he had participated in during his teenage years, but this time presumably, to kill the pain. Someone who shared in those binges was Alice Cooper. "Bernie, Cooper and I always used to watch Monday night football together when Bernie was working with Alice and then afterwards we would play pool and drink beer. I can still remember one evening at a club called 'On The Rox' in Los Angeles, which was a private club above the Roxy Theatre. It had taken over from the Troubadour as the place to go for new up and coming acts, Bernie and Alice ended up filling each other's boots with booze," remembered Larkham.

It was much the same when it came to smuggling drinks into the Dodger games: "In those days there was a ban on taking any hard liquor into a sports stadium," added Larkham, "so to overcome it, Alice would simply put some whisky into Coca-Cola bottles and then he had the chauffeur bring it in so we could drink whiskey and coke." It all seemed a totally bizarre way to carry on, but to Bernie and everyone around him, it seemed quite normal. The price of fame, it seemed, was starting to take its toll.

♫

Once again, Larkham was given the task of designing the album cover for *Rock of the Westies* and worked with Terry O'Neill, who had now become the official photographer, to take some shots of Elton and the band. The photographs that were to become the inner sleeve introduction to the band were taken at Caribou. "You will notice that I'm scowling on my photo," recalled Quaye. "The reason is that the photographer woke us up early to take photos, and having my photo taken early was the last thing I wanted to do. I had been up all night, and I had previously put a full day in the studio, plus the ranch was at high altitude, so you are short of breath and tired. I didn't want to do it, but they took it, and that is why I am scowling."

O'Neill also took the shot of Elton that subsequently became the front cover. "*People* magazine had sent him to take some pictures of Elton John recording at Caribou, and the front cover picture was an outtake of those pictures," confirms Larkham. "It was at breakfast, and as he was taking the shot, a cat came up and started eating Elton's cereal!"

Once the album was completed, the master tapes were taken back to the UK by Dudgeon for mixing. "Gus Dudgeon and I got on really well," recalled Gandy. "He used to ring me up as he liked smoking a bit of dope and in those days I knew every dealer on every street corner. So, whenever Gus came back from America, he would go straight into the studio, because he just loved getting back to the tapes, give me a call and I would go and meet him with some stuff."

When he came back with *Rock of the Westies,* he went into Trident Studios and started mixing them. "He called me up and told me to get to the studio with some stuff, and we spent time together rolling joints, and playing the music. When it was finished, Gus turned to me and said, 'This is going to go straight to No.1 in the album charts in a couple of months' time' and sure enough it did. With Elton, you couldn't get any higher really. It was extraordinary, just sitting with the guy who was mixing the sounds that were going to be No. 1. Gus made the sound of Elton John, he had been around since the early sixties. He knew his stuff and how to get the best out of the sounds."

♪

The first dates in the US for the new band were at the Troubadour in Los Angeles where it had all begun six years earlier. In many ways, it was Elton honouring the agreement made by Doug Weston and Ray Williams during the first appearance at the venue to come back and play. These gigs were benefits for the Jules Stein Eye Institute and represented a good way to get battle hardened for the imminent *Rock of the Westies* tour to support the album. Elton appeared on three consecutive days from 25 -27 August 1975, playing a total of six shows. The opening night was a gala performance with tickets selling for $250 which included entrance, a signed hardback programme, a champagne and buffet dinner and complementary limousine parking. The other gigs were priced at a more modest $25, and were only available through a postcard lottery. Elton played a total of nineteen songs that covered the five years of his career since his first performance at the club, and was appropriately billed as Five Years Of Fun.

"The highlight though, was at Dodger Stadium," said Quaye. "We all appreciated the historical significance of these gigs as we were the first band after The Beatles to play there. But then Wembley was a huge deal because it was one of the first rock shows at Wembley. We did a lot of firsts at the time. We were the first band to sell out Madison Square Garden for seven nights in a row and we were the first band to do four-hour shows, which was unusual at that time when you think people like Elvis were only on stage for about sixty minutes. Our fans were certainly getting their money's worth."

Rehearsals for the American leg of the tour were held in Washington DC. "Maryland was close to Washington, and we found out that Elvis was playing there," continued Quaye. "We all trooped out there to see him. He was a little podgy around the waist by this point in his career and after the show Bernie and Elton were invited backstage to meet him, but when they returned they said that he was really exhausted and wasted." Quaye couldn't believe how bad the gig was. The Keith Jarrett Trio were in Washington, so they all sneaked off after the Elvis gig to see them. It was more in keeping with their type of music; more so than Elvis was at that time.

Before the Dodgers gig, the shocking reality of Elton's fragile state resulted in an overdose of pills, seen as an alledged attempt to commit suicide which was largely blamed on the stresses and strains he was under in both his professional and personal life. "The day before the gig, we were all up all night having these meetings in the hotel discussing what we were going to do," recalled Quaye. "We weren't sure whether he was going to live because the doctors had to pump his stomach because he had taken so many pills. I had his mum and grandma [who were over in LA for the Dodgers gigs] asking me to talk to him because they kept saying I was his friend. I always got dumped with that one – 'Can I talk to him?', but it was no good. Sure I was a good friend of the family and in the beginning we would stay at each other's houses at Frome Court or in Finchley, so we knew each other well. His mother thought I could influence him. He would go running around his house saying, 'I'm going to be a star' and his mum would always say 'Talk to him Caleb, you are his friend'." The fact is, though, things were different now. Quaye and Elton had moved on, and Elton could not be persuaded or be influenced by anyone.

The news of his alledged suicide attempt also shocked Terry O'Neill. "I had no idea he had tried to kill himself a few days before. During the rehearsals for the gig, we were all, including Elton, playing football, and I found out that night that he had apparently tried to commit suicide. I only saw one side of him, which was someone who had wit, a sense of humour, and was very intelligent. I didn't see the down side of his life."

Despite hospital treatment, and Elton being in a 'difficult place', having alledgedly seriously tried to kill himself this time, as opposed to the less convincing attempt at Furlong Road a few years earlier, he amazingly, still went on stage, and played Dodger Stadium. Talk about 'The Show Must Go On'! Even more amazing is that the gig turned out to be one of the highlights of the tour and would go down in history as one of the defining concerts of the seventies.

"When we were due to play Dodger Stadium, we were all asked to meet at Elton's house in LA which was previously owned by Greta

Garbo," remembered Quaye. "We had a bunch of limos waiting for us with a police escort and we went to the gig. We had rehearsed there the previous day. It was a fantastic gig, possibly the best one I have ever done. We set up on the stage and Elton had curtains put up to hide the set so we could all come on without anything having to be moved. The other bands played in front of the curtains. They got Cal Worthington, who was a famous Cowboy-type car dealer from LA who hosted TV shows in the States, and he went on the stage with a huge lion. During his commercials, he would introduce his dog called Spot which was really a lion. He and his lion were a cult thing in the States, but backstage they had the lion in a cage. We all had trailers and we were all out of our minds on stuff. At one point there was a big commotion going on with roadies running around, screaming and shouting; apparently, the lion had got out of his cage and was roaming around somewhere backstage. All the musicians were told to get back in the trailers, because the lion had escaped and the roadies were trying to catch it. It was an old lion so it was grouchy and I am not sure whether it had any teeth left, but it was growling away and dust was getting kicked up, but they finally cornered him and put him back in his cage."

"Everyone who was anyone," recounted Pope, "was backstage: Cary Grant, Billie Jean King (who did backing vocals with a choir) and many other celebrities from the film and music industries. The stage had rollers which operated automatically, so when we went on and were ready to play the rollers were switched on and moved us all to the front of the stage. I cannot properly describe the feeling I had, but it sent tingles down my spine that made me cry. People had queued up for three days just to get tickets and then had queued up another three days to get to the front of the stage. Elton was over the moon; everything about the gig was perfect, we couldn't put a foot wrong. If the piano had split in half the crowd would still have been with us. If I never did anything else in my life and if I just had those two days, I would have been chuffed."

Now that he was the official photographer, one of the most important jobs Terry O'Neill was given was to document the event from every angle of the stage and his pictures certainly did that. They are today regarded as perhaps the most immortal images ever taken of Elton; they are still considered the best of their kind. "John Reid used to call me to take pictures all the time. I was working with people like Tom Jones and Engelbert Humperdinck. That's when John Reid had seen what I was doing and asked me to take some pictures of Elton as he had heard of my reputation as a rock photographer. I will never forget the Dodger Stadium concert though - it was the greatest gig of all time. I had an assistant who worked with me in America, and I told him, I was going on stage and he tried to stop me. I said, I couldn't resist it, so I went on stage, and started taking pictures. There were about 75,000-80,000 people there, so I said I must get that picture. So I crept up and took it but I found then that I was stuck on stage, as the song he was singing had ended. Elton spotted me and told the crowd who I was, and apologised. He said 'He gets in everywhere', and cleverly made a joke of it. I took photographs throughout the gig, of both Elton and of the rest of the band. A couple of days later I was at a party that John Reid had arranged and I found Elton in an alleyway crying. I asked him what was up, and he said he and John had split up. I didn't know what to say so I left him."

♫

At the end of the *Rock of the Westies* Tour the band took some time off and then they met up again in January 1976 to make the next Elton John album, *Blue Moves*. Elton by now had done three albums at Caribou and was ready to do something else. "We went to Toronto and worked at Gordon Lightfoot's studio for three or four weeks on *Blue Moves*," remembered Passarelli. "Davey Johnstone and I had a big suite and it was party central; it was a great time. Caleb and Roger stood their ground and helped me overtake the rules that Gus Dudgeon had about overdubbing. They wouldn't take any shit from him and so they made it clear that they wanted to make more of a live record. *Blue Moves* had much less overdubbing than Gus was used to and he fought it a lot. I always thought he had it in for me as he just loved Dee Murray and so did I, but I didn't make the decision to let him go. I know a lot of fans found it difficult when Dee was left out and I took the hit for that. I met with Dee in London before the Wembley gig and he was a great guy and his playing was fantastic but he was just blown away by not playing with Elton and I don't blame him. During that time it was just a blur because it happened so quick."

By this time the pressure of recording and touring constantly since 1970 was beginning to take its toll on Elton. "He was just starting to get high at Caribou, we were partying but we weren't out of it," recalled Passarelli.

By the time Elton came to record *Blue Moves* in 1976, it was public knowledge that Bernie and Maxine had gone their separate ways. It was probably the reason why the lyrics reflected Bernie's feelings at the time, so much so that tittle-tattle emerged that Elton was already considering using a different lyricist, which eventually paved the way for Gary Osborne.

According to the stories that were in circulation at the time, Elton considered the lyrics to be too downbeat and in some cases, too morose, even though the album would produce the exquisitely heart-breaking 'Sorry Seems To Be The Hardest Word'. It was even likely that the album title came from the mood and lyrics of the songs although, in some quarters it was said the title was doffing the cap to Joni Mitchell's 1971 album *Blue* of which Elton was a huge fan.

When they reached Toronto for the recording sessions, they stayed in the hotel for about a week without going to the studio, except to check on the equipment and the instruments. It seemed Elton had decided to go back to basics. Instead of the limousines and choppers taking them to and from the studio, they were walking everywhere which had its drawbacks. "One day we came out of the hotel in Toronto to go to the studio," recalled Quaye, "we had been driven everywhere prior to this, but we were walking down the street, and the next thing we know, there is a mob chasing us. We literally had to run for our lives, across roads and dodging traffic. When we reached the studio, we were shouting for the studio staff to let us in but they thought we were a bunch of fans and refused. We did manage to convince them in the end before we got lynched." And people say America is violent!

The next time they went out walking, Elton decided that he didn't want to be recognised so he put a track suit on and he bought an ice hockey mask. "We were staying in this beautiful hotel just down the road from the studio, but to reach it you had to cross a dual carriageway," remembered Pope. "He would try to go incognito, but we were dressed like musicians: respectable but we were obviously not going to work in a bank. There was Elton with a tracksuit on and an ice hockey mask, thinking that he was not going to get recognised walking down the road. This was alright for the first week and everything was cool, but the second week there was a holiday in Toronto and the kids were out of school. They knew the Elton John Band was staying in this hotel and how could they not notice Elton? So they used to chase us down the road. I used to walk because I was the drummer and no-one knew who I was."

As for the studio time, the days were long and again there were a lot of drugs being passed round. However, as Caleb Quaye recalled, "The sessions were good, and the band was tight, but the songs started to be different. At the time, we were not at all focussed on the relationship between Maxine and Kenny and the impact it had on Bernie, because we were just focussed on the music and the album, working on our respective parts. But Elton couldn't start writing songs without getting the lyrics first. It was amazing that as soon as Elton got Bernie's lyrics that he was able to interpret them as well as he did. Bernie's life was not in a good place at the time and it was reflected in his lyrics; but Elton was able to create a double album from them. To get the musicians to be so involved and sensitive to the songs was equally amazing. I was playing this song, and I'm thinking Bernie must be seriously fucked up, and then I realised that Kenny had gone off with his wife."

Kenny Passarelli took up the story: "We were young and restless. It was a very emotional time in a sense that my relationship with Maxine was going on covertly and so the *Blue Moves* record was very difficult for me emotionally. Bernie and I had become friends instantly and he was not the sort of person who had many friends. We just connected and when I met Maxine we connected as friends and as two Americans as well. The marriage was a bit spotty when we met; they got married very young and they were both in the Hollywood set. Bernie was doing what he wanted to do and she was doing what she wanted to do. It was strange, instead of me thinking about what I was doing and changing my approach when we first started to connect, we started a relationship instead but we were young and I'd never been in love before. We were together for seven years after that so it was far from being a fling. The consequence for me was that I was on the shit list for a while. So emotions were high, and I am explicitly described in 'The Years Between Seventeen and Twenty'. When I was playing the bass line during that song it was pretty heavy. I was around Bernie enough to see how upset he was about his marriage falling apart but he didn't know in the beginning that I was involved. It was difficult to watch what he was going through as his marriage was breaking up, me knowing that I was on the other side. No-one steals anyone else they make up their own mind what they want to do. The heavy thing was that a record was being made and Elton was also breaking up with John Reid and everything was falling apart. Everybody was breaking up and going in all directions and at times I felt I was the catalyst that was causing all this. You can feel the emotions in 'Sorry Seems to Be The Hardest Word'. I knew what was going on but no one else knew and it was hard. When I think back it was very stressful. I'll never forget the look in their eyes at the play back of the album; there was some kind of energy. I remember looking at Caleb's wife at the time. She looked at me and then looked at Maxine and then looked back at me and she knew and I knew right then that they knew. I remember that Roger Pope told me the rumour that I was having an affair with Raquel Welch because although I didn't have an affair with her I did go over to meet her and I just let them believe what they wanted to believe. Raquel Welch was one of the best movie stars at the time and a beautiful woman. I didn't have an affair with her but I let them believe that I did. Roger and I were very close and he never made any judgments about me even when it all came out. It was a lot for Maxine and Bernie to come to terms with; they met and got married very young and moved from California to a cottage in Lincolnshire and then to a mansion in Surrey and a mansion in LA and by the time I met Maxine she was still only 22 and I was 24. We were just a bunch of kids and they were rich and famous; it was a lot for them to take in. The entire record was incredibly emotional, incredibly difficult and when I look back on it and go through it track by track it was heavy, a real big weight on me and Bernie although he was in Barbados at the time. When we did 'Don't Go Breaking My Heart' it was the only light hearted part of the album and Bernie actually gave me the written lyrics."

♫

Similar to the sessions for *Rock of the Westies*, Elton again included the band in the creative process, on songs like 'Tonight' and 'Sorry Seems To Be The Hardest Word'. Pope insisted that the songs were played slowly without drums. James Newton Howard had just received the first polyphonic Moog synthesiser, mainly because he was friendly with Bob Moog, and he was working on some new and innovative sounds.

"He used it on *Blue Moves*," Quaye explained, "so we would meet in hotel rooms with James and his synthesiser, working on different sounds. Prior to the polyphonic synthesiser you could only play a synthesiser, one note at a time. We were all writing songs, and I was credited with some songs on *Blue Moves*. There was a lot of creative stuff going on during the making of the album but it was under a lot of pressure."

Outside of recording, the band had some good times though - one being Pope's birthday. "The band bought me a rug, and Elton got me a waistcoat, and a cake made into a drum kit. I gave Elton the first piece of cake and while he was chewing it we could hear this squeaking sound. He was chewing the polystyrene sheet that separated the slices; we all fell about laughing but Elton took it in good spirits."

Elton also found what he thought was a new partner, and swiftly fell in love. "I wasn't close to Elton, but he used to cry on my shoulder sometimes." said Pope. "I remember in Toronto, he fell in love with an ice hockey player and gave him a Porsche. The bloke just fucked off with it. He came crying to me saying he didn't know what to do and I asked him why he did it. He couldn't remember the registration number or even the colour, all he kept saying was it didn't matter." He just wanted his new partner back.

" 'Don't Go Breaking My Heart' was the very last number to be recorded at the *Blue Moves* album sessions in Toronto," continued Pope. "Elton said, I've got one more number and we all said 'For fuck's sake, we've been playing all week.' We were not too happy about it." According to Quaye, "We'd just done *Blue Moves,* and Elton did this song that he had written for Kiki. Kiki and Elton were not in the same country when they recorded the vocals, as Elton did the vocals in Toronto, and Kiki overdubbed hers in the UK."

Kiki said, "We had discussed doing a duet for a while because people weren't doing it much in the seventies and we all liked Tammy Terrell and Marvin Gaye. I was originally just going to sing a couple of words on a song with Elton but Gus said we couldn't do it. Elton recorded the song, singing both sets of lyrics at first and then I put my vocals on later. I was in London with Gus, and Elton was out of the country. I listened to the two voices of Elton, and just recorded my version. Gus dubbed it together and that was it. At the time I thought it was a pleasant song but nothing special. It was the least input I'd had on a song, and my job was just to make it sound like I was in a duet with Elton John. We filmed a video of the song for *Top Of The Pops* which was just me and Elton messing about really. It was nothing staged and we were miming. I remember Elton was feeling very self-conscious because he was not used to standing up. When it got to No.1 [in the long hot summer of 1976], there was huge excitement, and we were all thrilled: the world was at our feet. I just remember being chuffed, and my parents were very happy. We were travelling a lot and performing, so it was all a bit of a whirlwind. I was invited to guest on the 1976 tour which culminated in seven nights at Madison Square Garden and did the song live. I flew my parents over and Davey did the same. We all got on very well together."

The gigs were going well, but Elton was showing the strain of burning the candle at both ends. After all this time and all that he had been through, Elton was frazzled out; he just couldn't do it anymore. Before the last gig at Madison Square Garden, John Reid was once again left with letting the band know that it would be the last gig they would be playing with Elton. Incredibly, they were told before going on stage, which seems a high risk strategy if you want to get the best out of a band.

"We were told that the band was going to be disbanded on the last night," recalled Quaye. "It was depressing as the band was really tight by then. We were told about twenty minutes before we were due to go on stage, that this would be the last gig for the band. We didn't have time to respond to it, because we had to go on. We went through the motions and just did the gig. The crowd was just going crazy, but we knew it was the end. Elton had just had it and had come to the end of the road; he had succumbed to the pressure and his own internal issues."

Roger Pope was seriously angry. "By now I couldn't give a fuck whether there was 20,000 people in the place or not. Elton could see I was angry before we went on, and kept repeating he was sorry; I was calling him a lot of names. When I went on and played, I was just scowling at Elton all the time, and hitting the cymbal as hard as I could."

Pope and his wife Victoria were staying at the Waldorf Astoria, as was his mother and Pope had spent a lot of money arranging it all. "I wrecked the hotel room afterwards. I went mental. Ray Cooper tried to calm me down and he went and told Elton that he needed to sort something out because I was going to wreck the place." In the end he sent Reid, who gave the band a bonus royalty point for *Blue Moves*.

"I have never forgiven Elton for what he did at Madison Square Garden. For Roger it was more difficult than for me, because at that time I was living in the States and he wasn't," said Quaye. "He had spent a lot of money, having flown his family over from the UK, so it was really embarrassing for him. The whole band was just so depressed."

When Pope got back to the UK, he went into the Rocket Record Company and, having got drunk first, was abusive to Reid and Elton. After that Pope was excluded from sessions with Rocket and never worked with Elton or Reid again. "The band was great," reflected Pope, "it was like working with Sinatra; he had to have a great band and Elton was the same. They loved the music and it was an incredible time but that excitement has gone now and will never be repeated."

After the Elton John Band finished, Pope was invited to join Davey Johnstone's new band, China, who were recording an album in Munich. "I did that recording but I didn't enjoy it. They wanted me to go on the road but I didn't like the music they were doing. I then got a phone call from Phil Collins asking me to join Genesis (Collins had taken over the vocals and the band needed a second drummer for live work), but I turned them down too as I didn't like what they were doing. Eventually I joined Hall and Oates in America, with Quaye and Passarelli and had significant success on tour with them."

Pope leaves us with a happy memory of his time with Elton though. In the spring of 1976 they all embarked on 'The Louder Than Concorde, But Not Quite As Pretty' tour in the UK. "I remember being in Manchester the day Southampton beat Manchester United in the FA Cup Final [May 1 1976, and it was a big upset]," shudders Pope. "The atmosphere was not that good, and to make it worse, the weather was miserable, as it was raining. We started playing when suddenly the Chief of Police came on stage, and told us that we had to stop, because there was a bomb scare. We couldn't go into the dressing rooms; we just had to get out. There were five thousand people standing outside in the pouring rain and they had just lost the FA Cup Final too. Elton had told them all before leaving the venue that they shouldn't worry as he would still play his whole set, even if it lasted all night. We went outside with no coats on, and half an hour later, we were told that it was a false alarm and we were let back in again. We went back on and I was absolutely soaked. Elton introduced the band and where we came from. He got to me and of course I was from Southampton. You have never heard a boo like it! The audience had already worked out where I was from and I had seen all these toilet rolls everywhere. I told my roadie to get me a dustbin lid and when Elton said Southampton I stood up and put the dustbin lid in front of my face - there were toilet rolls flying everywhere. I then did a drum solo and everything was fine."

But not every night was as eventful as that gig. Quaye remembered the tour for the musical freedom he was given: "When we were on tour, much to Elton's credit, there was always room for freedom of interpretation even though we played the same songs every night. We could improvise the songs just to keep them fresh and so we would jam during songs. This was one of the qualities that he wanted back in the band, the ability, especially with Roger and me, to get into jams, and take the music to other places."

If Elton's dismissal of the musicians seems harsh, a possible reason may be found in an interview he gave to Chris Charlesworth when he dropped a bombshell. He was going into semi-retirement. He therefore had no need for a permanent band. In fact he played less than a dozen gigs in the next year, 1977, and most of those were with Ray Cooper as a duo.

"However, without the music and performance," noted Reid, "he had nothing to concentrate his energy on so, with Gary Osborne, he turned to more drugs and alcohol. He took it to excess."

13

A Single Man

In 1977, Elton John was, by his workaholic standards, in semi-
retirement; Elvis Presley had left the building permanently; and the
British music scene was as complacent as ever. The popularity of Glam
Rock, under which Elton was now branded, was waning and its fallen
King, Marc Bolan, was dead. However, the storm clouds were gathering
and the music scene was going to be given a much-needed shot in the
arm, or a wild descent into anarchy, depending on which side of the
musical fence you sat.

The emergence of the punk rock scene was set against the backdrop of
a nation in conflict and throughout the latter part of the seventies it was
getting worse. There was high unemployment, national strikes involving
dustmen, miners and postal workers, general civil unrest, a long summer
drought that led to water shortages which culminated in the much
publicised Winter of Discontent. Overall, it seemed that the 1970s had
created a disillusioned youth culture, which was anti-establishment, and
was now looking for a way to vent its frustration. Enter the Sex Pistols.

You could be forgiven for wondering why a book on Elton John is
veering off into the realms of punk but, like the sacking of Rome by the
barbarians, the bastion of Denmark Street was breached by the punks, not
that too many people noticed.

The music publishers of the fifties and sixties had left Denmark Street
for the West End by the time the Sex Pistols pogoed into view. Malcolm
McLaren, not renowned for putting his hand in his pocket, coughed up

£1,000 deposit on rehearsal space above a shop at 6 Denmark Street, suggesting he could see a future for his wayward charges. This space was owned by Bill Collins, father to Lewis Collins who found fame as tough cop Bodie in the 1970s TV show *The Professionals*. The rehearsal space was, by all accounts, pretty dingy, and the smell of blocked drains permeated the room. No matter, it was somewhere to fine-tune their songs and, for Pistols' guitarist Steve Jones and bassist Glen Matlock, somewhere to live at the time. Johnny Rotten was something of an artist and drew caricatures of the band of the band on the walls with a marker pen.

The Pistols disdain for tradition luckily didn't extend to the Gioconda Cafe and, as so many had done before them, they sat and talked about their futures over coffee there.

On 8 October 1976, EMI signed the Sex Pistols to a two-year contract and on the 26 November of the same year, released 'Anarchy In The UK', produced by Chris Thomas who had previously worked with decidedly non-punk acts such as the Beatles, Roxy Music, Pink Floyd, Procol Harum and, of course, with Elton as early as 1968.

There was little doubt that punk rock would permeate the nation's consciousness one way or another. However, this probably happened sooner than it might have, due to another Tin Pan Alley stalwart, Eric Hall, who, by 1976, was a plugger for EMI. Hall was the catalyst who secured the Sex Pistols a spot on the *Today* show, a regional news programme broadcast on Thames Television for London viewers, hosted by the hapless Bill Grundy. On 1 December 1976, in a career-wrecking episode for Grundy, he interviewed the band and several of their camp followers, such as Siouxsie Sioux, lost the plot and ultimately his job.

Hall recalled an event that became etched into the whole nation's consciousness via *The Daily Mirror*'s famous front page headline 'The Filth and the Fury'. "The producer had a regular pop video slot on the programme and he wanted a video of Queen which he hadn't ordered early enough to get clearance and so he wanted me to try and get it cleared 24 hours before the show was due to go out. I asked him to give me 24 hours and I would see what I could do. Unfortunately the guy at the clearance department was a bit of a jobs-worth, and because we hadn't given the required four days notice, he wouldn't give clearance. I went back and told the producer, who was now desperate to fill the schedule for the show that evening. He asked me about the Sex Pistols who were rehearsing somewhere for a tour. I said that I didn't think they were suitable even though I had promoted their record because I had to, it was my job; I didn't think it was very good. I tried to put him off but he said he wanted to take a chance. So I said to him tell Bill Grundy to make sure they didn't have a liquid lunch or they wouldn't be good for the show, and I would have a word with the boys and Malcolm McLaren. I called Malcolm at the rehearsal place and told him that I had a promotional spot that evening and was he interested. He asked me if it was *Top Of The Pops* and I said, No, it was the *Today* programme for Thames Television."

McLaren was not impressed and at first told Hall that he wasn't interested and he didn't want to interrupt the bands rehearsal for it. Hall countered with: "I told Malcolm that it was good exposure and any publicity is good publicity; he said the boys would do it if they received all the trimmings of the stars at EMI; he wanted a limousine to take them to the studio and salmon sandwiches and champagne on the journey. I told Malcolm it was a fifteen minute journey and by the time they had popped the corks they would be there, but he insisted and I gave it to them."

Little did Hall know what would follow and the impact a small regional news programme would have on the music business. The swearing that came out of that interview, encouraged, some say, by Grundy, who had consumed his own liquid lunch, led to punk rock exploding upon an unsuspecting nation and the Sex Pistols becoming a national phenomenon, which culminated in the release of 'God Save The Queen' on A&M Records, in the year of the Queen's Silver Jubilee. Just like Elton John, David Bowie and Marc Bolan before them, the Sex Pistols had taken the Tin Pan Alley music scene in a totally different direction, and away from the now ailing fortunes of the glitter and glam stars such as Mud, Sweet and the Bay City Rollers.

♪

Although punk music grabbed the headlines for a while and gave the music business a much-needed reality check, it can be argued that it made little lasting impact and it was back to business as usual when the Pistols imploded in 1978. The other big mid-70s movement was Disco, with artists like Donna Summer, Chic, Gloria Gaynor, and Eurovision winners, Abba. Also producers and composers like Giorgio Moroder and Pete Bellotte. Punk was all anger and anti-establishment, but Disco too had its political side with its multi-racial message, the acceptance of marginalised communities such as gays and the sexual liberation of women. You could argue, and many have, about which musical genre left the greater legacy.

As punk and disco took hold of the music scene in the UK, Europe and America, Elton took a break from the stresses and strains that successive tours and albums had taken on him. During a time when homosexuality was still taboo, Elton had admitted to being bisexual in an interview with *Rolling Stone* magazine in August 1976. This caused a backlash from the American record buying public, in particular, who plagued the offices of the magazine with anti-Elton messages, even going so far as burning his records: the traditional response of those who persecute others.

Although it was well known in the business that Elton was gay, it was little known by the record buying public. "Even though Elton had stated he was bisexual, and everyone in the music business knew he was gay, being gay was still a stigma in the late seventies in British society," recalled Andy Hill, the son of George Hill who ran the Northwood Hills pub and whom Elton employed as his PA. In doing this Elton was generously acknowledging past kindnesses by George. "All the time I was working with Elton and John Reid, it was obvious he was gay, but I just ignored it; you knew where you stood with John and I got on with him. He was an aggressive man and I remember when I was in Rocket the temporary receptionist had obviously cocked up a call, and he literally hurled her down the stairs. That's what got him into trouble in the end, in New Zealand, he was arrested and he went down for it."

Reid had allegedly had an argument with a journalist in a nightclub over the availability of whisky at a press launch and had knocked him to the floor; Elton was accused of grabbing his shirt and both Reid and Elton went up before the Magistrates in Auckland and Reid was jailed for over a month. Elton was discharged.

Hill continues, "Tony King was so obviously gay, but he was okay and we had a laugh. Elton would turn up to football matches with a Swiss 'girlfriend' closely by his side, to keep up the facade of his sexuality, and at the same time, attempt to try and prevent any bad crowd reaction, especially the opposition fans, who could be quite a distraction in the small grounds."

During his break, Elton spent his time between Windsor and America, and generally enjoyed a party lifestyle, with Gary Osborne, Andy Hill, John Reid, Tony King and a galaxy of stars on both sides of the Atlantic. As well as working at Rocket, Elton now had more time to concentrate on his other passion, Watford Football Club. He had become a director in 1974, along with Vic Lewis. But he was not content with being a small shareholder, he was hell bent on being the chairman, and insisted that Reid be a director as well, as then he would have a powerful ally. This meant another board member had to make way, so it was goodbye to Vic Lewis. "Elton was prepared to pay any price to become chairman and that made negotiations very difficult. The current chairman was happy to continue, and therefore we paid a high price for his shares," recalled Reid. "I knew nothing about football, and really didn't want to be a director, but I felt I had no choice, someone needed to make sure Elton was protected."

Elton became top dog and set about making Watford FC one of the best football clubs in Britain. "The first task was for us to find a manager but without telling me he started talks with Bobby Moore, who was coming to the end of his career with Fulham FC, [and was England's captain at the 1966 World Cup Finals]. I got a call from Don Revie, who was the new England Manager and a successful club manager at Leeds United," continued Reid. "He told me what Elton had done, and advised me that Moore was not the right manager for Watford and I should look at Graham Taylor, who was much more suitable for the task. I was not sure how I was going to tell Elton about his mistake but, as luck would have it, Elton contacted me, and said that he had changed his mind about Bobby Moore and could I tell him that the deal was off. It was yet another example of Elton not being able to face telling people bad news, so I called Moore and told him that we didn't want him as manager and, being the gentleman that he was, he accepted the rejection gracefully."

Reid and Elton turned their attentions to Lincoln City boss Graham Taylor and despite Reid's dogged negotiation skills Taylor did very well out of the deal. The relationship between manager and chairman was, in many ways, a match made in heaven and very successful. Within five years, Watford were plying their trade in the top division instead of the fourth; an incredible achievement.

Throughout Elton's chairmanship, he would often use his own money to buy players and fund events, but this was beginning to take its toll on his bank account, and it gave Reid the opportunity he needed to get Elton back into the music scene, as it was the only way at the time to raise the money needed to fund the club to the level he wanted.

Elton's continued friendship with Muff Winwood outside of the music business led to Elton introducing Winwood to Watford FC. "I was a keen football fan and I used to travel back to the Midlands to watch my favourite team, West Bromwich Albion," recalled Winwood. "One day Elton asked me why I kept going back to the Midlands to watch football when I could go with him to watch Watford, so I did. We both used to stand behind the goal with all the other supporters in those early days. I was taken aback by the whole thing, because Watford were in the third division, and I hadn't seen much of that level of football as West Bromwich Albion were in the first division. But I got taken in by it, and started going regularly with Elton. A few years later Elton came round to see me and said he was going to buy Watford FC. I was surprised when he told me he was the chairman and asked me to be on the board. At first I turned him down and I kept refusing for about eighteen months, but then eventually I agreed. In fact, I ended up staying on the board, even when Elton left. I enjoyed it and learned a lot. They were at the top of the first division and it was an exciting time. Elton really shook up the football community as he was quite bizarre."

Andy Hill agreed, "He was a true Watford fan, and for the charity *Goaldiggers* he would turn up in his Watford kit and he took great pride in wearing it." One of Hill's jobs was to get Elton to the away games by helicopter, or arrange to have him driven to the ground. "I would have to plan it weeks ahead because of his schedule, but he tried to avoid missing any game; it was very much part of his life. Even when Elton was overseas he would phone in for the results and it was not uncommon for him to listen to an entire game over the telephone lines. I would be on the phone listening to it and doing a commentary for Elton. He always used to regularly meet the players, and although they were successful, they didn't make much money. They wouldn't be allowed out after Wednesday before a game, but after the game they all socialised together and with Elton. He used to hire the top floor of a pub just down the road from the ground, and after the match they would all go into the pub until after closing time."

Taylor was a very professional manager, and he never let the Elton factor interfere with his running of the club. "He didn't even like Elton going into the dressing room," remembered Tony King. "He wanted the Watford team to be normal guys, with a normal lifestyle and for them not be affected by Elton's way of life. Taylor was the leading light, and he had the knack of making average players good. They were so much fitter than the other sides, and scored most of their goals in the last fifteen minutes of a game. Elton gave him money for players but not that much by today's standards. It got to the point where Elton was putting more and more money into the club, but getting little for it."

♪

After *Blue Moves*, Elton hadn't made any more records, and was concentrating on the now ailing Rocket Record Company, producing an album with a band from Scotland called Blue, who had a hit single with the classy 'Capture Your Heart'. He was determined not to let Rocket fail altogether, and still believed in the philosophy behind it. Even though Reid was less than enthusiastic about Rocket, at least it meant Elton stayed with his musical interests.

Things, however, were destined to change when one night in 1976 Kiki Dee told Gary Osborne she was going to Elton's for dinner and he had asked her if Osborne would like to join them. Osborne agreed and along with his wife, Kiki, and actor Peter Wyngarde, best known for his role as Jason King in ITV's *Department S,* headed out to see Elton at his residence in Woodside. The dinner went well and, soon after, Osborne reciprocated inviting Elton to his home.

From these two invitations, Osborne and Elton would become good friends and Osborne soon found himself in the Rocket fold, where he became an accepted member of the team, and signed a publishing deal for his songs.

Osborne was often seen with Elton at many of the Watford functions as their friendship developed. "We used to go to the Watford Garden Party at Woodside every year. There were three-legged races, egg and spoon races, and a five-a-side pitch where he would organise a game between the player's kids and the directors of the club. I remember we entered the three-legged race once. I was very thin at the time and he was chunky. If there were ever two people mismatched for a three-legged race, it was us. We fell over before we got very far."

Elton and Clive Franks were also about to start work on the next Kiki Dee album, and roped Osborne into writing some of the lyrics. "I was asked to write two lyrics for the Kiki Dee album, one with Kiki and Davey, called 'Into Eternity', and one with Kiki and James Newton Howard, titled 'Sweet Creation'. Elton liked these two lyrics. He was also a fan of the 'Amoureuse' lyric because he had picked it for Kiki to record. Elton was living in London at the time and not writing, because having retired, he had no album to write for, but he used to say to me quite often. 'We'll write together one day,' and I used to say 'Don't say that because if it doesn't happen you will feel embarrassed. I understand that Bernie is your writing partner and I am working on this thing called *The War Of The Worlds* with Jeff Wayne, which I think is going to do quite well, so let's just be friends and leave it at that'." Around that time, Bernie was living in LA, and working with Alice Cooper on an album titled *From The Inside*.

With musician and lyricist spending so much time together, it was probably inevitable that a song would happen between Elton and Gary, and it did. Osborne related how this little piece of musical history came about: "One day he sat down and played me this tune, and I told him what a lovely tune it was. He asked if I would like to write a lyric for it. I was very respectful about Bernie, as I thought he was a very good writer, and a fellow lyricist, and he had always been very complimentary about 'Amoureuse', so I asked Elton how Bernie would feel about it. Elton said he wanted to change, 'With Bernie, it's words first, and this is tune first, and that's not his thing.' Now with me it was different, I don't work that way. I am not a poet, I am a lyricist. So what he did with me was to give me a tune and then tell me what he wanted to say. My style suited Elton at that particular time, because he had been writing with Bernie for years, and had always been constrained by Bernie's lyric. So suddenly now, he was getting a little tune in his head, that he gave to me, and a few days later, I went back to him and he had a song. So there I am trying to argue against doing this lyric, but really what I wanted to do was to jump over the piano and kick him out of the house, and start working on it immediately. He said, 'I've played this to Bernie, and he hasn't come up with anything', but I have a suspicion that he was just saying that to make me feel better about doing it. So he left the house at about 2 in the morning, and I started working on it there and then and finished it a couple of days later. That was a song called 'Shine on Through'. We went in to demo the song, and while we were doing that, he wrote another tune, and he said 'Try this', and when we were demoing that tune, he wrote another one and so on. 'Shine on Through' was to re-launch Elton's musical career and he was even invited onto the prestigious *Morecambe And Wise* television show to promote it."

Elton continued to spend a great deal of his time with Gary Osborne, and they started writing together, with the encouragement of John Reid, who wanted Elton back in the world of music earning his corn. "I was incredibly useful to John Reid, who was concerned that his star act had retired, and was going through a chilly period with Bernie where he did not want to record and write," said Osborne. "He loved the idea of me hanging out with Elton, because I was writing, and it might lead to him writing, which is exactly what happened."

Much of the resulting work with Osborne did exactly what Reid wanted. It led to a new studio album and Elton's emergence out of his semi-retirement. "He would have come out of retirement eventually, but it was an open-ended retirement. He didn't say 'I'm not working until a set date', he just said 'I'm not doing it anymore', and therefore John was managing an artist who had just retired, and there was no future in that," said Osborne.

'Shine on Through' would become the catalyst for the writing and recording of his next album, *A Single Man*, which brought Elton's appetite for writing and recording back again. Reid, who was still worried about financing his star act, had Osborne to thank for that. Over a five year period, Elton and Osborne wrote thirty or forty songs together; album tracks, singles, songs for films, and songs that they never even demoed. "Frankly, just to have written one song with Elton John, and to put that on my CV was brilliant," raved Osborne. "I had no desire to replace Bernie Taupin in any way; although that was the way it looked at first."

Despite the new breath of fresh air that Osborne brought to Elton and Reid, they still wanted the Rocket label to be more than just Elton John's label, so they recruited Eric Hall, the plugger *par excellence* as talent scout. "I agreed to promote Elton's latest single, his duet with Kiki Dee, which resulted with me being offered a prime job with Rocket and its publishing arm, Big Pig Music. It was such a big hit that he asked John Reid to get me. At the time, he was concerned that every time Rocket had a hit it was associated with Elton John, even if it was a Kiki Dee hit, it was on Elton's label. Because it was a newly formed label and they didn't want it to be known as just Elton John's label (even though he loved it being called that really), Elton brought me in to find new talent and I did. The first act I signed was Judie Tzuke, and we had a hit with 'Stay With Me Till Dawn'. Then I signed the original Blue, and had a hit with them in the UK and USA, and then with Pete Waterman's production company, I signed The Lambrettas, who had a hit with 'Poison Ivy'. So I went to Rocket to bring artists to the label, and I was successful."

Elton also wanted to build up his publishing side and to get people to cover his songs and, again, he turned to Hall to accomplish that aim. "I heard that Bobby Crush [a popular pianist] was making an album, so I called the record company and suggested that the album should be *Bobby Crush Sings Elton John*. His manager thought it was great, and so did I, as I would be selling anything from twelve to fifteen songs by Elton John to him. I called Elton in St Tropez, and told him that I was selling his songs and what I had done. He went mad. I couldn't understand it, I kept explaining that I had sold fifteen covers of Elton John songs, so what was the problem? The fact was that he hated the idea of his songs being covered by Bobby Crush, and he told me to stop it coming out. But I was just doing my job and selling songs. I called John Reid and told him what had happened. He said, 'You'd better get on to them and tell them that you will pay every penny back that was spent on the project.' I said, 'I can't do that even if I wanted to', and so no, I didn't, and the album was released in 1980 on Celebrity Records, and did very well for both Crush and Elton."

Prior to joining Elton and Rocket, Eric Hall was working for Phil Solomon, who had been instrumental in the emergence of pirate radio with Radio Caroline, at Major Minor Records and had a hit with 'Mony, Mony' by Tommy James and the Shondells. "And then," recalled Hall, "I went to work for Don Arden as a plugger or promotions man working with The Move, ELO and Wizard. The Move became the Electric Light Orchestra, because of Jeff Lynne and Roy Wood. Then Roy and Jeff fell out after the first ELO single, and the resultant settlement led to Roy forming Wizard and Jeff keeping ELO. EMI had started a new label and I was asked by Roy Featherstone to be the promotions man for it. Everyone in the business knew about a new band called Queen and how good they were, so I told Roy that I would join EMI if they signed Queen. He was reluctant at first because of the money they were asking for them." Queen were duly signed, however, the move from Don Arden to EMI was not to be that straightforward, especially for Roy Featherstone.

"The next thing I had to do was tell Don Arden that I was giving my notice in. Don was notorious and was known as the Al Capone of the music business, and he said to me, 'What do you mean, you're leaving? You love it here.' and he tried to persuade me to stay. Don then went to see Roy Featherstone with a rifle and said you either tell him you don't want him anymore, or there is a bullet in here for you. Roy called me after his meeting with Arden, and said 'I can't employ you because Don Arden is going to shoot me if I do.' I told Roy to ignore it, that he was all mouth, and he wouldn't shoot him, and so I joined EMI."

In addition to taking Queen to EMI, Hall also takes the credit for signing Steve Harley, Pilot, Be Bop Deluxe, Mr Big and Tavares to the label. And soon after that, he was to meet John Reid. "Queen's first manager was Jack Nelson," continued Hall, "that's when they were initially signed to Trident before EMI. The band were not happy with some of the deals that were agreed by Nelson, and were looking for new management. Freddie would frequently mix with Elton and John Reid, and they became friends, and so he went back to the rest of the band, and told them that he wanted to sign for John Reid Enterprises and work with Reid. The relationship, however, was short lived, because John promised them the world, but when they signed he was difficult to get hold of, the same happened with Neil Sedaka; he was so busy with Elton John that he didn't really have the time to spend with anyone else."

Hall went on to promote all of Queen's songs, and became a good friend to the band and with Freddie Mercury in particular. "Freddie wrote a song about me as he really fancied me," laughed Hall. "I was in Luxembourg with them doing a promotional tour for their second record. We were staying in the Holiday Inn in Luxembourg and, at 2 in the morning, I received a knock on the door. I asked who it was, and a voice said, 'It's Freddie. I want to talk.' I said, 'We've got to get to sleep as we have a busy day tomorrow with radio shows.' Anyway this went on for a while, and it ended up with him asking me whether he could sit by the bed and hold my hand and that is what happened."

"On another occasion," recalled Hall, "Freddie called me up, and said he had just finished the new single and he wanted to play it to me. We met up at EMI studios and he played me 'Killer Queen'.' I told him the song was a monster and it would make No. 1 easily. He said, 'No my dear, you're not listening,' I said, 'No Freddie, I am listening, and it's a great song', and he kept saying 'No, no listen again, hear the lyrics', and so I heard it a third time, and then he said that the song was about me, 'You're a Killer Queen', he told me. I must say I was always generous with my expenses at EMI and so I enjoyed good hotel rooms, champagne and good food and I could hear the resemblance in the lyrics."

♬

Much of Elton's life after *Blue Moves* came out, was spent between his homes in Windsor, Los Angeles plus the occasional visit to New York. While music was never far away, much of the time was spent socialising with people like Michael Jackson, who was a close friend of one of Elton's entourage. Photographer David Nutter and Rod Stewart were among the most regular visitors to Elton's home in LA. "We stayed in LA and played tennis a lot," recalled Andy Hill. "The friendship Elton had over there was mainly with Rod Stewart, and his crowd. They had a love-hate relationship, and were always playing games on each other, like who was the richest. Overall, Elton had his own little way of life with the likes of Tony King. Rod liked to go out for a beer and a curry in the evening with his band and I'd go with them. Elton would be out with Tony King and his friends. Whenever Rod went back to Elton's for dinner, he would always get out the best cutlery and crockery to show Rod how rich he was. On one occasion to get his own back, Rod brought some cheap wine and changed the labels to make it look expensive: and Elton couldn't tell. It was always a good laugh. On another occasion, they were in a famous department store in the States when Rod noticed a lady assistant selling men's cologne. On asking her what she had to do to get commission, she said she had to sell as many bottles of cologne as she could. In a bidding war between Elton and Rod she earned a lot of commission, and Elton and Rod walked away with at least five hundred bottles of the stuff."

Both Rod and Elton used to be regulars in the Northwood Hills pub with Rod's band and Linda Lewis. In one tipsy session, the pair bet each other a fortune on the toss of a coin. But one practical joke that backfired, as far as Elton was concerned, was the one that involved his beloved Rocket Records. "We had a board meeting for Rocket Records in LA, and he was told it was going to be a fancy dress party," remembered Hill, "and he fell for it. He turned up in roller skates, a dress and a wig. It was the year-end financial meeting with all the accountants and he got really upset at that."

Although he was no longer on stage or consciously in the public eye, Elton was still wearing outrageous clothes simply because he wanted to be different. He had different coloured shoes and socks on at the same time, and he didn't care where he was or who spotted him, and he was equally as outrageous on Concorde as he was at a local restaurant. "There was a restaurant that we used to go to in New York, where they had a dress code. Rod walked in with a suit and tie on, but with white shoes, and the waiter said he wasn't complying with the dress code, but let him in anyway. Then Elton followed behind with shorts, cap, a red trainer on one foot and a white trainer and the other. I could see the waiter thinking 'There goes the dress code', but Elton was still a very shy person, and his way of overcoming it, was to be outrageous", laughed Andy Hill.

One of his frequent nightspots was Studio 54 in New York, opened in April 1977 by Steve Rubell and Ian Schrager. The nightclub soon became the home to some of the most diverse people, from writers to musicians, to everyday people of all ages, sexes and ethnicities. With this exposure to Disco, through clubs like Studio 54, Elton joined forces with Thom Bell, who was noted for his work with The Stylistics, to create a Disco/Philly Sound.

The result would later be called *The Thom Bell Sessions*, which was recorded in the latter part of 1977 and not originally planned for release, although it did surface a couple of years later. "He did a couple of recordings with Thom Bell which was great fun." continued Hill. "The sessions were recorded in New York, where Bell had a studio and a couple of staff. It seemed Elton was much better away from the UK. During the time we were out in America we did two weeks with Thom Bell and he was more relaxed with what was happening. Thom had met Elton in LA first and they played through some songs together, then we went to New York. What was put down in the studio and what Thom actually sent to Elton in the end, was different to what Elton had expected as Thom had made a lot of changes in the mixing, but Elton allowed it to be released."

Much to Hill's surprise, he ended up doing backing vocals on 'Are You Ready For Love', as they didn't have any singers at the time. Another surprise during this period was working with Bonnie Raitt, who would be a regular visitor to Elton's house in LA, rehearsing songs. "We were in New York with John Reid and Tony King, and Elton played us a song he had demoed called 'Amigo'. It was never released as a single or on an album, but it was one of the best piano solos he had ever done in my opinion," said Hill. "One of Elton's favourite things though, would be the regular jaunts to the local pubs and clubs to watch the up-and-coming bands, and keeping an eye on the new music scene that was emerging. We used to go into Tower Records all the time and fill trolleys with records, as he must have every album and single going. Back at Windsor, I remember, there was a library of records."

It was also during this period that Elton was still getting lyrics coming through from Bernie on the telex in Elton's house in LA, but nothing ever became of them, and Elton had stopped writing with them. "He just wanted a change, including a change in his life. His music life was so narrow up to this point, so he just wanted a change in the way he was writing and wanted to write with other people." said Hill.

Back home in the UK, Elton still considered Fred and Sheila as his bedrock and a sanctuary. They brought him back to reality, and his roots. "Whenever Elton was in LA, his stepfather and mother went with him, and stayed in his guest house." recalled Hill. "In fact, they used to go everywhere with him; they were his best friends. His Granny even used to live in the gatehouse at Windsor. Fred and Elton were always bickering, and there were some heated discussions, but it was a close knit family still, despite his fame."

Elton used to have a guest book in his house at Windsor, and the people who were in it were a real Who's Who of the film and music worlds. Elton used to love telling Hill who he had met and seen in person. Despite his own fame, he would still get a real buzz, and a pride, from meeting those people and sometimes he was in awe of them, but always very honoured to meet them. On one occasion, however, one of his idols, did not return the honour: "We went to see Eartha Kitt, and after the show, Elton asked if he could meet her, so her people agreed, and we went backstage, On meeting Eartha, she said to Elton 'Who are you?' She really made him feel very low."

The next album came out of the friendship Elton shared with Gary Osborne. *A Single Man* came out without any of Bernie's lyrics on it and, despite what some may have thought, it wasn't a conscious decision to exclude him, and nor had there been a falling out according to Gary Osborne. In fact, following *A Single Man*, both Bernie and Osborne collaborated with Elton on the next four albums. "It was just that Elton had retired and Bernie wanted to live in LA, and therefore Bernie just started working with other people. They had been working together for a long time. It was not a conscious decision for them to stop working together, but what was a conscious decision was that Elton wanted to try writing the music first for a change, and I think we made some great songs that way."

Indeed, writing with Osborne, brought a new dimension to Elton's usual song writing format. "It was a new way of working for him. What he used to say was that it was like a stopper coming out of a bottle and all these tunes came flowing out then I turned them into songs. Sometimes I did a good job, and sometimes I didn't do such a good job. But some, I am very proud of, like 'Madness', which is about a terrorist outrage, and 'Shooting Star', which Elton particularly liked. I didn't try to be too clever; my job was just to make a tune sound as good as I could make it sound. So if he gave me something that was jaunty, tongue in cheek, with a jokey feel to it, I would come up with a song like 'Big Dipper', and if he gave me a tune like 'Madness', with the whole arrangement so dramatic and so intense, then I got to write something intense.

"That's exactly what I do when I write a lyric. I describe the tune to myself. And if the tune is romantic and wistful, you get a romantic and wistful song such as 'Blue Eyes'. If the tune rocks, then so does the lyric. That's what I do. With 'Big Dipper', he wrote the tune and came up with the title. So my thought process was, 'What's the best thing that could happen on this big dipper? Well, you might meet somebody you like, you might go up on the big dipper, and you might get a blowjob.' I didn't say it in so many words, but that was it. I said to Elton, 'I am going to write you a poofy song, about a sexual encounter on a Big Dipper', and he said, 'Oh that's good, I'll get the Watford football team to sing on it' so I said 'If you can sell that to them and Graham Taylor you're bloody clever!' But they agreed, and they loved it, because they loved him."

The album was recorded at Dudgeon's Mill Studio in Cookham, which is where Dudgeon had now set up home, both privately and professionally. The Mill was a state-of-the-art facility with quadraphonic sound, which is how the new album would be mixed. Clive Franks was slated to produce the album with Elton and also play bass guitar as Elton hadn't got a band any more. Stuart Epps, who was now working for Dudgeon in the studio, was assisting with the engineering work. "It was great to be working with Elton again and he was in good form. Although not working with Bernie, the lyrics were a bit strange again. 'Hello Campers' was one of the prospective songs for the album, but luckily it didn't make it."

Once again, Buckmaster was brought in to do the string arrangements and it was almost back to the first team that Elton had worked with. However Buckmaster's role was somewhat weakened as he was drafted in just to set the orchestrations to a pre-determined sound instead of his previous role with the *Elton John* album for which he had complete control of all the arrangements.

Franks met with Buckmaster a few weeks before recording and briefed him, so he had plenty of time to write the scores. Unfortunately, just days before the scores were due to be delivered, Buckmaster inadvertently spilt ink all over them. He said it was the cat's fault, so he and Franks spent the next couple of days, working day and night, to get them ready for the recording sessions. Another previously-used session musician, BJ Cole, was asked to join Elton at the sessions, for the track 'Georgia'. By this time, Cole remembered Elton as being less humble about his control of the music and the final sound. The mutual respect he had back in the earlier 'Madman' sessions had gone, but according to everyone present, it was still great to work with him.

"It wasn't as memorable as 'Tiny Dancer'," said Cole, "and my part was essentially an overdub rather than being part of the overall creative process as it had been during 'Tiny Dancer'. I remember being in the studio, which had a deep pile carpet, and having to get a piece of card, so I could get to the pedals, which were sinking into the carpet."

One song that was recorded during the sessions was the hit 'Song For Guy', written on the same day as the death of a 17-year-old messenger boy, Guy, at Rocket Records following a motorcycle accident. Elton waited until the end of the album sessions before recording the song. Dudgeon set up a rhythm box to accompany Elton's piano, and Epps started the tape rolling. Elton was making mistakes and getting very angry and impatient; but he would not give in, and insisted on doing more takes.

The final take was going well, and Elton hadn't made any mistakes, but Epps and Franks were getting very concerned that there wasn't sufficient tape to finish the recording. The song went on and on, and getting better and better, but Franks and Epps were getting more and more worried. "If the extremely unthinkable happened and I ran out of tape before he finished, my life wouldn't be worth living," recalled Epps. "Just as it looked like I was dead, he played an outro and the last chord then as the last chord died away the tape ran out. Clive and I nearly died anyway from relief."

Even though Elton had returned to recording, his live performances were few and far between, and were confined to charity functions with the encouragement of Reid and Osborne. "In early 1977, the only concerts we were doing were charity ones," confirmed Hill. "We went to Hawaii, and into a bar, and they were raising money for 'Save The Whale', so he said, tomorrow night set up a piano, and I'll do a couple of hours and, by word of mouth, the place was packed."

He also decided to do a concert for the *Goaldiggers Charity* that he had come involved with, due to his deep passion for football. Its aim was to create football pitches for children throughout the UK. The board included television personalities such as Jimmy Hill and Eric Morecambe, alongside Elton and Reid. However, he had no band. Johnstone and Newton Howard had formed their own outfit called China, so Elton decided he would get them to do it.

"Davey was, and still is, one of my closest friends," said Osborne, "and at that stage, Davey and Kiki were living together in LA, so when they came to England they stayed with me. I was a successful session singer, so I had been doing all the backing vocals on songs like 'Lamplight' and 'Gonna Make You A Star' for David Essex. I was also singing on a lot of jingles, and was on the telly all night and day, singing about Abbey National, Midland Bank, Ultra Brite, gas, electricity and the like. I also sung on songs like 'Sugar Baby Love' by The Rubettes, 'You Left Me Just When I Needed You Most' by Randy Vanwarmer, and 'You Can Make Me Dance' by Rod Stewart and The Faces. Rod and The Faces were my mates, because my band had toured supporting them, and my brother-in-law was the drummer Kenney Jones."

"So Elton asked me to do the backing vocals, and since I was also a vocal booker, he got me to book a couple of other singers for this one charity gig. I booked the two best singers that Britain had at that time, Chris Thompson who sang on 'Blinded By The Light' for Manfred Mann's Earth Band, as well as 'Thunderchild' on *The War Of The Worlds* album. Chris was living with a wonderful singer called Stevie Langer, and I had worked with both of them on sessions before. Stevie now does all the vocal coaching for boy bands, but she had a great ballsy, bluesy voice. Davey had always sung backing vocals for Elton, so we had a good vocal blend."

"During the rehearsals for the gig that was arranged to take place in November 1977, Elton was enjoying it so much that he did say to me, at one point, 'I'm going to announce the end of my retirement during the concert'. He also asked me, Chris and Stevie if we would go out on the road with him. I thought, 'Fuck me, would I like to go out on the road with Elton John?' I was on cloud nine. But just before the show, he was in a foul mood. I can't remember what it was about, but something happened backstage. He started ripping up the place and kicking around the flowers that had been sent to him. He kicked one of them, a big floral display and it did a cartwheel and landed face down in an amusing way. Elton had a wonderful sense of humour even when he was in a rage. In the midst of his fury, he had to ask his PA Bob Halley, whose bouquet he had kicked. It turned out to be the one that Bob himself had sent. Elton loved that."

Osborne didn't know about all the fuss going on backstage, because he was with the rest of the band in another dressing room. "The show is going on, and I am standing there and absolutely loving it," explained Osborne. "10,000 people were going crazy, and I was singing some great songs. I was waiting for the announcement that Elton was about to make his comeback and go back on the road and that we were the guys that he would be touring with, but then he said exactly the opposite. 'I'm never going to perform again' and I couldn't believe it, I'd been sacked before I had even started. He was very pale and pasty at that gig, and he wore black; a black bomber jacket and beret and I think he'd probably had a skin-full the night before. I went to see what had happened afterwards, but Bob said he was in a foul mood so I left him alone."

Elton was true to his word, and didn't do any gigs after that point, until his comeback on the *Single Man* tour, but continued to support the charity through the proceeds of a single that could only be bought through mail order called 'The Goaldiggers Song', and various charity football matches, which included guests from the music and film industries.

After the release of *A Single Man,* Elton emerged fully from his hiatus, and announced a world tour to promote his new album. As part of the tour in 1979, Elton was invited to go to the Soviet Union. He agreed, as he would become the first western rock star to tour the USSR. John Reid, together with Gosconcert, the USSR state agency responsible for entertainment, agreed that Elton - along with his long time percussionist Ray Cooper - would play Leningrad, followed by a concert in Moscow. These would essentially be a repeat of the gigs Elton and Cooper played at the Rainbow Theatre in London for the Queen's Jubilee eighteen months earlier that had re-kindled Elton's desire to tour again.

The Jubilee shows were arranged following a commitment Geoffrey Ellis made to the Queen's Jubilee Entertainments Committee, Sub-Committee on which Ellis was co-opted as the representative for popular music. As Ellis was still at Rocket, and John Reid was keen to get Elton back to work, the gigs were agreed, but on a more intimate basis with just Ray Cooper accompanying Elton on percussion for the second half of the set, the first being just Elton and his piano.

The opening night, of six consecutive gigs, was attended by Princess Alexandra and her husband, the Honourable Angus Ogilvy, who both thoroughly enjoyed the show alongside their hosts John Reid and Ellis. In fact, the Princess was so amazed at Elton's energy on stage that she asked him, after the show, whether he was taking any stimulants! The gigs were a success, and a signal for John Reid to organise an extensive *Single Man* tour, but in small intimate venues with just Elton, his piano and Ray Cooper providing percussion. The tour started in Glasgow in March 1979 and included six consecutive nights at the Theatre Royal Drury Lane, which saw fans queuing all night for the few tickets available, and eventually the tour went around the world, ending in America, and was billed as 'Back in the USSA' in the aftermath of the successful tour of the Soviet Union.

The Soviet shows were not as financially rewarding as a normal Elton John tour, but at least Gosconcert had arranged for all the transport and accommodation to be paid for by the Soviet regime. Not that they were staying in the plushest hotels or using the most luxurious transport. Only twelve of Elton's normally large entourage were allowed to travel. So the dozen strong party, including Ellis, Elton's parents and two journalists, took the arranged flight to Moscow on the Soviet airline, Aeroflot - not the carrier with the greatest safety record at the time.

When they landed, they were welcomed in typical Soviet style, and escorted by two female escorts, and a handsome young male called Sacha, to a train which included an additional carriage that was normally reserved for senior officials of the Soviet state. The carriage was small, and there wasn't enough room for all the entourage to have a cabin each, so there was some doubling up of compartments. Once the train reached Leningrad, the party were escorted to the less-than-palatial hotel and Elton prepared for the gig. The concert hall had excellent facilities, but Elton was playing to a select audience, hand-picked by the Soviet government from approved families and schools. They were instructed to be on their best behaviour.

That, however, was to be short-lived, and after a brief spell of polite applause during the start of the gig, Elton soon had them whipped into a frenzy with his music and energetic stage antics, which included standing up and kicking away his piano stool and playing. This caused much distress to the Soviet government onlookers, who warned Elton not to do it again, because it was damaging Soviet property. Elton ignored them and it became a deliberate part of his act.

After the gig, Elton was heralded a great success, and became an overnight sensation in the Soviet Union, creating yet another fan base. The next gig was in the Soviet capital Moscow, but before leaving Leningrad, Elton and his entourage had some time off and were escorted around the Hermitage Museum, and given the rare privilege of seeing some of the splendid gold and bejewelled artefacts from the past; something that even the Soviet people were not allowed to witness.

When the group reached Moscow it was in the peak of a heat wave and the hotel, which was not much better than the one in Leningrad, didn't have a very efficient air conditioning system which made it uncomfortable for everyone in the party. The gig went much the same as the Leningrad show, with a hand-picked audience. The after show entertainment was much more relaxed. The hotel was allowed to adopt a more cosmopolitan attitude and offered private drinks parties provided the customers paid in US dollars and were out of view from Soviet citizens.

Throughout the trip, Elton had a good time and was in high spirits. Part of this attitude was possibly due to the friendship he developed with Sacha and Elton confided to Ellis that he was somewhat smitten. To Elton's dismay, Sacha introduced him to his wife and children after the Moscow gig. The *Single Man* gigs were deemed a great success and Reid and Osborne hoped it would lead to the re-emergence of Elton John and a full band, once again.

When it came to the next album, *Victim Of Love*, Elton returned to the disco floor. It was produced by Pete Bellotte, fresh from his success with Donna Summer. He coincidentally, had known Elton during his days as Reg in Bluesology at the Star Club in Hamburg.

However, by this time, the disco movement was in decline, and was pushed even further into the background by a fight back from rock fans, who were rebelling against the disco culture. This culminated in a riot in Comisky Park in Chicago in July 1979, which has since been labelled, 'The day that disco died'. The album only reached 35 in the Billboard 200, and is probably the least successful album amongst those Elton had released during the period since *Empty Sky*. It was a strange album, because it didn't include any songs that were penned by Gary Osborne or Bernie Taupin. In fact, it only featured Elton on vocals, with session musicians being used for the recording.

And with that rather disappointing album, the 1970s came to a close. Sir Elton's career continued to rack up some most notable achievements in the decade that followed the demise of Tin Pan Alley, such as returning to his roots to re-form his classic line-up of Nigel Olsson, Dee Murray and Davey Johnstone, and giving his song writing a more versatile approach by using lyricists other than Bernie Taupin. However, many of his old friends and work colleagues (some of whom provided valuable insights for this book) have since become simple acquaintances and some may argue, that he lost much of the creative input that was provided by the characters that had helped build his career, that is open to debate.

If it has, it certainly hasn't affected his popularity. In fact, he has since built a new following who seem to know very little of the Elton John of the 1970s. This is partly due to Elton's willingness to reinvent himself and try different things, which takes him to musical markets he might not otherwise touch. As a senior member of rock's aristocracy he has always been on hand to help the emergence of other prolific singer-songwriters, such as Kate Bush. He still keeps in touch with today's music, always appearing to be very much in tune with the likes of current acts, such as the Scissor Sisters, Rumor, Lady Ga Ga and Plan B. Stuck in the past he is most certainly not. Equally, however, it would be hard for anyone to deny that it was his early years that shaped the man and his music.

If, like me (the author), you heard 'Rocket Man' for the first time in 1972, you may have thought, as I did, that Elton John came into the pop world fully formed, little realising the years of hard graft and frustration that led him to his well-deserved success. You would almost certainly not have been aware of Tin Pan Alley and its influence, either on popular music or on Elton himself. Yet without Tin Pan Alley, one can only take a guess which direction Reg Dwight's life or career might have taken.

Looking back over his most formative years is, as Terry Carty, Elton's colleague at DJM, correctly noted, like looking back to where it all began. Not only for Elton, but others before him, and since. "It all stems back to the Beatles and Tin Pan Alley. If it wasn't for the connection between Dick James and George Martin, and then Brian Epstein, DJM would not have had the publishing for the Beatles, and it was likely that DJM would have failed, and there would have been no Elton John."

♪ ♪ ♪

Gigology

Bluesology

My sincere thanks go to Nick Warburton for supplying a lot of the dates after scouring the pages of local UK newspapers. Other acts on the bill are in italics.

1965

09 March *Bo Street Runners*	100 Club, London
16 March *Bo Street Runners*	100 Club, London
06 April *Bo Street Runners*	100 Club, London
13 April *Bo Street Runners*	100 Club, London
15 April *Dae-B-Four*	Elms Club, South Harrow
20 April *Dae B-Four*	Elms Club, South Harrow
29 April	Elms Club, South Harrow
06 May	Elms Club, South Harrow
13 May	Elms Club, South Harrow
20 May	Elms Club, South Harrow
27 May	Elms Club, South Harrow
08 June *Bo Street Runners*	100 Club, London
July Audition for Roy Tempest Agency	The State Cinema, Kilburn
03 December *supporting Major Lance*	Flamingo Club, London
03 December *supporting Major Lance*	The In Place
04 December *supporting Major Lance*	Manchester
05 December *supporting Major Lance*	Dungeon Club, Nottingham
06 December *supporting Major Lance*	Rochester
07 December *supporting Major Lance*	Birdcage, Portsmouth
08 December *supporting Major Lance*	Bromley Court
09 December *supporting Major Lance*	Paddington, London
10 December *supporting Major Lance*	Durham University
11 December *supporting Major Lance*	Middlesborough
12 December *supporting Major Lance*	Stramarsh, Glasgow
14 December *supporting Major Lance*	Harlow, Essex
15 December *supporting Major Lance*	Discs a Gogo, London
16 December *supporting Major Lance*	Cromwellian, London
16 December *supporting Alan Price Set*	Marquee, London
17 December *supporting Major Lance*	Stockport, Tabernacle
18 December *supporting Major Lance*	Cue Club, Paddington
18 December Bluesology only	New All Star Club, London

19 December *supporting Major Lance*	Flamingo, London
19 December Bluesology only	El Partido, Lewisham, London
20 December *supporting Major Lance*	Cooks Ferry Inn, Edmonton, London

1966

04 January *supporting Patti La Belle and the Bluebelles*	Ready Steady Go
05 January *supporting Patti La Belle and the Bluebelles*	Scotch of St James, London
06 January *supporting Patti La Belle and the Bluebelles*	Cue Club, Paddington
07 January *supporting Patti La Belle and the Bluebelles*	Stramash, Glasgow
08 January *supporting Patti La Belle and the Bluebelles*	Oasis, Manchester
09 January *supporting Patti La Belle and the Bluebelles*	Flamingo, London
10 January *supporting Patti La Belle and the Bluebelles*	Scene at 6.30
11 January *supporting Patti La Belle and the Bluebelles*	5 O'Clock Club
11 January *supporting Patti La Belle and the Bluebelles*	Cromwellian, London
12 January *supporting Patti La Belle and the Bluebelles*	Discs A Gogo
14 January *supporting Patti La Belle and the Bluebelles*	Ready Steady Go
14 January *supporting Patti La Belle and the Bluebelles*	All Star Club
14 January *supporting Patti La Belle and the Bluebelles*	Flamingo Club, London
15 January *supporting Patti La Belle and the Bluebelles*	The Dungeon Club, Nottingham
15 January *supporting Patti La Belle and the Bluebelles*	Mojo Club, Sheffield
16 January *supporting Patti La Belle and the Bluebelles*	Plaza, Birmingham
19 January *supporting Patti La Belle and the Bluebelles*	Whole Scene Going
07 February *supporting Doris Troy*	Cavern Club, Liverpool
10 February *supporting Edwin Starr*	Cue Club, London
11 February *Doris Troy*	El Partido, Lewisham
11 February *with Herbie Goins and Nightimers*	Cue Club, Paddington
12 February *Doris Troy*	Oasis, Manchester
12 February *Doris Troy*	Twisted Wheel, Manchester
12 February *with Manchester Playboys/Doris Troy*	Oasis, Manchester
13 February *with The Chessmen/Doris Troy*	Flamingo, London
18 February *with Caribbean Show Band/ Doris Troy*	Club West Indies, London
18 February *supporting Doris Troy*	Golders Green, Refectory
19 February *with Captain First/Doris Troy*	New All Star Club, London
22 February *with Spencer Davis Group*	Marquee, London
1 to 31 March *with Linda Laine and the Sinners*	Top Ten Club Hamburg
12 April *with Manfred Mann*	Marquee, London
22 April *with Sands*	Marquee, London
03 May *supporting Patti La Belle and The Bluebelles*	The Birdland
04 May *supporting Patti La Belle and The Bluebelles*	Scotch of St James, London
05 May *supporting Patti La Belle and The Bluebelles*	Ram Jam, Brixton
06 May *supporting Patti La Belle and The Bluebelles*	Ricky Tick, Windsor
07 May *supporting Patti La Belle and The Bluebelles*	New All Star Club, London
08 May *Patti LaBelle/Polekatz*	Oasis, Manchester
09 May *supporting Patti La Belle and The Bluebelles*	Whisky a Go Go, London
13 May *Patti La Belle/The Gass*	Flamingo, London
14 May *Patti LaBelle/Ram Jam Band*	Twisted Wheel
17 May *Patti LaBelle/The Clayton Squares*	Marquee, London
17 May	Whisky a Go Go, London
21 May	Cue Club, Paddington
21 May *Patti La Belle/The Ultimates*	Rhodes Centre, Bishops Stortford
03 June *supporting The Inkspots*	West Ruislip RAF Camp
04 June *supporting The Inkspots*	Douglas House, London
04 June *supporting The Inkspots*	New All Star Club, London
05 June *supporting The Inkspots*	Plaza Ballrooms, Birmingham
07 June *supporting The Inkspots*	Whisky a Go Go, London

10 June *supporting The Inkspots*	Orchid, Purley
10 June *supporting The Inkspots*	New All Star Club, London
11 June *The Inkspots/Alan Bown Set*	Twisted Wheel, Manchester
12 June *supporting The Inkspots*	Riverboat, Gainsborough
13 June *supporting The Inkspots*	Douglas House London
15 June *supporting The Inkspots*	Riverboat, Gainsborough
16 June *supporting The Inkspots*	Locarno, Streatham
17 June *supporting The Inkspots*	Royal, Tottenham
18 June *supporting The Inkspots*	Marcam Hall, March
18 June *supporting The Inkspots*	Mojo Club, Sheffield
25 June	Marquee, London
08 July *with VIPs*	Marquee, London
14 July *with The Move*	Marquee, London
31 July	National Jazz & Blues Festival, Windsor
06 August *with The Soul Agents*	Marquee, London
11 August *with The Move*	Marquee, London
20 August *with The Soul Agents*	Marquee, London
29 August	Nottingham Blues Festival, Sherwood Rooms
September	Papagayos, St Tropez, France
06 September *with The Action*	Marquee, London
26 September *supporting Jimmy James and The Vagabonds*	Marquee, London
29 September *supporting Edwin Starr*	Twisted Wheel
07 October *with Gary Farr and the T Bones*	Marquee, London
20 October *with The Move*	Marquee, London
29 October *with The Herd*	Marquee, London
29 October *with David Bowie & The Buzz/LJB The Action*	Shoreline, Bognor Regis
12 November *with The Herd*	Marquee, London
?? November	Cromwellian, London
November/December	Sweden
11 December *supporting Little Richard, Alan Price Set*	Saville Theatre London
24 December	Cavendish Club
30 December *supporting Long John Baldry/ Good Goods*	Marquee, London
31 December *Long John Baldry*	Blue Moon, Cheltenham

1967

31 January *Long John Baldry*	Klooks Kleek, West Hampstead
18 February *Long John Baldry/Soul Concern*	Links Pavilion, Cromer
24 February *supporting Edwin Starr*	California Ballroom, Dunstable
17 March *Long John Baldry Show/Timebox*	Marquee, London
03 April *Long John Baldry Show*	The Feathers, Ealing
21 April *Long John Baldry Show/Timebox*	Marquee, London
22 April *Long John Baldry Show*	California Ballroom, Dunstable
2 May *Long John Baldry Show*	Klooks Kleek, West Hampstead
11 May	Klooks Kleek, West Hampstead
01 June *Long John Baldry Show/Peppers Machine*	Clouds, Derby (Derby College Rag Week)
09 June *Long John Baldry Show/C-Jam Blues*	Marquee, London
17 June *Long John Baldry/Soul Concern*	Links Pavilion, Cromer
14 July *Long John Baldry Show*	California Ballroom, Dunstable
16 July *Long John Baldry Show*	Starlight Ballroom, Greenford
21 July *with The Fix*	Twisted Wheel
28 July *Long John Baldry Show/ The Workshop*	Marquee, London
11 August *Long John Baldry Show*	Bluesville '67 Manor House, London
14 August *LJB Show/Jimmy Powell & The Dimensions*	Marquee, London
20 August *Long John Baldry Show*	Carlton Ballroom, Birmingham
26 August	New Star Club, London

29 August	Sherwood Rooms, Nottingham
03 September *Long John Baldry Show*	Beau Brummel Club, Nantwich
10 September *Long John Baldry Show*	Hotel Leofric, Coventry
12 September *Long John Baldry Show*	Klooks Kleek, West Hampstead
15 September *Long John Baldry Show*	Marquee, London
30 September *LJB Show / Dr. Marigolds Prescription*	California Ballroom, Dunstable
19 October *Long John Baldry Show*	Marquee, London
23 November *Long John Baldry Show / Nite People*	Marquee, London

1968

02 January *Long John Baldry Show*	Club Casino, South Shields
05 January *Long John Baldry Show*	Silver Blades, Streatham
07 January *Long John Baldry Show*	Mr Smith's Club, Manchester
30 January	Brave New World, Portsmouth
03 February *Long John Baldry Show*	Manchester College
14 February *Long John Baldry Show*	Victoria Club, Liverpool
23 February *LJB Show / Soul Finger*	Clockwork Orange, Chester
22 March *Long John Baldry Show*	Mecca, Basildon, Essex
26 March *LJB Show / Look Twice*	Mr Smith's Club, Winsford
30 April *LJB Show*	Marquee, London
05 May *Long John Baldry Show*	Garrick Club, Leigh
06 May *Long John Baldry Show*	Towers Club, Warrington
07-11 May *Long John Baldry Show*	Garrick Club, Leigh / Towers Club, Warrington
25 May *Long John Baldry Show*	Bosworth Park, Leicester
01 June *Long John Baldry Show*	York Race Course
04 October *supporting Paper Dolls w / Scott Walker, Casuals*	Astoria, Finsbury Park
05 October *supporting Paper Dolls w / Scott Walker, Casuals*	Odeon, Manchester
06 October *supporting Paper Dolls w / Scott Walker, Casuals*	Gaumont, Bradford
09 October *supporting Paper Dolls w / Scott Walker, Casuals*	ABC, Edinburgh
10 October *supporting Paper Dolls w / Scott Walker, Casuals*	City Hall, Newcastle
11 October *supporting Paper Dolls w / Scott Walker, Casuals*	Odeon, Birmingham
09 November *supporting Paperdolls*	California Ballroom, Dunstable
16 November *Paper Dolls / Music Hath Charms / Barries Magazine*	Links Pavilion, Cromer

* Elton's last gig with Bluesology was the show on 26 March but for the sake of completion, the remaining gigs the band did have also been included.

Elton John

Elton did not tour in 1969 but concentrated on session work. He reportedly went on stage with Hookfoot and they played some songs from *Empty Sky* but finding out which of these gigs he played at is virtually impossible as even the band can't remember. The only dates known are the radio sessions listed.

1968

28 October	Aolian Hall BBC Studio 2, London, UK
27 November	BBC Maida Vale Studio 4, London, UK

1969

11 July	Aolian Hall BBC Studio 2, London, UK
28 July	Camden Theatre, London, UK
30 September	BBC Maida Vale Studio 5, London, UK

1970

03 March	TV Studios – 'Hits a Go Go', Switzerland
25 March	The Revolution Club, London, UK
26 March	Aolian Studios BBC Studio 2, London, UK
02 April	BBC Studios, Top Of The Pops, London, UK
05 April	John Peel Concert, The BBC, London, UK
06 April	Dave Lee Travis Show, London, UK
21 April	The Roundhouse, London, UK
07 May	The Roundhouse, London, UK
09 May	Slough College, Slough, UK
22 May	BBC Television Centre, London, UK
05 June	The Marquee Club, London, UK
17 June	Lyceum Ballroom, London, UK
21 June	The Roundhouse, Chalk Farm, London, UK
25 June	(Stuart Henry Sounds of The 70's) Playhouse Theatre, London, UK
26 June	St Mary's College, Twickenham, UK
03 July	Haverstock Hill Country Club, Hampstead, London, UK
04 July	Speakeasy, London, UK
11 July	Knokke Festival, Knokke, Belgium
13 August	Playhouse Theatre, London, UK (Bob Harris Sounds of The 70's)
14 August	Krumlin Barkisland, Halifax, UK
15 August	Krumlin Barkisland, Halifax, UK
25 August	Troubadour Club, Los Angeles, California, USA

26 August	Troubadour Club, Los Angeles, California, USA
27 August	Troubadour Club, Los Angeles, California, USA
28 August	Troubadour Club, Los Angeles, California, USA
29 August	Troubadour Club, Los Angeles, California, USA
30 August	Troubadour Club, Los Angeles, California, USA
08 September	Bay Arena, San Francisco, California, USA
11 September	Electric Factory, Philadelphia, Pennsylvania, USA
12 September	Electric Factory, Philadelphia, Pennsylvania, USA
19 September	The Playboy Club, New York, USA
05 October	Royal Albert Hall, London, UK
29 October	Boston Tea Party, Boston, Massachusetts, USA
30 October	Boston Tea Party, Boston, Massachusetts, USA
31 October	Boston Tea Party, Boston, Massachusetts, USA
06 November	Electric Factory, Philadelphia, Pennsylvania, USA
07 November	Electric Factory, Philadelphia, Pennsylvania, USA
08 November	The Mill Run Theatre, Baltimore, Maryland, USA
12 November	Fillmore West, San Francisco, California, USA
13 November	Fillmore West, San Francisco, California, USA
14 November	Fillmore West, San Francisco, California, USA
15 November	Santa Monica Civic Auditorium, Los Angeles, California, USA
17 November	A&R Studios, New York, USA (live recording of *17.11.70* album)
19 November	The David Frost Show, New York, USA
20 November	Fillmore East, New York, USA
21 November	Fillmore East, New York, USA
22 November	University Of Bridgeport, Bridgeport, Connecticut, USA
23 November	Glassboro State College, Glassboro, New Jersey, USA
25 November	Auditorium Theatre, Chicago, Illinois, USA
26 November	Music Hall , Cleveland, Ohio, USA
27 November	East Town Theatre, Detroit, Michigan, USA
28 November	East Town Theatre, Detroit, Michigan, USA
29 November	Guthrie Theatre, Minneapolis, Minnesota, USA
02 December	War Memorial Coliseum, Syracuse, New York, USA
04 December	Anaheim Convention Centre, Anaheim, California, USA
05 December	Swing Auditorium, San Bernadino, California, USA
11 December	The Andy Williams Show, New York, USA
20 December	The Roundhouse, London, UK

1971

02 January	Mothers, Birmingham, UK (Formerly The Carlton Ballroom)
03 January	Pavilion, Hemel Hempstead, UK
08 January	Haverstock Hill Country Club, Hampstead, London, UK
10 January	Guildford Civic Hall, Guildford, UK
11 January	Winter Gardens, Cleethorpes, UK
13 January	City Hall, Hull, UK
15 January	Southampton University, Southampton, UK
16 January	Loughborough University, Loughborough, UK
27 January	Philharmonic Hall, Liverpool, UK
29 January	University of Lancaster, Lancaster, UK
30 January	Regent Theatre Concert Hall, Brighton, UK
31 January	The Fox, Croydon, UK
01 February	Cooks Ferry Inn, Edmonton, London, UK
05 February	Students Union Main Hall, Coventry, UK (Lanchester Arts Festival)
06 February	Leeds University, Leeds, UK
09 February	Bumpers Nightclub, London, UK
12 February	Stirling University, Stirling, UK
13 February	Stratchclyde University, Glasgow, UK

14 February	Kinema Ballroom, Dunfermline, UK
20 February	Newcastle City Hall, Newcastle, UK
24 February	Imperial College, London, UK
26 February	Brunel University, Uxbridge, UK
27 February	Bradford University, Bradford, UK
01 March	Tivoli Gardens, Copenhagen, Denmark
03 March	Royal Festival Hall, London, UK
06 March	Leicester University, Leicester, UK
13 March	Kingston Polytechnic, Kingston Upon Thames, London, UK
14 March	Colston Hall, Bristol, UK
20 March	University College, London, UK
27 March	Dagenham Roundhouse, Dagenham, UK
21 March	Fairfield Hall, Croydon, UK
02 April	Loews Theatre, Providence, Rhode Island, USA
03 April	Boston Music Hall, Boston, Massachusetts, USA
07 April	The Spectrum, Philadelphia, Pennsylvania, USA
08 April	Fillmore East, New York, USA
09 April	Fillmore East, New York, USA
10 April	Fillmore East, New York, USA
11 April	Painters Mill Music Fair, Owings Mills, Maryland, USA
13 April	Auditorium Theatre, Chicago, Illinois, USA
14 April	Auditorium Theatre, Chicago, Illinois, USA
15 April	Auditorium Theatre, Chicago, Illinois, USA
16 April	University Of Detroit Fieldhouse, Detroit, Michigan, USA
17 April	Veterans Memorial Auditorium, Columbus, Ohio, USA
18 April	Cincinnati Music Hall, Cincinnati, Ohio, USA
20 April	Civic Auditorium, Omaha, Nebraska, USA
21 April	Memorial Coliseum, Portland, Oregon, USA
23 April	Agrodome Theatre, Vancouver, British Columbia, Canada
24 April	Centre Coliseum, Seattle, Washington, USA
01 May	Hawaii International Centre, Honolulu, Hawaii, USA
09 May	Civic Auditorium, San Francisco, California, USA
11 May	Memorial Auditorium, Sacramento, California. USA
12 May	Convention Centre, Fresno, California, USA
14 May	Convention Centre, Anaheim, California, USA
15 May	Arizona Veterans Memorial Coliseum, Phoenix, Arizona, USA
16 May	Denver Municipal Auditorium, Denver, Colorado, USA
17 May	University Of Colorado, Boulder, Colorado, USA
19 May	Civic Centre Music Hall, Oklahoma City, Oklahoma, USA
20 May	Sam Houston Coliseum, Houston, Texas, USA
21 May	Municipal Auditorium, San Antonio, Texas, USA
22 May	Fair Park Music Hall, Dallas, Texas, USA
23 May	Fair Park Music Hall, Dallas, Texas, USA
24 May	Tarrant County Theatre, Fort Worth, Texas, USA
26 May	The Warehouse, New Orleans, Louisiana, USA
28 May	Curtis Hixon Auditorium, Tampa, Florida, USA
29 May	Jai Alai Arena, Miami, Florida, USA
30 May	Coliseum, Jacksonville, Florida, USA
04 June	Kiel Auditorium, St. Louis, Missouri, USA
05 June	Ellis Auditorium, Memphi, Tennessee, USA
06 June	Convention Centre, Louisville, Kentucky, USA
08 June	Municipal Auditorium, Atlanta, Georgia, USA
10 June	Carnegie Hall, New York, USA
11 June	Carnegie Hall, New York, USA
12 June	Cleveland Arena, Cleveland, Ohio, USA

13 June	Rhode Island Auditorium, Providence, Rhode Island, USA
16 June	Merriweather Post Pavilion, Columbia, Maryland, USA
18 June	Farm Show Arena, Harrisburg, Pennsylvania, USA
08 July	Liseberg Park, Liseberg, Sweden
31 July	Crystal Palace Bowl, London, UK
26 August	Onondaga War Memorial, Syracuse, New York, USA
27 August	Unknown Venue, Wildwood, New Jersey, USA
28 August	Convention Hall, Asbury Park, New Jersey, USA
30 August	Marcus Amphitheatre, Milwaukee, Wisconsin, USA
02 September	Performing Arts Centre, Saratoga Springs, New York, USA
03 September	Onondaga War Memorial, Syracuse, New York, USA
04 September	Rochester War Memorial, Rochester, New York, USA
06 September	The Greek Theatre, Los Angeles, California, USA
07 September	The Greek Theatre, Los Angeles, California, USA
08 September	The Greek Theatre, Los Angeles, California, USA
09 September	The Greek Theatre, Los Angeles, California, USA
11 September	The Greek Theatre, Los Angeles, California, USA
12 September	The Greek Theatre, Los Angeles, California, USA
15 September	Convention Centre, Las Vegas, Nevada, USA
16 September	Fairgrounds Pavilion, Reno, Nevada, USA
05 October	Shibuya Kohkaido, Tokyo, Japan
06 October	Shibuya Kohkaido, Tokyo, Japan
07 October	Kosei Nenkin Hall, Osaka, Japan
08 October	Kosei Nenkin Hall, Osaka, Japan
10 October	Shinjuku Kohsei Nenkin Hall, Tokyo, Japan
11 October	Shinjuku Kohsei Nenkin Hall, Tokyo, Japan
16 October	Subiaco Stadium, Perth, Australia
24 October	Kooyong Stadium, Melbourne, Victoria, Australia
26 October	QLD Tennis Courts, Brisbane, Australia
29 October	Western Springs Stadium, Auckland, New Zealand
31 October	Sydney Festival, Sydney, New South Wales, Australia
21 November	Coventry Theatre, Coventry, UK
22 November	Free Trade Hall, Manchester, UK
24 November	De Montfort Hall, Leicester, UK
26 November	Winter Gardens, Bournemouth, UK
27 November	ABC Theatre, Plymouth, UK
28 November	Colston Hall, Bristol, UK
03 December	Town Hall, Birmingham, UK
04 December	Dome, Brighton, UK
05 December	Fairfield Hall, Croydon, UK
10 December	City Hall, Newcastle, UK
11 December	ABC Theatre, Stockton On Tees, UK
16 December	Town Hall, Leeds, UK
17 December	City Hall, Sheffield, UK
24 December	City Hall, Sheffield, UK

1972

05 February	Royal Festival Hall, London, UK
19 February	University of Lancaster, Lancaster, UK
20 February	Shaw Theatre, National Youth Theatre, London, UK
23 February	Exeter University, Exeter, UK
24 February	Town Hall, Watford, UK
26 February	Waltham Forest Technical College, Waltham Forest, London, UK
27 February	Shaw Theatre, National Youth Theatre, London, UK
01 March	The Music Hall, Aberdeen, UK
02 March	Caird Hall, Dundee, UK

03 March	Kelvin Hall, Glasgow, UK
04 March	Empire Theatre, Edinburgh, UK
12 March	Frankfurt Theatre, Frankfurt, Germany
14 March	Sporting Club, Monte Carlo, Monaco
15 March	Sporting Club, Monte Carlo, Monaco
17 March	Unknown Venue, Hamburg, Germany
19 March	Deutschlandhalle, Berlin, Germany
20 March	Frankfurt Theatre, Frankfurt, Germany
21 March	BBC Studios, Top Of The Pops, London, UK
27 April	Convention Centre-Baylon Uni, Waco, Texas, USA
28 April	The Sam Houston Coliseum, Houston, Texas, USA
29 April	Sun Bowl, El Paso, Texas, USA
30 April	Austin College, Austin, Texas, USA
02 May	Merriweather Post Pavilion, Columbia, Maryland, USA
03 May	Notre Dame, South Bend, Indiana, USA
04 May	Unknown Venue, East Lansing, Michigan, USA
05 May	Memorial Gym, Kent State University, Cleveland, Ohio, USA
06 May	St. John Arena, Columbus, Ohio, USA
07 May	Millett Hall, Oxford, Ohio, USA
08 May	Aire Crown Theatre, Chicago, Illinois, USA
09 May	Aire Crown Theatre, Chicago, Illinois, USA
10 May	Assembly Hall, Urbana, Illinois, USA
12 May	Southern Illinois University, Illinois, USA
13 May	Northern Illinois University, Illinois, USA
14 May	University of Wisconsin, Madison, Wisconsin, USA
15 May	St Cloud University, Minneapolis, Minnesota, UA
16 May	University of Texas, Austin, Texas, USA
03 June	Crystal Palace Bowl, London, UK
26 August	The Guildhall, Portsmouth, UK
27 August	Shaw Theatre, London, UK
31 August	City Hall, Newcastle, UK
01 September	Free Trade Hall, Manchester, UK
03 September	Fairfield Hall, Croydon, UK
08 September	Green's Playhouse, Glasgow, UK
10 September	New Theatre, Oxford, UK
17 September	Shaw Theatre, London, UK
26 September	Cornell University, Ithica, New York, USA
27 September	Music Hall, Boston, Massachusetts, USA
28 September	Music Hall, Boston, Massachusetts, USA
29 September	New Haven Arena, New Haven, Connecticut, USA
30 September	The Spectrum, Philadelphia, Pennsylvania, USA
01 October	Memorial Auditorium, Rochester, New York, USA
02 October	The Forum, Montreal, Quebec, Canada
05 October	Maple Leaf Gardens, Toronto, Ontario, Canada
06 October	Cobo Hall, Detroit, Michigan, USA
07 October	Memorial Auditorium, Buffalo, New York, USA
09 October	Nassau Coliseum, Uniondale, New York, USA
11 October	Illinois State University, Horton Fieldhouse, Normal, Illinois, USA
12 October	Cultural Centre, Wichita, Kansas, USA
14 October	Iowa State University, Ames, Iowa, USA
15 October	Municipal Auditorium, Denver, Colorado, USA
17 October	Anaheim Convention Centre, Anaheim, California, USA
18 October	Hawaii International Centre, Honolulu, Hawaii, USA
20 October	Seattle Centre Coliseum, Seattle, Washington, USA
21 October	Community Theatre, Berkeley, California, USA

22 October	Convention Centre, Anaheim, California, USA
23 October	The Forum, Los Angeles, California, USA
24 October	The Forum, Los Angeles, California, USA
25 October	Berkeley Community Theatre, Berkeley, California, USA
26 October	Civic Plaza, Tucson, Arizona, USA
27 October	Sports Arena, San Diego, California, USA
30 October	Palladium, London, UK
01 November	Oklahoma State University, Stillwater, Oklahoma, USA
02 November	Assembly Centre, Tulsa, Oklahoma, USA
03 November	Fairgrounds Arena, Oklahoma City, Oklahoma, USA
04 November	Municipal Auditorium, Kansas City, Missouri, USA
05 November	Memorial Auditorium, Dallas, Texas, USA
08 November	Texas A and M, College Station, Texas, USA
09 November	Municipal Auditorium, San Antonio, Texas, USA
10 November	Louisiana State University, Baton Rouge, Louisiana, USA
11 November	Mid South Coliseum, Memphis, Tennessee, USA
12 November	Memorial Auditorium, Nashville, Tennessee, USA
13 November	Scope Auditorium, Norfolk, Virginia, USA
14 November	University Of Alabama, Tuscaloosa, Alabama, USA
15 November	Atlanta Coliseum, Atlanta, Georgia, USA
16 November	Charlotte Coliseum, Charlotte, North Carolina, USA
17 November	Civic Centre, Charleston, West Virginia, USA
18 November	Hampton Roads Coliseum, Hampton, Virginia, USA
19 November	Carnegie Hall, New York, USA
20 November	Carnegie Hall, New York, USA
21 November	Civic Centre, Baltimore, Maryland, USA
22 November	State Farm Arena, Harrisburg, Pennsylvania, USA
24 November	Jacksonville Coliseum, Jacksonville, Florida, USA
25 November	Jai Alai Arena, Miami, Florida, USA
26 November	Bay Front Centre, St.Petersburg, Florida, USA

1973

20 January	Carneige Hall, New York, USA
24 February	Starlight Rooms, Boston, UK
25 February	Greens Playhouse, Glasgow, UK
28 February	Town Hall, Birmingham, UK
01 March	DeMontfort Hall, Leicester, UK
02 March	Empire Theatre, Liverpool, UK
03 March	Empire Theatre, Liverpool, UK
06 March	Guildhall, Preston, UK
07 March	City Hall, Newcastle, UK
09 March	City Hall, Sheffield, UK
10 March	Leeds University, Leeds, UK
11 March	Leeds University, Leeds, UK
12 March	Imperial College, London, UK
15 March	Colston Hall, Bristol, UK
16 March	Dome, Brighton, UK
17 March	Winter Gardens, Bournemouth, UK
18 March	Guildhall, Southampton, UK
22 March	Sundown, Edmonton, East London, UK
23 March	Sundown, Edmonton, East London, UK
24 March	Sundown, Brixton, South London, UK
25 March	Coventry Theatre, Coventry, UK
26 March	Hard Rock, Manchester, UK
27 March	Hard Rock, Manchester, UK
11 April	Sport Palace, Napoli, Italy

12 April	Sport Palace, Rome, Italy
13 April	Vigorelli Velodrome, Milan, Italy
14 April	Community Stadium, Firenze, Italy
15 April	Bologna Stadium, Bologna, Italy
18 April	Sport Palace, Torino, Italy
19 April	Sport Palace, Genova, Italy
24 April	Marquee Club, London, UK
25 April	Marquee Club, London, UK
15 August	Municipal Auditorium, Mobile, Alabama, USA
16 August	The Sam Houston Coliseum, Houston, Texas, USA
17 August	Hemisphere Arena, San Antonio, Texas, USA
18 August	Cotton Bowl, Dallas, Texas, USA
19 August	Arrowhead Stadium, Kansas City, Missouri, USA
23 August	Metropolitan Sports Centre, Minneapolis, Minnesota, USA
24 August	Chicago Amphitheatre, Chicago, Illinois, USA
25 August	Chicago Amphitheatre, Chicago, Illinois, USA
26 August	Iowa State Fairgrounds, Des Moines, Iowa, USA
28 August	University of Special Events Centre, Salt Lake City, Utah, USA
30 August	Portland Memorial Coliseum, Portland, Oregon, USA
31 August	Seattle Centre Coliseum, Seattle, Washington, USA
01 September	Balboa Stadium, San Diego, California, USA
02 September	The Coliseum, Denver, Colorado, USA
03 September	University Arena, Albuquerque, New Mexico, USA
04 September	Big Surf, Phoenix, Arizona, USA
07 September	Hollywood Bowl, Los Angeles, California, USA
08 September	Long Beach Arena, Long Beach, California, USA
09 September	Oakland Coliseum, Oakland, Maryland, USA
10 September	The Coliseum, Vancouver, British Columbia, Canada
17 September	International Centre, Honolulu, Hawaii, USA
21 September	Greensboro Coliseum, Greensboro, North Carolina, USA
22 September	Braves Stadium, Atlanta, Georgia, USA
23 September	Madison Square Garden, New York, USA
24 September	Nassau Coliseum, New York, USA
25 September	Boston Gardens, Boston, Massachusetts, USA
28 September	The Spectrum, Philadelphia, Pennsylvania, USA
29 September	Richmond Coliseum, Richmond, Virginia, USA
30 September	Civic Centre, Baltimore, Maryland, USA
03 October	University of Dayton Arena, Dayton, Ohio, USA
04 October	Kiel Auditorium, St Louis, Missouri, USA
05 October	Cobo Hall, Detroit, Michigan, USA
06 October	St John Arena (Ohio State University), Columbus, Ohio, USA
07 October	Indiana University Assembly Hall, Bloomington, Indiana, USA
09 October	Civic Arena, Pittsburgh, Pennsylvania, USA
11 October	Mid South Coliseum, Memphis, Tennessee, USA
12 October	Mid Tennessee State University, Murfreesboro, Tennessee, USA
13 October	University of Tennessee Stokely Athletic Centre, Knoxville, Tennessee, USA
14 October	Hampton Colliseum, Hampton, Virginia, USA
18 October	Memorial Stadium, Auburn, Alabama, USA
19 October	University of Georgia, Athens, Georgia, USA
20 October	Hollywood Sportatorium, Hollywood, Florida, USA
21 October	Ben Hill Griffin Stadium, University of Florida, Gainesville, Florida, USA
25 October	U.G.A Coliseum, Atlanta, Georgia, USA
27 November	Colston Hall, Bristol, UK
29 November	Belle Vue, Manchester, UK
08 December	Empire Theatre, Liverpool, UK

10 December	The Apollo Theatre, Glasgow, UK
11 December	The Apollo Theatre, Glasgow, UK
12 December	City Hall, Newcastle, UK
15 December	American School, London, UK
16 December	Town Hall, Birmingham, UK
17 December	Town Hall, Birmingham, UK
20 December	Hammersmith Odeon, London, UK
21 December	Hammersmith Odeon, London, UK
22 December	Hammersmith Odeon, London, UK
23 December	Hammersmith Odeon, London, UK
24 December	Hammersmith Odeon, London, UK

1974

01 February	Budokan, Tokyo, Japan
02 February	Budokan, Tokyo, Japan
03 February	Kosei Nenkin Hall, Osaka, Japan
04 February	Kosei Nenkin Hall, Osaka, Japan
05 February	Kosei Nenkin Hall, Osaka, Japan
07 February	Kyuden Kinen Tallkukan, Fukuoka, Japan
08 February	Yubin Chokin Hall, Hiroshima, Japan
09 February	Kyoto Kaikan, Kyoto, Japan
10 February	Festival Hall, Osaka, Japan
11 February	Civic Hall, Nagoya, Japan
13 February	Shinjuku Kohsei Nenkin Hall, Tokyo, Japan
21 February	South Melbourne Football Ground, Melbourne, Australia
28 February	Western Springs Stadium, Auckland, New Zealand
14 March	Randwick Racecourse, Randwick, Australia
18 March	WACA Grounds, Perth, Australia
05 May	Watford Football Club, Watford, UK *Watford F.C Benefit Concert*
18 May	Royal Festival Hall, London, UK *Invalid Children's Aid Society Benefit*
27 May	Empire Pool Wembley, London, UK

North American Tour with Kiki Dee

25 September	Dallas Convention Centre, Dallas, Texas, USA
26 September	Hofheinz Pavilion, Houston, Texas, USA
27 September	Municipal Auditorium Mobile, Alabama, USA
28 September	Memorial Coliseum, Tuscaloosa, Alabama, USA
29 September	Louisiana State University, Baton Rouge Louisiana, USA
03 October	The Forum, Los Angeles, California, USA
04 October	The Forum, Los Angeles, California, USA
05 October	The Forum, Los Angeles, California, USA
08 October	The Forum, Los Angeles, California, USA
09 October	Cow Palace, San Francisco, California, USA
10 October	Oakland Coliseum, Oakland, California, USA
12 October	Seattle Centre Coliseum, Seattle, Washington, USA
13 October	Seattle Centre Coliseum, Seattle, Washington, USA
14 October	Pacific Coliseum, Vancouver, British Columbia, Canada
15 October	Memorial Coliseum, Portland, Oregon, USA
26 October	Hawaii International Centre, Honolulu, Hawaii, USA
27 October	Hawaii International Centre, Honolulu, Hawaii, USA
30 October	St. Louis Arena, St. Louis, Missouri, USA
31 October	Civic Centre, St. Paul, Minnesota, USA
01 November	Chicago Stadium, Chicago, Illinois, USA
02 November	Chicago Stadium, Chicago, Illinois, USA
03 November	Ohio State University, Columbus, Ohio, USA

04 November	Cleveland Coliseum, Cleveland, Ohio, USA
08 November	Greensboro Coliseum, Greensboro, North Carolina, USA
09 November	Stokely Athletic Centre, Knoxville, Tennessee, USA
10 November	The Omni, Atlanta, Georgia, USA
12 November	Civic Arena ,Pittsburgh, Pennsylvania, USA
13 November	Cincinnati Gardens, Cincinnati, Ohio, USA
14 November	Olympia Stadium, Detroit, Michigan, USA
15 November	Olympia Stadium, Detroit, Michigan, USA
17 November	The Forum, Quebec, Montreal, Canada
18 November	Maple Leaf Gardens, Toronto, Ontario, Canada
20 November	Boston Garden, Boston, Massachusetts, USA
21 November	Capitol Centre, Largo, Maryland, USA
22 November	Capitol Centre, Largo, Maryland, USA
23 November	Veterans Memorial Coliseum, New Haven, Connecticut, USA
28 November	Madison Square Garden, New York, USA *Guest appearance by John Lennon*
29 November	Madison Square Garden, New York, USA
30 November	Nassau Coliseum, Uniondale, New York, USA
01 December	Nassau Coliseum, Uniondale, New York, USA
02 December	The Spectrum, Philadelphia. Pennsylvania, USA
03 December	The Spectrum, Philadelphia. Pennsylvania, USA
20 December	Hammersmith Odeon, London, UK
21 December	Hammersmith Odeon, London, UK
22 December	Hammersmith Odeon, London, UK
23 December	Hammersmith Odeon, London, UK
24 December	Hammersmith Odeon, London, UK

1975

21 June	Wembley Stadium, London, UK
29 June	Oakland Coliseum, Oakland, California, USA
20 July	Hughes Stadium, Fort Collins, Colorado, USA
09 August	Civic Auditorium, Santa Monica, California, USA
25 August	Troubadour Club, Los Angeles, California, USA
26 August	Troubadour Club, Los Angeles, California, USA
27 August	Troubadour Club, Los Angeles, California, USA
29 September	Sports Arena, San Diego, California, USA
01 October	Community Centre Arena, Tucson, Arizona, USA
02 October	Convention Centre, Las Vegas, Nevada, USA
03 October	Arizona State University, Tempe, Arizona, USA
05 October	McNichols Arena, Denver, Colorado, USA
06 October	McNichols Arena, Denver, Colorado, USA
07 October	Special Events Centre, University of Utah, Salt Lake City, Utah, USA
12 October	Pacifice Coliseum, Vancouver, British Columbia, Canada
13 October	Pacifice Coliseum, Vancouver, British Columbia, Canada
14 October	Memorial Coliseum, Portland, Oregon, USA
16 October	Centre Coliseum, Seattle, Washington, USA
17 October	Centre Coliseum, Seattle, Washington, USA
19 October	Coliseum, Oakland, California, USA
20 October	Coliseum, Oakland, California, USA
21 October	Coliseum, Oakland, California, USA
25 October	Dodgers Stadium, Los Angeles, California, USA
26 October	Dodgers Stadium, Los Angeles, California, USA

1976

29 April	Grand Theatre, Leeds, UK
30 April	Grand Theatre, Leeds, UK
01 May	Belle Vue, Manchester, UK

02 May	Guildhall, Preston, UK
03 May	Empire Theatre, Liverpool, UK
04 May	Empire Theatre, Liverpool, UK
05 May	De Montfort Hall, Leicester, UK
06 May	Victoria Hall, Hanley, UK
07 May	Civic Hall, Wolverhampton, UK
09 May	Fairfield Hall, Croydon, UK
11 May	Earls Court, London, UK
12 May	Earls Court, London, UK
13 May	Earls Court, London, UK
14 May	Baileys, Watford, UK
16 May	Odeon, Birmingham, UK
17 May	Odeon, Birmingham, UK
18 May	City Hall, Sheffield, UK
20 May	City Hall, Newcastle, UK
21 May	Usher Hall, Edinburgh, UK
22 May	Caird Hall, Dundee, UK
24 May	Apollo Theatre, Glasgow, UK
25 May	Apollo Theatre, Glasgow, UK
27 May	New Theatre, Coventry, UK
28 May	New Theatre, Coventry, UK
29 May	Gaumont Theatre, Southampton, UK
30 May	Odeon, Taunton, UK
31 May	Hippodrome, Bristol, UK
01 June	Hippodrome, Bristol, UK
03 June	Capitol, Cardiff, UK
04 June	Capitol, Cardiff, UK
29 June	RFK Stadium, Washington, Columbia, USA
30 June	Capital Centre, Largo, Maryland, USA
01 July	Capital Centre, Largo, Maryland, USA
04 July	Schaefer Stadium, Foxboro, Massachusetts, USA
06 July	The Spectrum, Philadelphia, Pennsylvania, USA
07 July	The Spectrum, Philadelphia, Pennsylvania, USA
08 July	The Spectrum, Philadelphia, Pennsylvania, USA
11 July	Pontiac Silverdome, Detroit, Michigan, USA
13 July	Greensboro Coliseum, Greensboro, North Carolina, USA
14 July	Charlotte Coliseum, Charlotte, North Carolina, USA
16 July	The Omni, Atlanta, Georgia, USA
18 July	Memorial Coliseum, Tuscaloosa, Alabama, USA
20 July	Freedom Hall, Louisville, Kentucky, USA
21 July	Market Square Arena, Indianapolis, Indiana, USA
24 July	Civic Centre, St Paul, Minnesota, USA
26 July	Chicago Stadium, Chicago, Illinois, USA
27 July	Chicago Stadium, Chicago, Illinois, USA
28 July	Chicago Stadium, Chicago, Illinois, USA
01 August	Richfield Coliseum, Richfield, Ohio, USA
02 August	Richfield Coliseum, Richfield, Ohio, USA
03 August	Cincinnati Gardens, Cincinnati, Ohio, USA
07 August	Rich Stadium, Buffalo, New York, USA
10 August	Madison Square Garden, New York, USA
11 August	Madison Square Garden, New York, USA
12 August	Madison Square Garden, New York, USA
13 August	Madison Square Garden, New York, USA
15 August	Madison Square Garden, New York, USA
16 August	Madison Square Garden, New York, USA

17 August	Madison Square Garden, New York, USA
17 September	Playhouse, Edinburgh, UK

1977

02 May	Rainbow Theatre, London, UK
03 May	Rainbow Theatre, London, UK
04 May	Rainbow Theatre, London, UK
05 May	Rainbow Theatre, London, UK
06 May	Rainbow Theatre, London, UK
07 May	Rainbow Theatre, London, UK
17 June	Shoreditch College Chapel, Egham, UK
01 August	Central Park, New York, USA
03 November	Empire Pool, Wembley, London, UK

1978

14 October	New York Plaza, New York, USA
20 October	RTL Studios, Paris, France
02 November	Hilton Hotel, London, UK

1979

05 February	Concerthaus, Stockholm, Sweden
06 February	Concerthaus, Stockholm, Sweden
07 February	Tivoli, Copenhagen, Denmark
08 February	Tivoli, Copenhagen, Denmark
10 February	Musikhalle, Hamburg, Germany
11 February	Congressgebau, Le Hague, Netherlands
12 February	Doelen, Rotterdam, Netherlands
14 February	Concertgebau, Amsterdam, Netherlands
15 February	Mozartsaal, Mannheim, Germany
16 February	Deutschen Museum, Munich, Germany
18 February	Kongresshalle, Berlin, Germany
19 February	Opera House, Cologne, Germany
20 February	Theatre De Champs Elysees, Paris, France
21 February	Theatre De Champs Elysees, Paris, France
22 February	Theatre De Champs Elysees, Paris, France
23 February	Theatre De Champs Elysees, Paris, France
24 February	Theatre De Champs Elysees, Paris, France
25 February	Theatre De Champs Elysees, Paris, France
26 February	Queen Elizabeth Hall, Antwerp, Belgium
27 February	Queen Elizabeth Hall, Antwerp, Belgium
01 March	Philipshalle, Dusseldorf, Germany
02 March	RheinMain Halle, Wiesbaden, Germany
03 March	Theatre Di Beaulieu, Lausanne, Switzerland
04 March	Theatre Di Beaulieu, Lausanne, Switzerland
06 March	Theatre De Verdure, Nice, France
07 March	Theatre De Verdure, Nice, France
09 March	Pavello del Joventud de Badalona, Barcelona, Spain
10 March	Pavello del Joventud de Badalona, Barcelona, Spain
11 March	The Real Madrid Pavilion, Madrid, Spain
17 March	Apollo Theatre, Glasgow, UK
18 March	Apollo Theatre, Glasgow, UK
19 March	Odeon Theatre, Edinburgh, UK
21 March	City Hall, Newcastle, UK
22 March	City Hall, Newcastle, UK
23 March	Guild Hall, Preston, UK
26 March	Whitla Hall, Belfast, UK

27 March	Whitla Hall, Belfast, UK
29 March	National Stadium, Dublin, Ireland
30 March	National Stadium, Dublin, Ireland
02 April	Theatre Royal Drury Lane, London, UK
03 April	Theatre Royal Drury Lane, London, UK
04 April	Theatre Royal Drury Lane, London, UK
05 April	Theatre Royal Drury Lane, London, UK
06 April	Theatre Royal Drury Lane, London, UK
07 April	Theatre Royal Drury Lane, London, UK
09 April	Dome, Brighton, UK
10 April	Dome, Brighton, UK
11 April	Gaumont Theatre, Southampton, UK
12 April	Gaumont Theatre, Southampton, UK
14 April	Hippodrome, Bristol, UK
15 April	Hippodrome, Bristol, UK
17 April	Oxford Theatre, Oxford, UK
18 April	Coventry Theatre, Coventry, UK
19 April	Assembly Rooms, Derby, UK
21 April	Hippodrome, Birmingham, UK
22 April	Hippodrome, Birmingham, UK
24 April	Apollo, Manchester, UK
25 April	Apollo, Manchester, UK
26 April	Apollo, Manchester, UK
01 May	Philharmonic Hall, Jerusalem, Israel
02 May	Philharmonic Hall, Jerusalem, Israel
03 May	Philharmonic Hall, Jerusalem, Israel
05 May	Mann Auditorium, Tel Aviv, Israel
06 May	Mann Auditorium, Tel Aviv, Israel
21 May	Great October Hall, Leningrad, USSR
22 May	Great October Hall, Leningrad, USSR
23 May	Great October Hall, Leningrad, USSR
24 May	Great October Hall, Leningrad, USSR
25 May	Rossya Hotel Concert Hall, Moscow, USSR
26 May	Rossya Hotel Concert Hall, Moscow, USSR
27 May	Rossya Hotel Concert Hall, Moscow, USSR
28 May	Rossya Hotel Concert Hall, Moscow, USSR
19 September	Gammage Auditorium, Tempe, Arizona, USA
20 September	Gammage Auditorium, Tempe, Arizona, USA
22 September	Community Theatre, Berkeley, California, USA
23 September	Community Theatre, Berkeley, California, USA
24 September	Community Theatre, Berkeley, California, USA
26 September	Universal Amphitheatre, Los Angeles, California, USA
27 September	Universal Amphitheatre, Los Angeles, California, USA
28 September	Universal Amphitheatre, Los Angeles, California, USA
29 September	Universal Amphitheatre, Los Angeles, California, USA
30 September	Universal Amphitheatre, Los Angeles, California, USA
02 October	Universal Amphitheatre, Los Angeles, California, USA
03 October	Universal Amphitheatre, Los Angeles, California, USA
04 October	Universal Amphitheatre, Los Angeles, California, USA
05 October	Universal Amphitheatre, Los Angeles, California, USA
06 October	Universal Amphitheatre, Los Angeles, California, USA
09 October	Northrop Auditorium, Minneapolis, Minnesota, USA
10 October	Northrop Auditorium, Minneapolis, Minnesota, USA
11 October	Auditorium Theatre, Chicago, Illinois, USA
12 October	Auditorium Theatre, Chicago, Illinois, USA
13 October	Elliott Hall of Music, W. Lafayette, Indiana, USA

15 October	Music Hall, Boston, Massachusetts, USA
16 October	Music Hall, Boston, Massachusetts, USA
18 October	Palladium, New York, USA
19 October	Palladium, New York, USA
20 October	Palladium, New York, USA
21 October	Palladium, New York, USA
23 October	Palladium, New York, USA
24 October	Palladium, New York, USA
25 October	Palladium, New York, USA
26 October	Palladium, New York, USA
27 October	Eisenhower Hall, West Point, New York, USA
29 October	Hill Auditorium, Ann Arbor, Michigan, USA
30 October	O'Keffe Centre, Toronto, Ontario, Canada
31 October	O'Keffe Centre, Toronto, Ontario, Canada
02 November	Tower Theatre, Philadelphia, Pennsylvania, USA
03 November	Tower Theatre, Philadelphia, Pennsylvania, USA
04 November	Constitution Hall, Washington District of Columbia, USA
05 November	Constitution Hall, Washington District of Columbia, USA
07 November	Grande Ole Opry House, Nashville, Tennessee, USA
08 November	Civic Centre, Atlanta, Georgia, USA
10 November	Moody Coliseum, Dallas, Texas, USA
11 November	Hofheinz Pavilion, Houston, Texas, USA
25 November	Hordern Pavilion, Sydney, New South Wales, Australia
26 November	Hordern Pavilion, Sydney, New South Wales, Australia
27 November	Hordern Pavilion, Sydney, New South Wales, Australia
28 November	Hordern Pavilion, Sydney, New South Wales, Australia
30 November	Festival Hall, Melbourne, Victoria, Australia
01 December	Festival Hall, Melbourne, Victoria, Australia
02 December	Festival Hall, Melbourne, Victoria, Australia
03 December	Festival Hall, Melbourne, Victoria, Australia
06 December	Entertainment Centre, Perth, Western Australia, Australia
07 December	Entertainment Centre, Perth, Western Australia, Australia

About the Author

Keith Hayward is the author of *Tin Pan Alley: The Rise of Elton John*. He is also a renowned music collector, expert and historian, who has met Elton John on several occasions and was Roger Pope's manager before his death in September 2013.

Elton John: From Tin Pan Alley to the Yellow Brick Road is his second book. He lives in West Sussex, England, and has travelled the world in his quest to document Elton's early life and career.

Index

Song titles in single quotation marks. Album titles, films, TV shows and printed publications are listed in italics.

235